CROSSBILL GUIDES

Eastern Andalucía

Córdoba to Cabo de Gata – Spain

Crossbill Guides: Eastern Andalucía – Córdoba to Cabo the Gata
First print: 2017

Initiative, text and research: Albert Vliegenthart, Bouke ten Cate,
Dirk Hilbers, Kees Woutersen
Additional research, text and information: John Cantelo,
Kim Lotterman, Antoon De Rycke
Editing: John Cantelo, Brian Clews, Cees Hilbers,
Riet Hilbers, Kim Lotterman
Illustrations: Horst Wolter
Maps: Alex Tabak
Design: Oscar Lourens
Print: Drukkerij Tienkamp, Groningen

ISBN 978-94-91648-10-6
© 2017 Crossbill Guides Foundation, Arnhem, The Netherlands

This book is produced with best practice methods ensuring lowest possible environmental impact, using waterless offset, vegetable based inks and FSC-certified paper.

The Crossbill Guides Foundation and its authors have done their utmost to provide
accurate and current information and describe only routes, trails and tracks that
are safe to explore. However, things do change and readers are strongly urged to
check locally for current conditions and for any changes in circumstances. Neither
the Crossbill Guides Foundation nor its authors or publishers can accept responsi-
billity for any loss, injury or inconveniences sustained by readers as a result of the
information provided in this guide.

Published by Crossbill Guides in association with KNNV Publishing.

KNNV Publishing   SAXIFRAGA foundation

www.crossbillguides.org
www.knnvpublishing.nl
www.freenatureimages.eu

CROSSBILL
GUIDES
FOUNDATION

4

Highlights of Eastern Andalucía

1 Visit Europe's only semi-desert region with its amazingly colourful badlands and canyons, dry riverbeds, shimmering plains and desolate villages.

El Colorado –
Hoya de Guadix

2 Visit the salinas and nearby desierto to find rare birds like White-headed Duck, Black-bellied Sandgrouse and Trumpeter Finch.

White-headed Duck

3 Search for wildflowers – each region, from the semi-deserts to the limestone mountains and the upper slopes of the Sierra Nevada, has a superb range of species.

Dune flora at Cabo
de Gata

4 Visit in early July, when you can see over 125 species of butterflies in two weeks.

Two-tailed Pasha

5 Put on the walking boots and take some long hikes in spectacular limestone mountains of Cazorla, Maria or Huétor.

Walking in the Alpujarras

6 Visit the roof of the Iberian Peninsula – the Veleta and Mulhacén mountains in the Sierra Nevada and marvel at the relict Alpine vegetation with the highest rate of endemic flora in Spain.

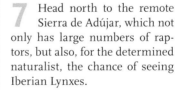

Sierra Nevada

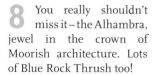

7 Head north to the remote Sierra de Adújar, which not only has large numbers of raptors, but also, for the determined naturalist, the chance of seeing Iberian Lynxes.

Iberian Lynx

The Alhambra

8 You really shouldn't miss it – the Alhambra, jewel in the crown of Moorish architecture. Lots of Blue Rock Thrush too!

About this guide

This guide is meant for all those who enjoy being in and learning about nature, whether you already know all about it or not. It is set up a little differently from most guides. We focus on explaining the natural and ecological features of an area rather than merely describing the site. We choose this approach because the nature of an area is more interesting, enjoyable and valuable when seen in the context of its complex relationships. The interplay of different species with each other and with their environment is astonishing. The clever tricks and gimmicks that are put to use to beat life's challenges are as fascinating as they are countless.

Take our namesake the Crossbill: at first glance it's just a big finch with an awkward bill. But there is more to the Crossbill than meets the eye. This bill is beautifully adapted for life in coniferous forests. It is used like scissors to cut open pinecones and eat the seeds that are unobtainable for other birds. In the Scandinavian countries where Pine and Spruce take up the greater part of the forests, several Crossbill species have each managed to answer two of life's most pressing questions: how to get food and avoid direct competition. By evolving crossed bills, each differing subtly, they have secured a monopoly of the seeds produced by cones of varying sizes. So complex is this relationship that scientists are still debating exactly how many different species of Crossbill actually exist. Now this should heighten the appreciation of what at first glance was merely an odd bird with a beak that doesn't seem to close properly. Once its interrelationships are seen, nature comes alive, wherever you are.

To some, impressed by the 'virtual' familiarity that television has granted to the wilderness of the Amazon, the vastness of the Serengeti or the sublimity of Yellowstone, European nature may seem a puny surrogate, good merely for the casual stroll. In short, the argument seems to be that if you haven't seen a Jaguar, Lion or Grizzly Bear, then you haven't seen the 'real thing'. Nonsense, of course.

But where to go? And how? What is there to see? That is where this guide comes in. We describe the how, the why, the when, the where and the how come of Europe's most beautiful areas. In clear and accessible language, we explain the nature of Andalucía and refer extensively to routes where the area's features can be observed best. We try to make Andalucía come alive. We hope that we succeed.

How to use this guide

This guidebook contains a descriptive and a practical section. The descriptive part comes first and gives you insight into the most striking and interesting natural features of the area. It provides an understanding of what you will see when you go out exploring. The descriptive part consists of a landscape section (marked with a red bar), describing the habitats, the history and the landscape in general, and of a flora and fauna section (marked with a green bar), which discusses the plants and animals that occur in the region.

The second part offers the practical information (marked with a purple bar). A series of routes (walks and car drives) are carefully selected to give you a good flavour of all the habitats, flora and fauna that eastern Andalucía has to offer. At the start of each route description, a number of icons give a quick overview of the characteristics of each route. These icons are explained in the margin of this page. The final part of the book (marked with blue squares) provides some basic tourist information and some tips on finding plants, birds and other animals.

There is no need to read the book from cover to cover. Instead, each small chapter stands on its own and refers to the routes most suitable for viewing the particular features described in it. Conversely, descriptions of each route refer to the chapters that explain more in depth the most typical features that can be seen along the way.

In the back of the guide we have included a list of all the mentioned plant and animal species, with their scientific names and translations into German and Dutch. Some species names have an asterix (*) following them. This indicates that there is no official English name for this species and that we have taken the liberty of coining one. We realise this will meet with some reservations by those who are familiar with scientific names. For the sake of readability however, we have decided to translate the scientific name, or, when this made no sense, we gave a name that best describes the species' appearance or distribution. Please note that we do not want to claim these as the official names. We merely want to make the text easier to follow for those not familiar with scientific names. An overview of the area described in this book is given on the map on page 15. For your convenience we have also turned the inner side of the back flap into a map of the area indicating all the described routes. Descriptions in the explanatory text refer to these routes.

 car route

 walking route

 beautiful scenery

 interesting history

 interesting geology

 interesting flora

 interesting invertebrate life

 interesting reptile and amphibian life

 interesting wildlife

 interesting birdlife

 visualising the ecological contexts described in this guide

8

Table of contents

LANDSCAPE

Mention a visit to eastern Andalucía to an average group of people and the reactions are predictable: it is far too hot in summer and too built up on the coast, but be sure to visit the Mezquita in Córdoba and the Alhambra of Granada. Responses of those more aware of nature are likely to include references to the Alpujarras (what a lovely region!) and the Sierra Nevada (splendid hiking!).

None of these reactions are wrong, but they do not do justice to what eastern Andalucía has to offer. The entire region has exciting wildlife to discover, with markedly different sub-regions each distinct from the next, reflecting the strong variation in climate, altitude, rainfall and geology that is such a salient characteristic of this region.

The region is easily accessed from the airports of Málaga or, better still, Almería. Hop into your rental car and exciting discoveries start already on the coastal marshes right outside the airport. Here you can 'bag' your first Purple Gallinules, Booted Eagles and Long Skimmers (an essentially African dragonfly species) a mere hour after touch-down! Beyond that, you're spoilt for choice – head out into the desert-like south-east of Andalucía or go northwest to explore the Sierra Nevada – the highest mountain of the Iberian Peninsula. Many visitors opt for the latter, connecting the sun-soaked beach and the ski pistes of the Nevada in a single day! Beyond the Nevada, there are superb woodlands and scrublands, vast steppe plains, barren karst plateaux and picturesque oak and olive groves. In short – options are endless and the extent of fine and wildlife-rich habitat is far too great to cover all in great detail.

Therefore, in this Crossbill Guide we've chosen to divide the region into geomorphological unities: the semi-deserts of the south-east, the Alpujarras and Sierra Nevada, limestone mountains to the north and west and the mountain-locked plains or Hoyas that separate them. The northwestern part of our area includes the upper Guadalquivir basin and the Sierra de Andújar, part of the Sierra Morena. Each has its own ecological story to tell, with different species of flora and fauna playing the lead role.

These areas are covered in two ways. First, in a descriptive section that explains the landscape, geology, flora and fauna and second, from page 113 onwards, in 20 beautiful routes and 19 sites which cover the most attractive habitats and host the most remarkable flora and fauna. In passing, we'll introduce you to the rich cultural history of the East-Andalucían landscape as well.

Dry, open pinewoods, gorges, steppe plains and deserts are the main ingredients of the little populated 'Wild East' of Andalucía. This is a view from the little visited Sierra de Baza.

12

Geographical overview

Andalucía is Spain's largest autonomous region and the one with the most diverse habitats and wildlife. Therefore, we decided to cover the the region in two separate guidebooks. The volume on the west focuses on the provinces of Huelva, Sevilla, Cádiz and most of Málaga, while this volume covers the provinces of Córdoba, Granada and Almería – roughly everything east of the line Málaga – Córdoba.
Andalucía is with 8.3 million inhabitants sparsely populated, especially when you consider that the majority of the population lives in the large cities of Sevilla, Málaga, Huelva, Córdoba, Granada, Jaen and Almería.
The most prominent feature of eastern Andalucía is the Sierra Baetica – a rugged mountain range that runs from the southwest to northeast, separating the arid southeast from the fertile basin of the Guadalquivir River. Several of the largest cities of East Andalucía (Córdoba, Andújar and Jaen) are situated in the Guadalquivir basin.
North of the Guadalquivir lies the Sierra Morena. Politically it is part of Andalucía, but geologically it belongs to central Spain. This wild region is basically a string of nature reserves, the easternmost of

Overview of eastern
Andalucía

which, Sierra de Andújar and Despeñaperros, lie within the scope of this book. The Sierra Baetica reaches its highest point at the Sierra Nevada, southeast of Granada. Further northeast, the Sierra Baetica disintegrates into a complex of smaller mountain ranges, like the Sierra de Huétor, Sierra de Baza, Sierra de María, Sierra Mágina and Sierra de Cazorla y Segura. Each of them sport large areas of woodland and scrub and wild cliffs and karst plateaux, which all are destinations well worth a visit. These sierras are separated from one another by plains, known as *depresiones* or *hoyas*. Some of them are fertile and lovely, like the Granada basin (in which the second-largest city of East Andalucía, Granada, is situated). Others, like the Hoya de Baza, Hoya de Guadix and Desierto de Tabernas, are impressively wild, empty, steppe-like in character and rich in birds and other wildlife.

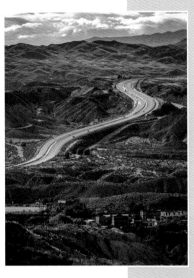

The Sierra Baetica and the *hoyas*, with the exception of the Granada basin, are sparsely populated. It becomes more crowded as you approach Almería, which is, after Córdoba and Granada, the third largest city in the area, with almost 200,000 inhabitants in 2014.

The Sierra Nevada with the Alpujarras form a formidable barrier between Granada and the sea to the south.

As the main towns are situated either northwest or southeast of the Sierra Baetica, the road network follows the mountain passes that connect the *depresiones* between the ranges of the Sierra Baetica. The main north-south connections are the A-45 Córdoba – Antequera – Málaga road and the E-902 Jaén-Granada-Motril. From west to east, there is really only one main connection: the A-92 that runs from Antequera (and further west, Sevilla) to Granada, where it crosses the pass between the Sierra de Huétor and Sierra Nevada to the Hoya de Guadix. At the town of Guadix, it splits. The north-east branch (N-342) crosses over to the Hoya de Baza and on to the Sierra María, while the A-92 bends south to Tabernas and Almería.

The N340 and E15 coastal motorway follows the mountainous south coast, connecting Almería with Motril and, further west, Málaga. Several small wetlands and rivers on the coast boast a distinctly African-influenced flora and fauna. It is also the gateway to the lovely Alpujarras, an attractive area for hikers.

The motorway through the Desierto de Tabernas. Empty landscapes and few but excellent roads characterise Eastern Andalucía.

14

Geology

From glacial *cirque* to desert basin, the geological variety of eastern Andalucía is the most extreme of the whole of Spain. Spain's highest peak, the Mulhacén of the Sierra Nevada (3,478 m), lies just a short distance away from the coastal plains. If you want to understand the high biological diversity of eastern Andalucía, start with the geology of the region.

A concise geological history of eastern Andalucía.
Before the Cenozoicum (c. 38 million years ago), the coast was at the foot of the Sierra Morena (A). As tectonic plates collided during the Cenozoicum, the Baetic Cordillera started to rise as a series of mountain ranges standing above straits, inlets and inland seas (B). The combination of further tectonic uplift and a dry climate desiccated the inland seas, leaving several high plains enclosed by mountains (C). As the land continued to rise, the Guadalquivir basin gradually filled up with sediments. Volcanic activity gave rise to the Cabo de Gata mountains, which locked in more shallow bays that gradually dried out. Flash floods carve steep gullies in the hoyas, creating 'badlands' in the Desierto(D).

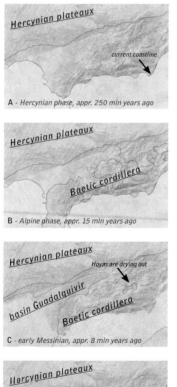

A - Hercynian phase, appr. 250 mln years ago

B - Alpine phase, appr. 15 mln years ago

C - early Messinian, appr. 8 mln years ago

D - Pliocene, appr. 5 mln years ago

In comparison to most areas in Spain, eastern Andalucía is rather young. For millions of years, when the Spanish central *mesetas* of Don Quixote were already formed, what became eastern Andalucía was still covered by a shallow ocean, known as the Tethys Sea. The plateau had its southern edge at present day Sierra Morena – the long, hilly range that stretches along the northern border of Andalucía up to the pass of Despeñaperros. Within the area described in this book, only the Sierra de Andújar and Despeñaperros are part of this old Hercynian shield.

In the Cenozoicum, some 38 million years ago, tectonic pressures gave rise to the Cordillera Baetica or Baetic mountain range – a range that has ever since dominated the geology, nature and history in this part of Spain.

Rise of the Cordillera Baetica

In terms of plate tectonics, Spain is neither European nor African. The peninsula is situated on a small 'micro' plate (micro being relative as the plate's surface covers the entire Iberian peninsula and a good chunk of its coastal waters). Some

40 – 13 million years ago, as
the African and Eurasian plate
moved towards each other, the
Iberian plate got crushed in
the middle, giving rise to the
Pyrenees in the north, and,
later, the *Cordillera* (or *Sierra*)
Baetica in the south. Like a car
caught in a multiple pile up,
the 'boot' and 'bonnet' of the
plate formed a gigantic crum-
ple zone, only one formed in
millions of years, rather than a
split second. In fact, the crash
is ongoing.

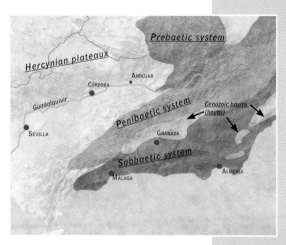

The three different
parts of the Sierra
Baetica.

Being much smaller and light-
er, the Iberian microplate (the car in this analogy) sustains most damage
– the collision zone gets folded like an accordion with ridges (the mountain ranges) and depressions (the *hoyas*). The Pyrenees have two distinct
zones, the Cordillera Baetica three, which are known as the *Prebaetics*,
the *Subbaetics* and the *Penibaetics*.

These Sierras are not three unbroken walls of mountains. Rather, it is a
series of ranges separated by lowlands (the *hoyas*) or low hills. Thanks
to this disjunct nature, the name Sierra Baetica is not much used and is
perhaps even unknown to you. However, some, if not all, of its separate
parts will certainly ring a bell: Sierra Nevada, Las Alpujarras, Sierra de
Cazorla and Sierra de María are all part of this huge Sierra Baetica range.
Further east, marine outcrops of the Sierra Baetica form the Balearic islands (Mallorca, Ibiza, etc.) while to the west the Sierra de Grazalema and
even the Moroccan Rif are part of the range.

Geologically, the Sierra Baetica is a very complicated mountain range.
The tectonic pressure and, at the same time, the rotation of the land
mass did not only fold the earth's crust into three distinct ranges, but
also caused the 'collision zone' to fracture. As the Iberian and African
plates crashed into one another and at the same time slid past each other,
the ranges became folded – the strain was so enormous that the bedrock
cracked. There are many of these fractures and most of them are what
geologists call strike-slip faults: fractures caused when plates move in opposite directions horizontally. As the crust fractures, the parts suddenly
surrender to the pressure and get displaced. This is why the Cordillera

Baetica consists of so many smaller and relatively isolated sierras – what once was a single range, broke and each piece shifted along the fault in a different location.

Different kinds of bedrock

The Hercynian shield of the mesetas of central Spain were formed between 370 – 290 million years ago. The rise of the Cordillera Baetica started about 40 million years ago. In the 250 million years (!)separating these events, the evolution of micro-organisms took a crucial step: the development of planktonic micro-organisms with calcareous exoskeletons – more commonly called shells. During this period everything south of what we now call Andújar was still ocean, but one in which layer upon layer of shells, mostly microscopic, were deposited to form a sea floor hundreds of metres thick. Over time, it was compressed to limestone. When the Cordillera Baetica rose up, the old bedrock was covered with a thick limestone blanket. As a result many of the constituent ranges of the Cordillera Baetica consist of these limestones. The Sierra de Cazorla y Segura is an example, as are the Sierras de Huétor and María.

Limestone is a comparatively soft and brittle type of rock. At the point where the collision between the plates was most intense, the highest mountains were formed. This happened in the Sierra Nevada and Alpujarras. Here the strains on the limestone layers were so intense that it cracked completely, allowing the tough old basement layer to resurface. This is why some (but not all) of the highest parts of the Sierra Nevada and Alpujarras form an island of the old Hercynian material.

Most limestones are easily recognisable: white, somewhat rounded, creviced rock, commonly with karst fields and steep cliffs.

The properties of the soil ultimately depend on the underlying rock which in turn largely dictates what kind of vegetation can grow at a site. Hence it should be no surprise that the landscape of some of the slopes in the Nevada – Alpujarras region remind of that of the Sierra Morena. However, in the Nevada and Alpujarras, the immense and prolonged pressures that accompanied the formation of these mountains changed (metamorphosed) the chemical structure of the bedrock, giving rise to schists, marbles, gneisses, conglomerates and quartzites – all metamorphic rock types that are formed under different conditions of pressure and from different base materials.

Infilling of the Hoyas

The Sierra Baetica's three major ranges – the Penibaetics, Subbaetics and Prebaetics – were separated by large inland seas and lagoons. The entire Guadalquivir basin was a long arm of the sea. In the Tortonian era (12 million years ago), the climate became drier. A little later, in the Messinian (7 million years ago), the water level in the Mediterranean dropped significantly. The sea was cut off from the Atlantic Ocean as the Strait of Gibraltar was closed by tectonic forces. Deprived from ocean water and with an evaporation far exceeding the inflow of water from rivers, the Mediterranean basin started to dry out – an event known as the Messinian Salinity Crisis.

The great valleys and depressions between the Penibaetica range and the Subbaetica range (see map on page 15), previously large brackish lakes or inlets of the sea, also started to dry out. Left behind were the thick layers of sediments that had been brought down by the often fast-flowing rivers that poured into them. Some of these ancient waterbodies were completely

The soil in the Guadalquivir basin is fertile, mostly consisting of riverine sediments. Consequently, it is a major agricultural region for olive and cereal production.

Although the soft sediments in the hoyas easily erode, they are not infertile. Hence the striking combination of barren eroded hills and gorges with olive groves and corn fields.

isolated from the sea (e.g. the Granada basin, the Hoyas de Guadix and Hoya de Baza), but the shallow bays in the southeast remained connected to the sea for a long time (e.g the Desierto de Tabernas and the lowlands of Cabo de Gata-Níjar). The latter were filled with marls, limestones and gypsum. Gypsum is a special kind of rock, both ecologically and economically of great importance. Spain is the fifth largest producer of this material in the world. The most superb area of gypsum (including its endemic flora) can be admired at the Yesos de Sorbas (see site C on page 132). The character of these hoya-landscapes is in large measure defined by the climate under which they were formed. Southeast Andalucía was (as it still is) in the rain shadow of the Sierra Baetica. As a result, the eastern hoyas simply dried out rather than being filled up by sediments (as happened in the Guadalquivir basin and the western depressions). Dried up seabeds have an odd type of soil, which holds the middle between loose sediments and solid rock. The high concentration of salts and the slow baking process, literally, created a very brittle type of sedimentary rock. Most of the surface material today stems from sediments from the end of the Messinian period. At that time, desiccation and extreme salinity had killed off most of

the corals, leaving only porite reefs from which many of the sediments found in the region were formed, especially near Tabernas and Níjar. Such sediments are typically very soft. The sparse, but heavy, rains that characterise the climate of this area (both the current and ancient) give rise to flash floods that cut through the bedrock like a knife. Hence the curious landscapes of the Desierto de Tabernas and the *hoyas*, where level plains are intersected by dramatic gorges, and, in places where water carved out many different channels, a labyrinth of table mountains and valleys. The many escarpments, sink holes and caves that were created this way, were of huge importance to the Palaeolithic inhabitants of the region as well as to wildlife – the latter still is the case.

The volcanoes of Cabo de Gata

Around 15 million years ago, volcanic activity stirred the sea south of eastern Andalucía. The coastline then ran along the southern base of the Sierra de Filabres. As the African and Iberian plate crushed into each other, the Sierra de Alhamilla rose up (creating the 'hoyas' of Desierto de Tabernas and Sorbas), but it also pushed the earth crust down into the mantle, where it began to melt. Further tectonic movements weakened the contact zone between the plates, where the new magma bubbled to the surface and created eruptions.

At first these were all submarine eruptions, which took place over a large part of the Alboran Sea (then much wider than the current version situated between Morocco and Spain). The eruptions took place over a large area from present-day Cabo de Gata to the Spanish enclave of Melilla.

Eventually, some 7 million years ago, the volcanoes rose above the sea at present day Cabo de Gata. At that time the volcanoes formed an archipelago, separated from mainland Andalucía. In between was a shallow, subtropical sea, full of coral reefs. The Sierra de Cabrera (which lies just north of Cabo de Gata) rose up only 5 million years ago from this sea. It is the youngest mountain range of mainland Spain. Fossilised reef banks can still be seen in the area, the most beautiful example being Mesa Roldán (just north of Cabo de Gata). Here an old reef sits on top of a volcanic hill. The submarine eruption lifted the entire reef up from the seafloor, where it now stands as a watchtower over the Mediterranean Sea.

New soils

The sparce rainfall today and during most of the recent history has created very little new sediment. Large sediment-filled lowlands and estuaries, such as those in western Andalucía, are largely absent in eastern Andalucía.

The exception is the bay of Almería, where the retreat of the coastline in combination with the deposition of material from the Rambla Morales has created a flat and relatively fertile land. Dunes, partially fossilised and exposed after the sea retreated, and partially young, have created some of the youngest land of present-day Spain.

Climate and weather

Although eastern Andalucía has a Mediterranean climate, the temperature and rainfall varies strongly from place to place. The Sierra Baetica is the cause of these differences. The range runs parallel to the prevailing westerly oceanic winds so rainfall decreases from west to east. The high mountains of the Sierra Nevada purge the last drop of water from the oceanic clouds, which quickly dissolve further east. The eastern lowlands of the province of Almería as a consequence, hardly receive any rain. Only when the wind blows east from the Mediterranean, there is a chance of precipitation, but these winds, passing over a sea rather than an ocean, are much drier. Hence this region is the driest of the whole of Spain, and the only area in Europe that is classified as semi-desert. Tabernas and Cabo de Gata are with barely 117 mm of rain the driest places in Europe.

Further inland on the plateaux, the climate is quite continental with, by Mediterranean standards, very cold winters and above average hot summers. Rainfall is sparse except higher up in the mountains of Cazorla and the Sierra Nevada. In winter much of the precipitation falls as snow. The southern coastal strip is again very different. Here the classic Mediterranean climate of hot and dry summers and cool and wet winters has a subtropical slant to it. Sheltered from the cool highlands of the interior, the south coast has above average mild winters, to which the occurrence of many African plants and animals testifies.

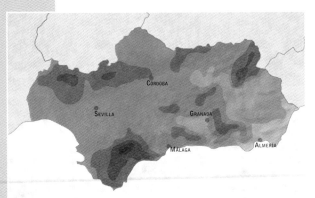

Precipitation map map of Andalucia

< 300 mm

300 - 500 mm

500 - 700 mm

700 - 1000mm

1000 - 1500 mm

1500 - 2000 mm

Habitats

Mirroring the dramatic topography and enormous difference in temperature and rainfall, eastern Andalucía has a broad range of habitats. There are large areas of steppes, Mediterranean woodlands and scrub, oak savannahs (dehesas), pine forests and karst plateaux – all wonderful and rich habitats, full of wildlife and with an attractive flora.

What is special about these habitats, is that they are 'reinvented' in each of the areas in the region. The steppes and badlands in the lowlands and volcanic Cabo de Gata are only superficially like those on the high sandstone plateaux of the Hoyas. The scrubland of the Sierra Morena is dominated by cistus bushes and thereby radically different from the gorse-and-rosemary scrub of the nearby Sierra de Cazorla which, in turn, barely resemble the thyme scrub of the Desierto de Tabernas nor the hedgehog broom scrub of the karst plateaux. Forests occur in all regions except the semi-deserts, but in the Sierra Morena it is mostly in the form of dehesa, while oak forests dominate the Alpujarras and pinewoods the limestone sierras. In short, the general theme is roughly the same all over, but the way the details have worked out is radically different.

Therefore we have chosen in this guidebook to set up our habitat descriptions a little differently than we usually do in the Crossbill Guides. Rather than focussing on a specific habitat (like scrubland, woodland, steppe) we focus on the various regions within eastern Andalucía. In the following chapters we cover semi-deserts and coastal habitats of the southeast (page 22), the Sierra Nevada and Alpujarras (page 29), the inland plains or *hoyas* (page 35), the limestone mountains (page 37), the Guadalquivir basin (page 43) and the Sierra Morena (page 45).

Cross-section through the habitats of eastern Andalucía.

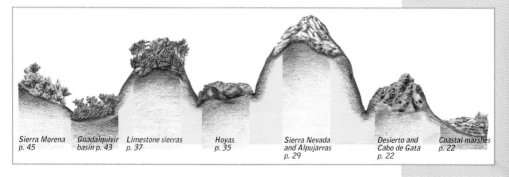

Sierra Morena
p. 45

Guadalquivir
basin p. 43

Limestone sierras
p. 37

Hoyas
p. 35

Sierra Nevada
and Alpujarras
p. 29

Desierto and
Cabo de Gata
p. 22

Coastal marshes
p. 22

LANDSCAPE

22

Cabo de Gata and Desierto de Tabernas – the arid southeast

> Routes 1, 2, 3 and sites A – F on page 130-134 are located in Cabo de Gata.
> Routes 4 and sites D and E on page 134 explore marshes and dunes on the coast
> of Almería.

Location of the semi-desert part of eastern Andalucía (light grey) with Cabo de Gata and Desiero de Tabernas (dark grey).

The south-eastern corner of Andalucía is exotic. This is the land of beautiful but forlorn desertscapes, empty plains, dramatic, red-coloured cliffs, sleepy villages. Desolate creaking farmhouse ruins complete the romantic poor-lonesome-cowboy image as exploited by 'spaghetti westerns' (see below). At the coast, empty beaches alternate with spectacular cliffs – a heritage of some dramatic geological and climatological processes that are radically different from those that shaped the rest of Andalucía (see geology chapter).

Sadly, the scenery is spoilt in some areas by unchecked urban development and agricultural polytunnels (*plásticos*). However, the Cabo de Gata nature park, Desierto de Tabernas, Yesos de Sorbas and, to a lesser extent, the Punta Entinas-Sabinar reserve have remained wonderful, desert-like

A forlorn landscape on the road out west from Tabernas.

coastal areas, If you pick your spots well, you'll find that the landscape, flora and wild-life of this area is astonishing.

Almería Province's aridity is obviously its de-fining element. It is the only part of Europe that can properly be classified as semi-desert. On average, the region receives 3,050 sun-shine hours and in large areas less than 200 millimetres of precipitation annually. This is not sufficient to support woodland, hence the hills and plains are cloaked in a scatter of dwarf shrubs and sturdy tussocks of esparto grass. In between is barren ground – it is only following a rainy spell that countless small annual plants pop up to bloom and set seed before the heat and drought takes the best of them again.

Ecologically, this region has more in common with North-Africa than with the lands directly surrounding it. The core range of much of the flora and fauna of this region lies on the other side of the Mediterranean Sea. Almería is an isolated 'island' of African desert in Europe, squashed between the Mediterranean moun-tains and the sea. Due to its eco-geographical isolation, the region also boasts an impressive number of endemic species, most of which are plants.

The south-east of Andalucía consists of low mountain ranges with plains in between. Some of the mountain ranges (e.g. Sierra de Alhamilla) are limestone forerunners of the Sierra Baetica, whereas others are volcanic (Cabo de Gata). The plains in between are for-mer inlets of the Mediterranean that gradually dried out. The soft sediments of these plains subsequently eroded by ancient rivers and flash floods into chaotic 'badland' landscapes of steep cliffs, table mountains with upland plains in between. The Desierto de Tabernas is a good example.

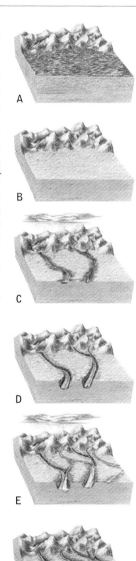

Formation of the hoya badlands. What start-ed as a shallow inland sea (A), became a plain after the water evaporated during the Messinian salinity crisis (B). Rivers that flowed down from the mountains (C) carved out gorges over the years (D). The typical climate of prolonged periods of drought, punctuated with short, heavy spells of rain caused many flash floods which carved out new river courses (E). As the bedrock is so dry and brittle, it easily erodes and new gorges connect-ing with the existing ones were created. This formed the maze of ridges and gullies that is now called a 'badland'. See also photo on page 35.

Spaghetti westerns – no more than a fist full of dollars

The badlands of Almería are more famous than you may have thought. They are, in fact, world-famous. Few people realise that when one is watching classic movies like The Good, the Bad and the Ugly, a Fistful of Dollars or Indiana

Jones and the Last Crusade, that the desert scenes were all filmed in the Desierto de Tabernas.

The authentic looking 'Western' landscape has drawn European film makers to the Desierto to use it as a substitute for the real thing. However, it was not the landscape alone that drew directors of spaghetti westerns (so called as most were Italian productions). Since wages were so low here during the Franco years, it was above all an economic choice to shoot the film here on location.

Spaghetti Western in mini Hollywood (route 5).

Rich diversity of semi-desert habitats

The desert conjures up images of uniform landscapes where the absence rather than presence of life is conspicuous. Nevertheless, many deserts are remarkably rich in wildlife and the semi-deserts of Almería are actually extremely biodiverse. There are two reasons for this. First, there is a large variety of habitats in a relatively small area – plains, slopes, cliffs, dry river beds (*ramblas* in Spanish or *wadis* in Arabic), dunes and saltmarsh at the coast. Second, most of these habitats reappear on very different substrates. In this geologically diverse region, there are sandstones, limestones, ultra-basic gypsums, basalt rock and

Cross section of the semi-desert and its habitats.

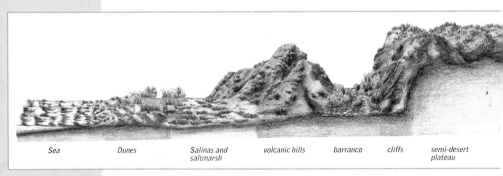

| Sea | Dunes | Salinas and saltmarsh | volcanic hills | barranco | cliffs | semi-desert plateau |

sediment beds. The botanic diversity, in particular, profits from this variety – a *rambla* in the sandstone *desierto* hosts quite a different set of plants than one in a basalt substrate, while life on a plateaux consisting of loose sediments is quite different from that on the gypsum soils. The birdlife is less influenced by soil conditions. The relatively small area of semi-desert in Spain, in combination with the isolation from the main African populations, means that only a relatively small number of African desert birds makes it to Almería. The most notable species are Dupont's Lark, Black-bellied Sandgrouse and Trumpeter Finch.

Dunes and saltmarsh

Today's coastal plains were once submerged in shallow bays of the Mediterranean. They gradually filled up with marine and river sediments. The marine origin of the plains is responsible for the fact that many of the soils in these lowlands have a high level of salinity. This in turn explains why the area is still in such pristine condition – in spite of the fertile soil, the salinity makes for unattractive conditions for crops.

On the coast, the lowlands are fringed with a line of dunes, In comparison to the dunes of west Andalucía, those of Almería are very modest in size. The limited tidal range (between 20 and 60 centimetres) and the prevailing off-shore winds form about the worst possible conditions for the formation of large dunes, hence they are no more than small sandy bumps along the beach (see routes 1 and 2).

This is enough, though, to change the conditions that govern the surrounding plains radically. A thin layer of freshwater underneath the sand allows a rich flora of both shallow-rooting freshwater plants and deeper-rooting saline species to develop. Curry Plant, Sea Medick, Sea Daffodil, Cottonweed, masses of Winged Sea-lavender, Coastal Reichardia* (*Reichardia gaditana*) and Pink Catchfly* *(Silene colorata)* are just a few of the wildflowers that brush the dunes with all imaginable colours in spring. The Tamarisk bushes usually house a few Common Chameleons and Stone Curlew also feels at home here.

Modest as they may be, the dunes have a striking impact on the hydrology. The dunes form a sufficiently resistant obstacle to block the feeble water flow of the ramblas into the sea, thereby creating shallow fresh and brackish lagoons just behind the narrow row of dunes. An example of such a lagoon is the Rambla de Morales (route 1). In some places, these lagoons have been put to use by humans as saltpans – e.g. at Cabo de Gata and the saltpans of Punta Entinas-Sabinar (routes 1 and 4). Both saltpans and natural lagoons are of great importance for marshland birds. The fertile soils

The salinas of Cabo de Gata form an important refuge for wetland birds (top), the most conspicuous of which is the Greater Flamingo (bottom).

are alive with invertebrates on which the resident Flamingos, Black-winged Stilts, Kentish Plovers and Slender-billed Gulls feast, as well as a whole array of migrating waders, gulls and terns. During migration, these are the places where the most exotic birds can turn up. The surrounding glasswort steppes are home to a variety of larks (especially Lesser Short-toed Lark), Spectacled Warbler, Stone Curlew and Black-bellied Sandgrouse.

The fresh or slightly brackish lagoons attract, above all, a specific type of waterfowl, which includes several highly endangered species like Marbled and White-headed Ducks and Crested Coot. The attractive Purple Gallinule occurs here as well. All in all, the coastal habitats of Almería are among the most attractive areas for birdwatchers in the entire region.

Plains

The maritime origin of the plains explains the local deposits of salt, and gypsum. In the saline soils, vegetation is not only very well-adapted to extreme drought, but also to high levels of salinity. Here, saltworts and glassworts dominate the soils, whereas elsewhere, on the sandstones, a low scrub or grassland dominates. The vegetation is patchy – tussocks of grass or bushes dot the plains, rather than forming an unbroken carpet of vegetation, as is the case in the steppes of the centre and west of the Iberian Peninsula.

The birdlife of these plains is very attractive, even though the numbers of birds are naturally low and the cryptic plumage and secretive behaviour of the most sought-after species make them a challenge to find. Characteristic birds of these plains are Black-bellied Sandgrouse, Stone Curlew, Spectacled Warbler, Black-eared Wheatear, Short-toed Lark, locally Lesser Short-toed Lark and – now very rare – Dupont's Lark. The situation is similar for the reptiles: a very distinct set of reptiles frequents these plains, which prefer the combination of open patches and shelter in the bushes. Spiny-footed Lizard is a very typical animal here, as is Ocellated Lizard and Spanish and Large Psammodromus. The most common snakes are Ladder and Montpellier Snake. Rabbit and Iberian Hare occur in low numbers.

The area around Sorbas (site C on page 132) is known for its deposits of high-quality gypsum, which were once in high demand. To botanists, the region is of interest for its special vegetation. Due to the fact that gypsum is water-soluble it is, much like limestone, susceptible to the development of karst (see Geology, page 18). Gypsum karst develops and degrades much faster than limestone karst because the solubility of gypsum is far greater than that of limestone. The gypsum karst in Almería however degrades very slowly due to the extremely low levels of precipitation. Therefore, the region around Sorbas is home to one of the world's best preserved complexes of gypsum karst. Like elsewhere, this karstic landscape has a remarkable hydrology with subterranean rivers and freshwater aquifers. Where these rivers or aquifers emerge on the surface, true oases can develop! These spots of course attract all manner of interesting flora and wildlife.

Slopes, cliffs and ramblas

Most life in the semi-deserts concentrates on the ramblas – riverbeds that are either completely dry or form a string of desiccating pools. Only during periods of heavy rainfall, these gorges carry off excess water towards the Mediterranean Sea. Because heavy rainfall is a rare occurrence in the region, these streams are dry for most of the year.

Patches of Oleander, Tamarisk, Giant Reed, Dwarf Fan Palm and saltwort are found here and there along the ramblas – tall vegetation that provides shelter from the sun and predators. These bushes are breeding sites for birds and a retreat for snakes, Ocellated Lizards and in some locations, chameleons.

Following the course of these ramblas is often the best, if not the only way to explore the rugged terrain. The Rambla de Tabernas (route 3) is the

The gently rolling strip of dunes near Cabo de Gata is not nearly as spectacular as the dunes on the Atlantic coast, but the flora here is just as attractive.

most well-known example. If you take your time to observe the life around the taller rambla vegetation, you will be able to witness the richness of these spots. The more open parts in the rambla sport a rich flora, best appreciated in early spring, from late March to early May. Many of the region's endemic wild-flowers occur here, such as Almería Sea-Lavender* *(Limonium insigne)*, Almería Toadflax *(Linaria nigricans)*, and the odd-looking and conspicuous parasites Yellow Cistanche and Maltese Fungus. The loose sediments offer the perfect retreat for the drought-adapted Natterjack Toad, which is quite numerous, although only found above ground when the wetter conditions make the environment less brutal for an amphibian. For butterflies too, the seclusion of the rambla, sheltered from wind, with plenty of nectar plants and a combination of sunny and shady spots, is ideal.

The steep, rocky slopes and cliffs around the ramblas form another wonderful habitat for naturalists. A walk through the ramblas is therefore a constant trade-off between looking down for plants, reptiles and butterflies, and up for birds.

The cliffs are first and foremost attractive for their birdlife. The most conspicuous species here is the Black Wheatear – a black bird with a white vent and rump that perches on rocks. Endemic to Iberia and North Africa, it has declined markedly in Spain, but is still common in the dry southeast. Listen too for the whining call and toy trumpet song of the Trumpeter Finch, another desert bird that breeds in mainland Europe only in the Cabo de Gata and Desierto de Tabernas. Ledges on and holes in the rock face offer breeding sites for Eagle Owl, Red-billed Chough, Kestrel and Bonelli's Eagle. The latter is one of the most common eagles in the area.

The ramblas and coastal cliffs of Cabo de Gata are different from those inland. The basalts offer fewer breeding sites for birds, but the plantlife is spectacular. The many gorges and dry river beds that cut through these lavas have created very scenic, secluded beaches between the cliffs, like the well-known Playa de Mónsul (route 2). The ramblas sport rare rock plants like Caralluma (Europe's only native cactus-like plant), and the endemic Cabo de Gata Snapdragon* *(Antirrhinum charidemi)*, Cabo de Gata Germander* *(Teucrium charidemi)* and Spanish Silk-vine* *(Periploca angustifolia)*.

Sierra Nevada and Alpujarras

Routes 16 to 19 and the Puerto de la Ragua (site A on page 204) are situated in the Sierra Nevada and Alpujarras.

The Sierra Nevada is a monumental landmark – impossible to miss. This massive mountain stands out like a giant, iced bridal cake in the landscape, dwarfing all the sierras around it. At 3,478 m its highest peak, the Mulhacén, is not only the highest of the Baetic mountain ranges, but also the highest peak on the entire Iberian Peninsula, Pyrenees included.

Location of the Sierra Nevada (dark grey) and Alpujarras (light grey).

The Sierra Nevada has a tremendous diversity in landscapes, flora and fauna. It is only 35 kms from the snowcapped mountains to the sunscorched steppes of the Hoya de Guadix and a similar distance towards the coast. Within this area there is every imaginable type of habitat: coastal marshes, steppes, Alpine bogs and snowfields and a large number of different woodlands and scrublands. Add to this the large variety in soil types (see geology section) and precipitation differences between the east and the west sides and you end up with an exceptionally high biodiversity.

Cross section of the Sierra Nevada and its habitats.

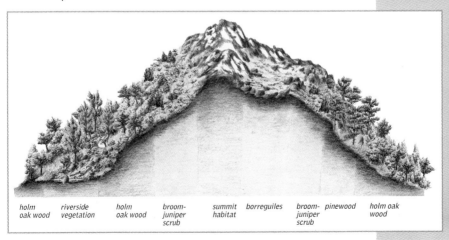

| holm oak wood | riverside vegetation | holm oak wood | broom-juniper scrub | summit habitat | borreguiles | broom-juniper scrub | pinewood | holm oak wood |

As in the semi-deserts, the diversity is enhanced by the many different types of bedrock. When the African and European plates collided, the tectonic pressure in this area was so intense that the ancient bedrock broke through the overlying layer of limestone. This created a giant outcrop of metamorphic, siliceous rock (which is over a billion years old in places) in the middle of a ring of much younger (200 million years old) sedimentary limestones. Whereas the surrounding sierras are all limestone ranges, the Sierra Nevada has both, although siliceous rock dominates.

So apart from being a deservedly famous area for hiking, the Sierra Nevada (and to lesser extent the Alpujarras), is a fascinating world for naturalists. The attraction is oddly twofold: on the one hand the Sierra Nevada boasts one of the continent's highest incidence of endemic flora and fauna, and on the other hand it is a meeting place of wide-ranging species from North-Africa, the Mediterranean, temperate Europe and even the Arctic.

Amongst high European mountain ranges, the Sierra Nevada is a bit of an odd one out. The classic vision of mountain ecosystems is to see the succession of vegetation from valley bottom to mountain peak as analogous to a journey from moderate latitudes towards the Arctic. In the Pyrenees for example, you'd proceed from Mediterranean scrub and forest at the base of the mountains to deciduous woodland (the temperate element) to the coniferous forest (which echoes the taiga) to the tundra-like Alpine pastures and snow fields. This image is very much engrained in our

View of the Sierra Nevada.

A Spanish Ibex on a borreguile or high altitude peatland in the Sierra Nevada (top). Borreguiles support a rich flora of endemic species, including Sierra Gentian* (centre) and Sierra Nevada Butterwort (bottom).

perspective as it is echoed in so many mountain ranges, from the Pyrenees and Cantabrian Mountains to the Alps, the Carpathians, the Balkan mountains, the Caucasus and beyond. But the Sierra Nevada is different. Although there are some remnants of 'northern' ecosystems in the highest reaches, the upper slopes form a very different kind of ecosystem.

The high Sierra Nevada

The Mediterranean climate with its summer drought and strong evaporation makes the summit of the Sierra Nevada more of a cold desert than giving it Arctic characteristics. Rather than sustaining boggy swards of grasslands, this upper zone is bleak and stony, with a thin scatter of small, tussocky dwarf shrubs and perennial herbs that grow in cracks and hollows sheltered by snow in winter. The landscape has been shaped by enormous glaciers, which dominated these mountains in the ice ages. With some practice, glacial cirques, valleys and moraines can all be discerned here.

This zone has the highest level of endemism (species that occur only in a specific area) of the entire Iberian Peninsula. Particularly the flora is unique. The rocky substrates are the habitat of endemic plants like the Sierra Nevada Violet* (*Viola crassiuscula*), Nevada Saxifrage* (*Saxifraga nevadensis*), Glacial Toadflax* (*Linaria glacialis*) and countless others.

If you visit the upper zone you cannot miss the beautiful, bright green patches of grassland in hollows and depressions, often fringing a mountain lake. The green grasses and sedges contrast sharply with the rocky surroundings. These are the *borreguiles* or high-mountain peatlands.

The *borreguiles* are a remnant of an Arctic ecosystem. Peat layers can only form and sustain themselves in areas where the vegetation is permanently soaked in water, either in frozen or liquid form. Thus, peatlands typically occur in cold areas where either evaporation is low or precipitation high – the high Alpine areas or the north, in other words.

Isolated from other peatlands since the ice ages, the borreguiles are the second hotspot for endemics, with plants like the much sought-after endemics Nevada Butterwort* (*Pinguicula nevadensis*) and Sierra Gentian* (*Gentiana sierrae*; see routes 17 and 19).

There is often a clear zonation in the *borreguiles* from the very wet lake's edge to a boggy centre and a dry outer rim. Each of these zones has its own unique plants.

The majority of the high mountain zone is dominated by siliceous rock. Only a small area consists of limestones. Here, a different vegetation is found.

Descending the slopes

The upper zone of the Sierra Nevada lies roughly above 2,800 m. Beneath it, between 1,800 m and 2,800 m, you'll find yourself in the hedgehog zone. The climate is not as extreme and hostile as on the highest peaks and the vegetation is more or less continuous. However, high solar evaporation and extreme drought in summer, favours a particular growth form of dome-shaped dwarf bushes, the 'hedgehogs'. As an ecosystem, the hedgehog zone is described in more detail on page 41.

The Nevada is not the only range that is high enough to reach into the hedgehog zone. In Andalucía, the Sierra de Cazorla, Sierra Mágina and Sierra de María also have extensive areas of this vegetation type. These are limestone mountains where the blue-flowered Hedgehog Broom plays a lead role. In the Sierra Nevada, the siliceous variant is most common. Here the yellow-flowered broom *Genista versicolor* dominates, together with Common and Savin's Juniper. Locally, where the soil is a little deeper and finer grained, a grassland appears with a fine flora.

Gullies and flowery patches are the best places to look for the unique butterfly fauna of the Sierra Nevada, which peaks in this altitude zone. Look for wind-sheltered patches of Nevada Thyme and *Jurinea* (the latter like a ground-hugging knapweed), which are two excellent nectar plants.

At high altitudes the Nevada Blue and the local race of Spanish Argus occur. Between 1,800 and 2,000 m, look for Apollo, Andalusian False Grayling and Black Satyr.

The birdlife in the two upper zones is not rich, but includes some special species, such as Alpine Accentor, Northern Wheatear, Rock Thrush, Black Redstart and Red-billed Chough. Towards the treeline, Black-eared Wheatear, Rock Bunting and Blue Rock Thrush appear.

View over Poqueira in the Alpujarras with the Sierra Nevada in the background (bottom). This is an excellent region for long hikes and to enjoy the rich butterfly fauna. The Spanish Marbled White is a common sight here in summer (top).

Beneath the tree line – the Alpujarras

In the Sierra Nevada, the tree line lies at about 2,000 m. On silicious soils, the junipers that mark the treeline gradually disappear as you descend, and holm oak trees take over. In the limestone areas, the natural forests are open stands with junipers and pines (mostly Austrian and Scots Pine – the latter a subspecies endemic to the Nevada). There is a marked difference between the south and north slopes. The gentle southern part of the range is known as the Alpujarras. Holm oak scrub and woodlands dominate on the dry slopes while in the more secluded or wetter western valleys, Pyrenean and Portuguese Oaks cover small areas. In between there are large areas of Mediterranean scrubland. You are now too low for the unique Nevada flora and fauna but the bright yellow clusters of broom are a feast for the eye and provide perches to typical Mediterranean birds like Woodchat Shrike and Black-eared Wheatear.

Lower still you enter the populated parts of the famous Alpujarras, with its rich history and culture. From the 8th century onward, the Moors developed the region economically, introducing silk farming and an advanced system of irrigation, the *acequías*, which keep the area lush and arable to this day (see history chapter).

The rivers in the Alpujarras are attractive. The riverine forests that accompany the many *acequias*, streams and rivers, consist of Pyrenean Oak, Chestnut and Ash – often majestic trees that dwarf the specimens on the slopes. Golden Orioles sing from within the crowns of these trees while the stream itself is the domain of Otters, Kingfishers, Grey Wagtails and Dippers.

Beneath the tree limit – the north slopes

From the summits of the Muhacén and Véleta you have a magnificent vista to the north that gives an immediate understanding of the difference between the north and south slopes. The north-facing ones are cooler and moister because they are turned away from the sun. Outcrops of limestone are more frequent and human influence less strong. These factors favour tree growth and the tree line lies on a higher altitude than on the drier southern slope, agriculture is less widespread, while a larger part of the land is forested. The natural pinewoods on limestone soil are frequent and are home to Crossbill, Firecrest, Citril Finch (recently arrived and still very local) and other conifer specialists. Further down, the pine plantations make way for holm oak woodlands and cistus scrub.

The Hoyas – inland plains

Route 5, 6 and the site on page 147 explore the hoyas.

The Hoyas of Baza and Guadix are the depressions between the Sierra Nevada, the Sierra de Baza and the
Sierra Mágina. Their landscape, flora, fauna and geological history bear many similarities to those of the
Desierto de Tabernas (page 22) in that both once con-
sisted of shallow bays and lagoons of the Tethys ocean
(the forerunner of the Mediterranean). They were gradually filled with marine and riverine deposits and then

Location of the hoyas
in eastern Andalucía.

raised above sea level by tectonic movements. The water evaporated, ex-
posing the fragile sediments of the former seabeds to the elements, allowing streams and rivers to carve mazes of ragged cliffs and steep ravines.
However, there are significant differences between the *hoyas* and the
semi-deserts of Almería. The *hoyas'* location inland, set between mountain ranges and on plateaux raised to a greater altitude, gives them a

El Colorado in Hoya
de Guadix. In some
areas in the hoyas, the
'plains' are so heavily
eroded that they form
a maze of gorges and
table mountains.

LANDSCAPE

distinctly continental climate with freezing winters and hot summers. The climate is not nearly as dry as that of the *desierto* and, since the *hoyas* are much older, the soil is much less saline.

These characteristics make the region suitable for arable farming. There are large stretches of fields and 'cereal steppe', alternating with patches of more natural grasslands, stony terrain, esparto-covered slopes and sand dunes.

Several rivers run through the plains, forming wet and nutrient-rich life veins in the otherwise arid land. Olive and almond groves and even the occasional dehesa add variation to the landscape, which is, with the high mountains continuously in the background, quite impressive.

Steppe birds are the main attraction of the hoyas. Black-bellied Sandgrouse, Stone Curlew, Thekla, Short-toed and Dupont's Lark are all present, although the latter is very rare. in contrast with the *desierto*, Lesser Short-toed Lark is scarce, while Calandra Lark is remarkably common. There are also good populations of Little Bustard and Montagu's Harrier, while Roller and Great Spotted Cuckoo reach some of their highest densities in Spain in the hoyas. Several rare plants and butterflies and a good range of reptiles complement the biodiversity and make these deserted plains attractive.

The flat steppe-like lowlands are fringed by rugged badlands. The cliffs are again the domain of Eagle Owls, Black Wheatears, Choughs and Rock Thrushes. In certain places, the reddish tint of the cliff faces evokes comparisons with Colorado (see route 5). The gorges are different from those in the Tabernas region. There are some dry ramblas, but quite a few permanent streams too. Lush riparian vegetation often accompanies these streams and rivers. The Río Gor (again route 5) is a beautiful example.

There are some fine steppe areas in those parts of the hoyas that have not been carved up by gorges. The Calandra Lark is a common species on such grasslands.

Cazorla, Mágina, María, Huétor and Almijara – the limestone mountains

Routes 6 to 12, 15 and 20 visit limestone mountains. The river habitat in limestone mountains features on routes 8, 9, 15, 20 and site A on page 212. For attractive woodlands and glades, try routes 8, 10, 11 and 15. The hedgehog zone features prominently on routes 5, 6, 7 and 10 17, while bird-rich cliff habitat is present on routes 8, 9 ad site A on page 167.

The Sierra Baetica has a complicated structure. This large mountain range stretches out from Tarifa across the south of Andalucía into Múrcia and beyond. Geologists distinguish three different ranges, the Prebaetic, the Subbaetic and the Penibaetic, with each formed in different ways. However, if you simply look at a map, you'll notice each of these chains are broken up into isolated mountain ranges, with large areas of plains or rolling hills in between them. These are the mountain ranges you'll see named on the maps: Sierra de Cazorla, Sierra Mágina, Sierra de Huétor, Sierra María, Sierra de Almijara, Sierra Nevada and Sierra de Alhamilla. The first five of these have, due to their calcareous bedrock, their altitude (roughly up to 2,000 metres) and their climate, roughly the same set of habitats and are therefore discussed together in this chapter (The Sierra Nevada, described on page 29 is much higher and has a more diverse bedrock, whereas the Sierra de Alhamilla, described on page 208, is much drier).

Location of the limestone sierras.

Cross-section of the limestone mountains and their habitats.

| olive groves and steppes | scrub and holm oak wood | riverside vegetation | holm oak wood | pinewood | karst plateau / hedgehog vegetation | gorge and cliffs | summit / hedgehog vegetation | pinewood |

What unites the limestone sierras is their ruggedness. Over millions of years, rivers have carved out deep ravines and caves. Erosion created magnificent cliffs and forbidding karst plateaux. The rocky slopes, most of which are unsuited for agriculture, are clad in woodlands of oak and pine, or are so dry that only a scatter of low scrub or steppe-like pasture is able to gain a foothold.

All these mountains share a similar vegetation zonation from the river-bed in the valley, oak woodland on the lower slopes that gives way to pine woodland higher up. Finally, on the plateaux, a type of very low and spiny dwarf scrub occurs that is special for the south and east of Spain and is known as 'hedgehog vegetation'. On all levels, except on the plateaux, there are large patches of Mediterranean scrubland where the soil is thin or the ecology has been disrupted.

As many of these Sierras are broken by lowland areas, it is easy (and sometimes unavoidable) for the visitor, to combine an exploration of the mountains with one of the lowland habitats too. In some areas, the lowlands are covered in olive groves or, at higher altitudes, groves of almonds, figs or cherries, which make for an attractive start of the excursion into the mountains. More exciting however are the lowlands near the Sierra de Almijara, Sierra de Baza and Sierra de María, where a wonderful area of steppe grassland and extensive arable land around the mountains offer great birdwatching and spectacular empty 'wild west' landscapes.

View over the Sierra Mágina. As with many other ranges within the Sierra Baetica, Mágina is an isolated range situated in a rolling countryside of steppes and olive groves.

Rivers

The upper part of the Guadalquivir and most rivers that feed it, spring from the limestone mountains. The winter snow and relatively high spring precipitation feed the streams well into summer, while the permanent sources of water, subterranean reservoirs, keep the streams going even in the driest months. The surrounding soil is, due to sedimentation, rich in nutrients, so the permanence of both water and nutrients makes the valleys true life lines, both for people and nature.

Many rivers are lined with a ribbon of riverine forest – a mixture of tall poplars, ashes and alders and thickets of willow. It forms an ideal habitat for Golden Oriole, Iberian Green Woodpecker, Nightingale and Hawfinch. The river itself is frequented by Grey Wagtails and, in some sierras, Dippers, which are here close to the southern limit of its range. Many rivers are rich in dragonfly species too. Western and Beautiful Demoiselles, Small Pincertails and Common Goldenrings are typical species on most rivers, but on some southern rivers (e.g. Río Chíllar – route 20) there is a score of even more localised and sought-after species.

Wherever the valley is wider or runs through an open depression, there are grasslands, which are, with increasing intensity of grazing, scrubby, flowery or a rather bitten down grassy sward. Almost regardless of their size and the state that they are in, such grassy places are hotspots. Early in the morning, deer and wild boar come down here to feed, followed, as the sun warms the air, by large numbers

Waterfall in the Sierra de Cazorla. The springs and mountain streams form an important habitat for dragonflies. Due to the isolation of these mountain ranges from similar habitat in temperate Europe, endemic local forms have arisen, such as this *nevadensis* subspecies of the Common Goldenring (bottom).

Golden Eagles breed in all the larger mountain ranges of eastern Andalucía.

of butterflies and owlflies. In the Sierra de Huétor alone, over 120 species of butterflies occur, and the other ranges do not lag far behind. Grassy, flowery spots and gullies, many of which are in river valleys or woodland glades, are the richest.

Woodlands, scrub and glades

The slopes of the limestone mountains are covered in a vegetation that is not easy to typify. From a distance, it looks like continuous woodland, but come closer and large areas turn out to be scrubland, mixed with patches of denser woodland, either pine or deciduous, or very open and park-like with glades and patches of scrub. The slopes are extremely varied, with different types of vegetation fading into one another without clear demarcation.

The natural vegetation of the limestone slopes in East Andalucía is widely considered to have been a dense Mediterranean woodland of oaks – Holm and Kermes Oak up to, very roughly, 1,000 metres, Portuguese and, locally, Pyrenean Oak above them and, higher still, stands of Austrian Pine from 1,800 m upwards. This image is deceptive. The extreme continental-Mediterranean climate in the mountains, with its bitterly cold winters and very hot and dry summers, are a stress test for trees. Particularly in the eastern Sierras, like Sierra de Baza and María, the climate is extreme. In the more sheltered and nutrient rich spots, trees grow very well, but where it is rockier or the soil is shallow, especially on south-facing slopes, trees have a difficult time. Even in a completely undisturbed state, shrubs rather than trees probably dominated in many areas. Grazing and the occasional forest fires often didn't allow succession to proceed past the shrub stage.

With the arrival of humans (who came early in these parts), the forest cover diminished. The grazing of animals, harvesting of wood and

increased the number of forest fires denuded many slopes. Only in recent decades, as people moved away from the mountains and pastoral-
ism sharply declined, have woodlands increased again. In addition, pine
plantations have been established in many areas. Ergo, although a very
general zonation of vegetation can be recognised, the appearance of any
single slope is more a reflection of local usage and history than a result of
general ecological conditions.

Meanwhile, flora and fauna fare very well under these conditions. The
countless micro-habitats on all of these slopes harbour a great diversity
of species. Whereas the deep interior of woodlands or the core of a uniform scrubland houses relative few plants and animals, the transition
zone between forest, parkland, scrubland, grassland and rock slope is
where diversity reigns. Many areas are an almost perpetual transition
zone.

The parkland areas, where tall trees, scrub and flowery grasslands meet,
are a hot zone for butterflies, birds, reptiles and mammals. Typical species here are Genet, Red Fox and grazing animals, including Spanish
Ibex. Citril Finch, Crossbill, Iberian Green Woodpecker, Rock Bunting,
Subalpine and Sardinian Warblers are a representative selection of the
possible bird species, while the list of butterflies is simply too long to
fully list here (but see butterfly section on page 103). Among the common and conspicuous wildflowers, are Grey-leaved Cistus, Western
Peony and Stinking Hellebore plus, more generally, various daffodils
and asphodels and a long list of orchids. Woodland glades in limestone
mountains are the single-most important orchid habitat in the whole of
Andalucía. You'll find excellent examples on routes 7, 8, 9, 11 and 15, both
for orchids as well as for butterflies.

Karst cliffs and the hedgehog zone

Many high altitude slopes and plateaux seem, from a distance, devoid of
vegetation. Upon closer inspection, the rocky soil is dotted with tussocks of
sturdy grasses and small, rounded spiny bushes, that are the plant version
of a hedgehog. This is the hedgehog zone, where the vegetation has adapted
entirely to a combination of poor soils, extreme winter cold, even more extreme solar radiation in summer, and a strong grazing pressure. Again, it
is difficult to say at what altitude the hedgehog zone replaces woodlands. In
completely natural conditions, this may not occur below 2,000 metres in
the western sierras and 1,500 metres in the east, but grazing pressure, fires
and tree felling have allowed it to thrive below 1,000 metres in the sierras
with the harshest conditions (e.g. Sierra de María).

The hedgehog zone is not that rich in species, but it abounds in endemic ones. After the cliffs (which are natural refuges for grazing animals), the hedgehog zone sports the highest number of endemic wildflowers in the limestone sierras. Many take the form of prostrate or dome-shaped, spiny or densely hairy bushes, adapted to minimising evaporation and grazing. The most conspicuous are the blue-flowering Hedgehog Broom and Savin's Juniper. There are not too many bird species at these altitudes, mostly Black-eared and Northern Wheatear (the latter at the highest altitudes), Rock Bunting, Red-billed Chough and Spectacled Warbler, with Golden, Short-toed, Booted and Bonelli's Eagles frequently patrolling above the plateaux.

Cliffs

Both for birds and wildflowers, cliffs are a hugely important habitat type. Several rock-dwelling birds breed exclusively on cliffs and rocky karst, such as Rock Thrush and Blue Rock Thrush, Alpine Swift, Crag Martin, Red-billed Chough, Black Wheatear, Eagle Owl, Griffon Vulture and Golden and Bonelli's Eagle. For the raptors, the south-facing cliffs, where warm air rises up, offer the best nest sites. Several plant species are exclusively found in rock cracks. Whereas the hedgehog plants have developed the capacity to fend off grazing animals, the cliff endemics have mastered the strategy of escape, seeking refuge on cliffs that even the sure-footed Spanish Ibex can't reach. Of the rare flora of the Sierra de Cazorla, the two most iconic plants, the Cazorla Violet and Eelgrass-leaved Butterwort* (*Pinguicula valisneriifolia*), occur exclusively on rocks (the latter on wet cliffs).

Beautiful old pine-woods in the Sierra de Cazorla (route 9).

The Guadalquivir basin

Endorheic lagoons in the Guadalquivir basin can be found on sites E and F on page 181-182. The Guadalquivir river and tributaries are part of route 14 and sites A and D on pages 178-180.

The name Guadalquivir originates from the Arabic *Al-Wadi-al-Kabir*, the mighty river. Indeed, with a length of 657 km, it is the longest river of Andalucía and since its entire course lies within the region, it is one of the most prominent landscape features of Andalucía. Many of the major cities, such as Andújar, Córdoba and Se-

Location of the Guadalquivir basin (light grey).

villa, sit on its banks or on those of its tributaries (Jaén and Granada). The Guadalquivir basin is a wide lowland area that separates the Sierra Morena to the north from the Sierra Baetica to the south. The river rises in the Sierra de Cazorla flows from the east through which the Guadalquivir runs from east to west. East of Sevilla, the river runs not in the centre of the basin, but along its northern rim. The basin is not flat, but a region of rolling hills, alternating with more level terrain near the rivers. In geologically recent times (see page 19) the Guadalquivir basin was a large shallow inlet of the sea which gradually became dry as tectonic upheaval pushed the land up and the rivers filled the basin with its sediments. Hence, the basin consists of young and fertile sediments which are a godsend for farmers in a country where good soil is scarce. Vast areas of olive groves clad the hills in the eastern Guadalquivir basin, interspersed with cotton, grain, rapeseed and sugar beets close to the river – the type of landscape a naturalist generally steers away from.

Indeed, of the great east-Andalucían regions, the basin of the Guadal-quivir is the least attractive, but it does have two great draws: small wetlands and remnant steppe habitat. The first come in two forms – endorheic lagoons and riverside marshes.

What defines endorheic lagoons is that they have no connection to the river system and thus no outlet to the sea. The inflow of water is either so variable, the bedrock so porous or evaporation so strong (or a combination of these) that on average as much or even more water disappears than that flows into the lagoon. Thus, endorheic lagoons are characterised by highly changeable water tables and many of them fall dry entirely during the

In many parts of the Guadalquivir basin, there seems to be no end to the olive groves (top). This landscape has little to offer to the naturalist. However, the rivers and some endorheic lagoons in this region are hotspots for flora and fauna, not least for water birds such as this Night Heron (bottom).

summer. As endorheic lagoons are isolated from other water bodies, it is hard or impossible for fish to colonise them naturally and as a result amphibians and certain species of aquatic plants often thrive. This shows in the birdlife too – several rare birds prefer these kind of lakes above other wetlands. The species composition varies greatly depending on both the water level (and amount of exposed muddy shore) and the natural salinity of the water, but typical species are Greater Flamingo, Little and Black-necked Grebe, Common and Red-crested Pochard and a variety of waders. The star birds however, are White-headed Duck, Purple Gallinule and Crested Coot (reintroduced). The lagoons are rich in dragonflies too.

Since agriculture requires a lot of water, the extraction of water has permanently dried out many former natural lagunas. However, many small reservoirs, constructed to ensure the water supply during the hot months, double as artificial 'endorheic lakes' (although often less attractive than their natural cousins). A particularly attractive example is the Laguna Grande (site E on page 181), once created to store water for irrigation but now a protected site. The bulrush and reed marshes and tamarisk thickets support a rich birdlife and there are excellent observation options. The Guadalquivir itself can be considered as a single, long linear wetland, even though it has, with the exception of a few spots, no protected status. The river meanders and has much higher water levels in winter and spring than in summer. These seasonal differences created wide riverbeds with exposed sand banks, reeds, poplar woods and thickets of willow and tamarisk – all ideal for breeding birds, Penduline Tit, Golden Oriole, Olivaceous Warbler and lots of herons. A very good spot is the confluence of the Jándula with the river (site A on page 178) and another is the Sotos de Albolafia in the heart of Córdoba city. Over 120 species of birds have been seen here and it is an excellent site for dragonflies (site D on page 179).

There are three important areas for steppe birds in the eastern section of the Guadalquivir valley. The first extends southeast of the Guadalquivir from near Mengíbar/Porcuna to Porcuna. Less common steppe birds like Great and Little Bustard, Black-bellied Sandgrouse are found sparsely here. The two other areas further east are Campiña de Cazalilla and, further east again, near Jódar. Stone Curlew, Montagu's Harrier and Roller occur somewhat more widely and are often found in the fields surrounding the endorheic lagoons.

The Sierra Morena

Routes 13, 14 and sites A, B and C on page 178-179 visit the Sierra Morena. In addition, each of the nature parks in the Sierra Morena has a limited number of walking options. You can purchase leaflets of these routes in the local visitors' centres (see page 218-219.

The Sierra Morena is an ancient range of hills and low mountains that extends for 450 km from the Portuguese border to the Sierra de Cazorla (which is part of the Sierra Baetica). As the Sierra Morena is geologically part of the mesetas of Central Spain, it is the natural border between Andalucía and the regions of Castilla-La Mancha and Extremadura. The entire range is remote and isolated, but only the eastern part, the rockiest and wildest, is covered in this guidebook.

The westernmost part of the range covered in this book is the Sierra de Hornachuelos, which lies in the west of Córdoba Province and is

Location of the Sierra Morena (light grey) and within it the smaller ranges of Sierra de Andújar and Despeñaperros (dark grey).

a seamless extension of the Sierra Norte in Sevilla Province. East of Hornachuelos, the Sierra Morena is lower and more hilly until, roughly north of the town of Andújar the mountains rise to over 1,000 m. This is the twin nature park of Sierra de Andújar and Sierra de Cardeña y Montoro – one of the largest, least populated and densely wooded parts of Andalucía. Further east again, close to where the E5 motorway links Andalucía to Castilla-la Mancha, the Sierra Morena reaches its eastern terminus. Here are the Parque Natural de Despeñaperros and Cascada de la Cimbarra – two much smaller areas with cliffs, beautiful water-falls and slopes with mixed woodland of oak and chestnut.

The bedrock of the Sierra Morena is poor, acidic and rather uniform, which is why these nature parks differ only in detail from one another. The bedrock consists of old schists, quartz and granite – substrates that are radically different from those of the limestone sierras, hence the natural world of the Sierra Morena has its own unique character. Its soils typically support only the growth of oak woodland and Mediter-ranean scrub, where, particularly in April-May, the pretty and conspicu-ous Gum Cistus and French Lavender are prominent.

As water doesn't easily penetrate the bedrock, countless streams run down the hills to join the larger rivers that, in the end, flow into the Guadalquivir. The Sierra Morena isn't very high and has no subterra-nean water reservoir to feed the rivers during the summer. Hence, most streams dry up, except for a few more secluded and larger ones at the base of the mountains. These are a true oasis during summer, lined with lush riverine vegetation. Dragonflies, reptiles, amphibians, birds and certain types of butterflies are all drawn to this habitat that, in spite of covering only a modest area, is among the most important and attrac-tive in the region. The best sites are on the edge of the Sierra de Hor-nachuelos with many butterflies and dragonflies, while the patches of agriculture attract uncommon birds like Roller, Great Spotted Cuckoo and Rufous Bush Robin.

The highest peaks of the Andújar are slightly damper and cooler than the surrounding area and support modest-sized woodlands of Portu-guese and Pyrenean Oaks as well as cliffs that form important breeding sites for birds.

Arable farmland and olives are limited to small pockets in valleys and plains. Most agriculture takes the form of extensive husbandry in de-hesas – parklike, open woodlands of Holm or Cork Oaks. This typical landscape that dominates large areas in western Spain and Portugal reaches its eastern limits here in the eastern Sierra Morena.

Dehesas have an extremely rich birdlife. Shrikes, Hoopoes, Bee-eaters, Azure-winged Magpies, Thekla and Woodlarks are all common. Even more in evidence are the birds of prey. Apart from the widespread and common Black Kites, Griffon Vultures, Booted and Short-toed Eagles, the Sierra Morena, and within our part especially Sierra de Andújar, has good populations of Black Vulture, Golden Eagle and Spanish Imperial Eagle.

As in many parts of Andalucía, most of the land in the Sierra Morena is private property. The large estates have a double function as agricultural and hunting areas. In the Sierra de Andújar, hunting is an important source of income, which is reflected in the large numbers of game. Red Deer, Fallow Deer, Wild Boar and Mouflon are, to varying degrees, common on the estates and fairly easily seen. The great mammalian attraction however, is the presence of two top predators: the Wolf and the Iberian Lynx. A small, isolated relict population of Wolf, the only one in southern Spain, persists in the Sierra Morena but the animals are very elusive, shy and hard to detect, let alone see. Views of the Iberian Lynx in contrast, are, with some luck and dedication, possible. Currently, there are only two populations remaining in the wild of this extremely rare and endangered species (although there are reintroduction programmes for various areas in Spain and Portugal) and the one of Andújar is the largest of them. The other population is in Coto Doñana. With a side show of Egyptian Mongoose, Otter and various other small carnivores, the Sierra de Andújar is probably the best spot to see wildlife in the entire region.

The landscape of the Sierra de Andújar consists largely of open holm oak woods with pastures and scrub.

History

Much like its nature, and largely for the same reasons, East Andalucía's history is extremely rich. This wealth can, for a large part, be attributed to the fact that Andalucía is the geographical meeting point of the continents of Africa and Europe.

Prehistory

Some 1.8 million years ago, the first hominids (*Homo erectus*) came from Africa. Western Europe's oldest hominid remains (1.4 million years old) were found near María. These and comparable finds have raised the theory that the Strait of Gibraltar was the first hominid entry point onto the continent. These settlers eventually evolved into the well-known Neanderthals, which would come to populate most of Europe. Many caves in Andalucía have yielded Neanderthal finds. An approximately 43,000 year old cave painting in the Cueva de Nerja in the Sierra de Almijara currently holds the distinction of having the oldest known hominid paintings and, with recent discoveries at Gorham's Cave on Gibraltar, the first known examples of Neanderthal cave art. This caused something of a stir as, hitherto, Neanderthals were widely considered intellectually incapable of such creativity.

As *Homo sapiens* colonised the continent from the east, Andalucía was one of the last regions where the Neanderthals persisted before they became extinct (perhaps they were driven to extinction by *Homo sapiens*). All the mountain ranges in eastern Andalucía have their share of Neolithic remains.

Early history

In the ages to come, humans would flourish in the region due to the mild climate and availability of arable land. Visible remains of human civilization can be found, amongst others, on the banks of the Río Gor near Gorafe, which was an important crossroads of trade routes from the late Stone Age and well into the Bronze Age (route 5). This period also saw the rise of the Tartessian culture in the west and the establishment of Phoenician and Greek trading posts along the Andalusian coast. There were agricultural settlements at the base of the mountains, such as the Sierra Nevada, where the soil was fertile and there was plenty of water.

The decline of the Phoenician culture and the rise of Carthage (itself once a Phoenician dependency) as a naval power in the region eventually ended the trade and the Tartessian culture disappeared with it. These events signalled the beginning of the rivalry between Rome and Carthage. After a series of battles, the Romans displaced the Carthaginians. Over the course of the next two centuries, the Romans conquered, Romanised and developed the entire Iberian peninsula, which they named *Hispania*. During the Roman days, the woodlands in the lowlands gradually gave way to cereal fields and olive groves. Spain's economy developed and bloomed and the peninsula became the primary source of wheat, wool, olives, wine and various metals to the empire. The territory of present-day Andalucía largely fell under the authority of the Roman province of *Baetica*. *Corduba* (Córdoba), *Basti* (near present-day Baza) and *Castulo* (near present-day Linares) were important regional centres. The Romans constructed their famous roads or *vías* which connected the Spanish cities with each other and with the other Roman provinces. One such road ran from the north through the Hoya the Guadix to Almería – a well-preserved stretch of it can be found in the Despeñaperros Natural Park (site C on page 179).

Roman power in the region started to decline in the 4th and 5th centuries. Among the reasons for this decline was an unmanageable migration of northern Germanic tribes into Roman territories. The first of these tribes to reach the Iberian peninsula were the Vandals. In 409 they crossed the Pyrenees and in 425, the Vandals ravaged Andalucía before eventually settling in north-Africa. The Visigoths followed and established a Christian kingdom which eventually covered the entire peninsula.

Moorish rule

In 711, the Visigoth Kingdom rapidly collapsed due to one of the most defining moments in Spain's history: the invasion of the Muslim *Umayyads* from North Africa. In this year, the Berber general Tariq Ibn Ziyad landed a Muslim army at Gibraltar, the name of which is derived from the Arabic *Jebel al-Tariq*, which means Tariq's Mountain). Although the Muslim army may just have been a raiding party, internal strife among the Visigoth nobility had led to great instability in the ranks of the Visigoth army. A year later, the Moors landed another army and swept through the entire Iberian Peninsula, conquering all but a narrow strip of land along the mountainous northern coast.

These events ushered in an age of Moorish dominance on the Iberian Peninsula that lasted in parts of eastern Andalucía for over 800 years (Even though they belonged to different peoples, all North-African Muslims were collectively referred to as Moors by the Europeans).

Córdoba became the capital and the Guadalquivir valley became the hub of Moorish power on the peninsula. *Al-Andalus*, as it was called then, started as a province but broke with the Damascus-based caliphate in 756 to become an independent Muslim state. The period that followed is considered to be the 'golden age' of economic prosperity and cultural enrichment. Córdoba became the largest and wealthiest city of both Europe and the Islamic world. Science and art flourished and the *Mezquita* (Great Mosque) of Córdoba became the symbol of the cultural and economic wealth of *Al-Andalus*. It was also a period of peace and, for the time, a high degree of religious tolerance. Many Christians and Jews lived in relative harmony with the Muslims.

The agricultural economy was greatly boosted when the Arabs brought silk production, sugar cane, citrus fruits and their extensive technical knowledge to the peninsula. Most famously, the Moors introduced the system of irrigation through small channels or *acequías* (derived from the Arabic *as-sāqiya*, which means water conduit). This irrigation system was most elaborate in the Alpujarras and some *acequías* of Moorish origin are still operational (see routes 18 and 19).

Start of the reconquista

In 1031, internal strife ended the Caliphate and its territory disintegrated into several smaller principalities called *taifas*. Meanwhile, in

---

The Despeñaperros pass

The beautiful Despeñaperros pass (site C on page 179) is the natural gateway between eastern Andalucía and Castilla-la Mancha. It is a strategic point protected on all sides by the mountains and has played a decisive role in various battles. One of them took place during the Reconquista. The Almohad Caliphate marched on the invading Christian forces. The kings of Castile, Portugal, Aragón and Navarre realised the gravity of the threat and united their armies, aided by numerous knights from elsewhere in Europe. The caliph's army was encamped on the southern side of the Despeñaperros pass. A local shepherd guided the Christian forces through the pass unseen and they were able to take the numerically superior Muslim army completely by surprise. In the ensuing Battle of Las Navas de Tolosa, the Muslims were completely routed. The caliph himself narrowly escaped capture and fled. During the Napoleonic wars, the Despeñaperros pass was the scene of another battle, this time between the French commander Dupont and the Andalucían army of Francisco Castaños.

the unconquered northern strip of the Iberian Peninsula a sextet of Christian kingdoms (Portugal, Galicia, Navarra, Castilla, Aragón and Asturias-Leon) began to cohere and resist the dominance of the Caliphate. The disintegration into *taifas* encouraged these kingdoms to invade the Muslims lands. In a desperate attempt to prevent being overrun by the Christians in the late 11th century, the *taifas*' princes called on the Berbers for military aid. This halted the Christian expansion but as the Berbers annexed the *taifas* into their own empire, the religious tolerance and economic prosperity ended.

In a long series of battles, the Iberian Peninsula would gradually be recaptured by the Christian kingdoms. This is the period of the *Reconquista* (literally, the recapture). Between the 13th and 15th century, the border was close to the Sierra María – los Vélez. Many *castillos* and fortifications remind of this period.

The final climactic act of the *Reconquista* was the marriage of Ferdinand II of Aragón and Isabella I of Castile in 1469. They, the *Reyes Católicos* (Catholic Monarchs) set their sights on completing the Reconquista. In 1492, after a ten year war, they forced the last Emir of Granada, Muhammad XII to capitulate.

A watchtower in the Sierra Mágina indicates that this was once a borderland between the Moorish caliphate and Christian kingdoms.

Esparto Grass

In eastern Andalucía's most arid regions, the vegetation is often dominated by an interesting plant: Esparto Grass (*Stipa tenacissima*). Because of its strong fibres, Esparto has been used throughout history for a variety of purposes. The earliest recorded use of Esparto dates back to the 6th millennium B.C. In 1958, 50 mummies were found in the Cueva de los Murciélagos in Albuñol, Granada along with esparto sandals, clothing and baskets. The famous Roman historian Pliny the Elder noted that the Roman Empire started cultivating Esparto primarily for rope making after the Second Punic War. The region in which the Esparto Grass was cultivated was called the *Campus Spartarius* (Rope Fields) and it is from this name that the word Esparto is derived. Esparto cultivation continued throughout the Middle-ages. The plants was known in *Al-Andalus* as *Halfa*.

It was only with the advent of synthetic fibres that the cultivation started to decline. Eastern Andalucía's extensive espartales (natural esparto fields) are left largely abandoned, although paper made out of esparto fibre is still highly valued in the printing industry.

Another common and typical species of grass is called False Esparto (*Lygeum spartum*). It is also widespread in the semi-desert areas. The fibre of this plant is similar to that of true Esparto and both plants have been used for the production of the fibres. It is only when the grasses flower that both plants can easily be distinguished from each other.

False Esparto Grass (left) and Esparto Grass (right).

Natural world and land use

The landscape and natural world the *Reyes Católicos* found in eastern Andalucía must have been a mixture of agriculture and husbandry in the plains and wild forests in the mountains. Cereal fields and olive groves dominated the fertile lands of the Guadalquivir basin, while almonds and cereals dominated the *hoyas* and mulberries (the larval food tree for silk moth caterpillars) and horticulture thrived in the Alpujarras. Here and there, mining was important, such as in the dry lands of Almería where in a few of the less hostile areas, a type of subsistence farming supported the few people that lived here.

Sheep were the most important form of livestock and were raised by a system of *transhumance*: in winter the animals grazed the lands at the base of the mountains while in summer, they moved, together with the herdsman and his family, up into the mountains.

The mountains themselves were largely wild and uninhabited. A 16th century account for the woodlands of the María mountains (one of the drier ranges) is that there were Ibex, Red Deer, Roe Deer, Wild Boar, Wolf, Iberian Lynx and even Brown Bears! The few uses of the mountains were hunting, bee-keeping, tapping resin and collecting mushrooms and wild, edible plants and herbs.

The expulsion of the Moriscos

Much changed following the subjugation of the last Emir, both in the towns and the countryside. First, all remaining Muslims were forced to choose between converting to Christianity, exile or death. The Moors who had chosen to remain in Spain would henceforth be referred to as *Moriscos* to denote their Moorish roots. Repeated *Morisco* rebellions against repressive measures centred on the Alpujarras, together with strategic fears over Ottoman expansion in Europe, persuaded King Philip III to decree the expulsion of all *Moriscos* (and Jews) on April 9th 1609. Over the course of a 5-year period, the vast majority of them were expelled or fled although there remained a small core of muslims into the early 1700s until extinguished by the inquisition.

The war and subsequent exiling of the *Moriscos* diminished the population of eastern Andalucía, which was replaced by people from the north – Aragón, Castile, Extremadura.

They brought with them their own customs, livestock and land uses. Sheep farming and transhumance grew in importance. The local *Oveja Segureña* sheep race from the Segura and María mountains is the pride of the region. It is renowned for its adaptation to the harsh mountain climate as well as for its tender meat, but actually it stems from a mixed flock brought in by settlers from Extremadura, Castile and Aragón. With the increase of the flocks, the mountains became more important. Forests were felled on a large scale. In this age of the great sea voyages, the wood was used for ship building. The remaining open land became the summer pasture for the flocks of sheep.

On the coast, things changed as well. Some of the exiled *Moriscos* and Jews would return with a vengeance as they joined the Barbary pirates. Based on the North-African coast, they were the scourge of the western Mediterranean well into the 19th century, attacking ships and raiding coastal towns. Many coastal villages were abandoned and an elaborate system of fortified towers and coastal forts was set up to counter the threat. In case of a raid, beacons on top of the towers would be lit, warning the local population and alerting the garrisons of the forts to the impeding attack. Numerous remains of these towers and fortresses can be found in eastern Andalucía (see routes 1 and 4 and site B in Cabo de Gata).

From 1700 to 1900

The Moriscos were the driving force behind the region's trade, agriculture and crafts. Their expulsion was a setback for the economy. A temporary one, though, as the region would soon profit from the riches from the American colonies, the import of which came almost exclusively through the Andalucían harbours. From the Americas, two new crops found their way onto the land – Sisal and the Prickly Pear. Both originate from the Mexican desert and were grown on a modest scale near Cabo de Gata. Sisal (route 1) is a type of Agava that produces strong fibers that were used as rope for weaving (in which, thanks to Esparto Grass, there was considerable expertise in Spain). The Prickly Pear is the food for the Cochineal, a scale insect which when dried and crushed, produces bright red carmine dye. As the name suggests the plant also produces edible fruits and, thanks to their armoury of thorns, serves as 'biological barbed wire' around fields.

In 1700, King Carlos II died without heir and the French king Louis XIV claimed the throne for his grandson, Philip, who subsequently became King Philip V of Spain. This threatened to make France the dominant power in Europe, so igniting, in the centuries to come, a series of wars and power struggles over this issue. The opening salvo, the War of the Spanish Succession (1701–1714), left eastern Andalucía relatively unscathed. Later Napoleon's determination to control Iberia led first to a Franco-Spanish invasion of Portugal and then to an invasion of Spain itself. Whilst the Anglo-Portuguese army fought conventional battles with the French, the Spanish waged what many regard as the first, and one of the most successful, partisan wars in history. It was here that the term *guerrilla* (small war) was first coined and its tactics defined. This brought much of the fighting to eastern Andalucía.

Although Spain was ultimately victorious in the conflict, the war had left the country in ruins. The economy was in shambles and the Spanish overseas colonies (except Morocco) had freed themselves from their oppressors and were lost for the Spanish economy. It did, however, transform the historical enmity between Spain and England into one of friendship and co-operation.

19th and early 20th Century Spain

Dynastic disputes, laced with tensions between liberal reformers and reactionary forces, resulted in an unsettled and even chaotic period for the hundred years following the accession of Isabella II in 1830. On the one hand supporters of her rival, Infante Carlos, opposed liberalisation, on the other hand, reformers pressed for far more. Neither were satisfied. This was to be the leitmotif for the next century or more with repeated uprisings and social disorder from both left and right.

The 'Disaster of 1898' saw Spain stripped of most of her remaining colonies. It also created still more demand for change and a growing tension between leftwing anarchism and rightwing fascism. Although Spain kept out of World War I, the Rif War in Morocco ultimately led to a military coup in 1923 under Primo de Rivera. Rivera's incompetence as a leader, particularly during the Great Depression (1929), both increased social tensions and discredited the monarchy resulting in the king abdicating and the establishment of a new Republic in 1931.

Civil war and Franco era

The tensions that had bedevilled Spain for a century would culminate in the outbreak in 1936 of the Spanish Civil War between the Republicans and the Nationalists, led by general Franco. At the onset of the conflict, eastern Andalucía (with the exception of Granada) was a republican stronghold. During the war, eastern Andalucía saw only minor military engagements. The Battle of Lopera (Jaén) became famous for the participation of the international brigades – military units fighting on the Republican side made up of volunteers from different countries. Also notable were the bombing of Jaén and the shelling of Almería by the German Navy (the Nazi regime backed Franco).

Franco's Nationalists came out victorious. Under the subsequent totalitarian regime, agriculture and forestry were modernised into large-scale, planned schemes. Large parts of the mountains, in particular areas in the Sierra Nevada and Sierra de Huétor, were planted with coniferous trees. The economic use of the mountains shifted from animal husbandry to forestry. Heavy industries, like automobile production were other important projects under Franco. The key industrial cities were outside eastern Andalucía and many people moved from the countryside to these cities.

With the defeat of his principle sponsors, Fascist Italy and Nazi Germany, in World War II, many expected Franco's regime to collapse. However, as the Cold War increased in intensity, Franco's strong opposition against the communists made him an ally to the western world. At first Franco had pursued a policy of self-sufficiency, restricting almost all international trade, but by the end of the 1950s, under the initiative of the Americans, Franco's economy opened up to the west-European countries. Although politically, Spain remained a pariah fascist dictatorship, the economy was restructured around international trade and services, with heavy industry and (beach) tourism as focal points. The *playas* of eastern Andalucía saw a relatively modest tourist development – the main tourist centres were around Málaga and on the east coast of Spain (Valencia, Catalunya).

After Franco's death in 1975, Spain joined the EU and became a democratic monarchy. Andalucía became one of Spain's 17 autonomous communities. Economically, the service sector (primarily tourism) grew

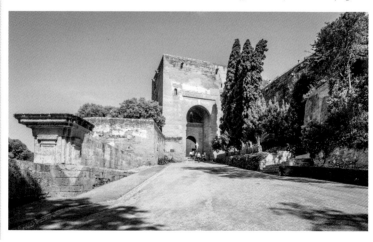

The Alhambra is, together with the Mezquita of Córdoba, the most iconic piece of Moorish architecture in Spain.

rapidly, as did the agricultural sector. With new drilling techniques and the development of cheap plastic polytunnels, the previously unattractive arid plains around Almería became the perfect location for growing peppers, tomatoes and cucumbers on an industrial scale. Almost overnight, the immense greenhouse horticulture spread out across these plains, heralding a new era, one in which we still live: the age in which landscape destruction, biodiversity depletion and environmental problems are in a political arms race with nature conservation and sustainable development efforts.

Nature conservation

Although in east Andalucía Green Tourism has become hugely popular, the area faces a number of serious conservation problems.
In the previous chapters we've shown that the immense diversity in climate and geology gave rise to a high number of different ecosystems, some of which are unique and sport their own flora and fauna. Eastern Andalucía is like an archipelago of ecosystems – each of its 'islands' are relatively small and isolated from places with similar conditions. Isolation of populations and small areas with special ecological conditions are the best conditions for, given time, the development of a unique flora and fauna. But at the same time the inevitably small populations are very sensitive to disturbance. Biologically, many parts of eastern Andalucía are a china shop with not one, but two bulls on the rampage: climate change and a changing land use.

Energy farming, tourism and intensive agriculture – a changing land use

Over the centuries, the landscape of Andalucía has seen its share of changes – the woodlands in the plains became cereal fields and steppes. Some of these later gave way to olive groves. Terracing and the development of the *acequías* allowed small scale agriculture and almond groves, even on steep hillsides. However, these changes were for the most part slow and low key, unlike the drastic changes that have taken place over the last few decades.
The massive, white sea of plastic greenhouses around Almería are the most blatant example of the ecological disaster wrought by 'development' in recent decades. Until the early 1970s, these plains were still open fields with small-scale sheep farming. Today an area of around

20,000 hectares has disappeared under plastic – thereby having the dubious honour of being the only man-made construction that is visible with the naked eye from the moon, discernible as a blinking white spot in the south of Europe. With its warm winter temperatures, good soil and plenty of sunshine, the Almería lowlands are perfect for growing cucumbers, tomatoes and other crops, when under plastic even in winter. The only limitation is the water supply. At the moment, water is pumped up from deep subterranean reservoirs. In spite of the plastic restricting evaporation, the water use is enormous and far exceeds that of the rainfall. Approximately 88% of water use is by agriculture in the Almería region as a whole.

Water use along the coast has also radically increased thanks to the tourism boom. In the middle of the 1960s, Franco declared many coastal areas as 'National Tourist Interest Space' and consequently tourist complexes expanded at the cost of dunes and coastal lagoons. Showers, swimming pools and, above all, water-devouring golf courses are exhausting the aquifers in the coastal region. As a result more and more illegal boreholes have been drilled to satisfy the need of freshwater. The government attempts to shut them down but has been met with fierce opposition.

The waste from the plastic horticulture is another big problem. The few wetlands at the coast are threatened by water polluted with garbage, pesticides and other toxic waste. Here the Squacco Herons have adapted to the new conditions by raising their chicks in largely plastic nests.

The government and agricultural companies are looking at technologies such as desalination plants to meet the water demand. Another hi-tech

The marshes of Cañada de las Norias is marooned in a sea of plastic polytunnels. The extent of these plastic greenhouses is such that they not only usurp the Great Wall of China as the only human structure reputedly visible from the moon but also that they have actually reflected so much sunlight back into space that, against a general increase in temperatures, here they have actually fallen by 0.3°C per decade.

solution is to place dark fabric across a patch of land to absorb the sun's heat. Such a 'heat island' causes a higher rainfall up-wind, mimicking the effect that cities have.

The farmlands in the interior have changed as well. The reduction in the size and number of herds has caused many grasslands, both in the mountains and the steppes, to revert to scrubland. In other places, the land use has been intensified. In some parts above the treeline in the Sierra Nevada, an increase of goat herding has caused overgrazing which threatens the characteristic Alpine flora. Large-scale ploughing in the steppes and pesticide use in the olive groves also causes problems.

Another thorny issue is the use of large areas for renewable energy. The long coastline with its sea breezes and endless hours of sunshine makes the area perfect for wind and solar energy. As much of the land is poor quality farmland, the change to energy-farming seems logical. Add to this the dire need to counteract climate change (the second bull in the china shop) and it appears to be a no-brainer. Hence Spain is now the second largest producer of wind energy in the world.

Sadly, clean, renewable energy comes at a cost. There is growing opposition to the blight they cause on the landscape. In addition, ill-placed wind turbines are a serious (and potentially deadly) hurdle for migratory birds and bats. Similarly, solar energy plants in steppe or semi-desert areas destroys the flora and fauna in the immediate area plus, at least for birds, reduces the amount of available habitat. Badly placed solar panel farms can wipe out the populations of steppe birds on a formerly bird-rich plain. NGOs like the SEO (the Spanish Birdlife partner), are fighting for a greater care in chosing the location of new solar and wind farms, avoiding sensitive migration routes and ZEPAs (Special zones for Bird Protection).

Climate issues

In 2007, the Sierra Nevada Global Change Observatory program began. The main objective is to assess biotic and abiotic information to identify the impact and effects of global climate change. The main results after five years indicate an increase in average temperature of 4.8°C by the end of the 21st century in the Sierra Nevada, a slight decrease in rainfall and a reduction in the duration of snow cover. These outcomes fit the general picture from other sources – eastern Andalucía is becoming hotter and drier. Soon the Sierra Nevada will cease to be 'nevada', at least in summer. Many of the plants in the high reaches, being relict species marooned after the end of the last ice age some 10,000 years ago, are now threatened with extinction. Butterflies and other insects that migrate to the higher altitudes, where their host plants grow will also be threatened. In this way the 'island' of cold-adapted biodiversity threatens to be swallowed by the 'sea' of warm-adapted Mediterranean ecosystems.

More revealing is that the Sierra Nevada Global Change Observatory identified change in land use as an important driver of change in Mediterranean mountains. In the 1950s, overgrazing and charcoal extraction artificially lowered the treeline, normally restricted only by temperature and drought. This had a positive effect on those plants and insects of high mountains that followed the treeline. With the abandonment of these rural activities, oak forests are reclaiming areas to the natural treeline, which itself is also climbing up as a result of climate change. As a result, the four summits of the Sierra Nevada saw an 8% decrease in botanical diversity over the last decades and that percentage appears to be accelerating.

Climate change also prompts the migration of species. Due to its geographical position Andalucía is one of the gateways from Africa to Europe and many species have made the leap across the Pillars of Hercules to colonise the European mainland.

New colonisers are often harmless – an addition to the local biodiversity even. Few naturalists would be concerned at the sight of yet another population of Violet Dropwings, Monarch butterflies or White-rumped Swifts. Every now and then, though, a coloniser, particularly those introduced by human agencies, turn out to be a disruptive species. By disrupting established systems, climate change makes natural regimes more vulnerable to such alien invaders.

Nature conservation efforts

Parallel to this gloomy prospectus of Andalucía's future is a more hopeful one. Nature conservation efforts in this area started early and have achieved a great deal. Many areas are protected under the Habitat Directive or Natura 2000, including the region's twelve nature parks and one National Park, the Sierra Nevada. Many NGO's work to counteract the threats and aim to protect the Andalucían wildlife and landscape. Among the more active organisations are the aforementioned SEO, the *Asociación Española de Entomología, Sociedad Española de Biología de Conservación de Plantas*, WWF-Spain and *Ecologistas en Acción*.

The need for vigilance is nowhere better illustrated than the Algarrobico hotel scandal. Built within the Parque Natural del Cabo de Gata-Níjar and in clear defiance of acts protecting the coast, it took over a decade before the Spanish supreme court declared this twenty story monstrosity illegal in February 2016.

The Spanish approach to nature conservation has overridingly been one in which conservation and economic development should go hand in hand. Conservationists fight against threats concerning poaching, construction of reservoirs, destruction of habitats and for restoration of populations, whilst at the same time arguing for sustainable alternatives of economic development. Ecotourism is one of these alternatives. You, eco-conscious visitor, are a weapon (or in more friendly terms, a tool) in the hands of conservation, as you bring a sustainable form of economic development. This is why so many natural parks have such excellent tourism facilities. On page 221 we give some tips on how to maximise your visit's utility for conservation and in promoting sustainable development (and how to do so in a most rewarding way).

Beware of Iberian Lynx crossing the road. Traffic is an important cause of death in what is one of this endangered species' last strongholds, the Sierra de Andújar.

Perhaps the stress on tourism and education also explains the strong emphasis on emblematic species. There are reintroduction and recovery plans for spectacular species like Lammergeier (in Cazorla – see box on page 86) Iberian Lynx (in Andújar), Crested Coot (in Entinas-Sabinar and Charca de Suárez), Spur-thighed Tortoise (In María – los Veléz) and the Pinsapo Fir (in Sierra Nevada).

The latter seems perhaps an odd-one-out. The Pinsapo (or Spanish Fir) is found only the western Sierra Baetica and in the north of Morocco. It is an ice-age relict that got stuck in these relatively cool mountains as the climate warmed (see our guidebook to western Andalucía for more details). Only 700 hectares of Pinsapo forest remained in 1964. As a result of careful forestry management this size is increased to 5000 hectares today, but experts judge that climate change weakens the species' resistance to fungal infections (a great threat today). Therefore, infected specimens are burnt to prevent the spread of the disease and Pinsapo trees have been replanted in Sierra Nevada and Sierra de Cazorla, away from the natural population and its damaging fungus.

FLORA AND FAUNA

In terms of biodiversity – the total number of species of flora and fauna – eastern Andalucía isn't just rich, it is exceptionally rich. After the world's rainforests, the Mediterranean climes are the most biodiverse terrestrial regions of the world. Worldwide, there are five regions with a Mediterranean climate. The largest one is the Mediterranean basin itself, with the others being in California, Chile, South Africa and southern Australia.

So the Mediterranean region in total hosts many species, but within this region, there are about a dozen diversity hot-spots, particularly for their plantlife. Three of these are to be found in Spain: the Spanish Pyrenees, the coastal mountain ranges of Catalonia and, of course, the Beatic mountains of Andalucía.

The bulk of the eastern Andalucían species are those with a Mediterranean distribution– that is those that encircle the Mediterranean Sea. For birds, reptiles and plants archetypal examples of this are the Sardinian Warbler, Montpellier Snake and the Olive Tree. The latter is often regarded as natural delineation of the Mediterranean ecozone.

These species are richly supplemented by a superb mix of cosmopolitan, Ibero-African and Alpine species, plus lots of local endemics.

To understand this rich melting pot of species, you need to go back in time and look at the geology and climatic fluctuations of the past. Around 6 million years ago, the Beatic mountains formed a string of ranges that were as much African as they were European (see map on page 14). At some point the Iberian Peninsula and Africa were connected through a land bridge across the current Strait of Gibraltar. At this time, the arid climate of south-east Andalucía developed and gave rise to similar habitats in North-Africa and parts of eastern Andalucía. Species of these arid zones on either side of the Straits are many – Wild Jujube Bush* (*Ziziphus lotus*) and Black Wheatear are just two examples. Likewise, some of the mountain plants are found on both sides of the current Mediterranean too. Glacial Eryngo* (*Eryngium glaciale*) is an example of a plant which can be found both in the Sierra Nevada and the Rif mountains in Morocco. Later, in the Quarternary era, a series of cold periods (glacials or 'ice ages') pushed many northern species down into the Mediterranean basin. In the warmer periods (interglacials), these species retreated onto the colder mountain tops which were 'island' refuges, which are therefore sometimes referred to as *Arks of Noah* that safeguard the cold-loving species in a 'sea' of hot lowland. Today, all European mountains are such

Purple Gallinules have increased enormously in Spain in the last few decades. Even in the small wetlands in the dry eastern half of Andalucía, you can admire this fabulous bird with relative ease.

Arks of Noah. The Snow Vole is a good example of one of its passengers – it occurs in the Sierra Nevada, Pyrenees, Sierra de Gredos and Cantabrian Mountains and further in the Alps, Carpathians, Abruzzi mountains and several high ranges in Greece. Glacier Buttercup is another one, occurring only in the very high ranges (Nevada, Pyrenees, Alps) and high up in the Arctic, in Iceland, Greenland and in northern Norway.

Where the simple comparison with Noah's Ark fails is that over tens of thousands of years in isolation, the populations started to evolve into new species. This is a gradual process that moves at a different pace in different species. Sometimes, new cold spells reconnected the isolated populations, resetting the speciation process. This reconnection process was less frequent in the mountains in the deep south, like the Sierra Nevada. Here isolation was greater which explains the exceptionally high level of endemic species and subspecies – the isolated populations have evolved into new species. Apart from wildflowers and beetles, the butterfly fauna of the Sierra Nevada shows a great number of endemics – species and subspecies unique to the Sierra Nevada. Other species are shared only with other mountains in Spain and / or Morocco.

Separated by only a short distance and a narrow sea, but united by a similar climate, new species continue to arrive in Andalucía from Africa at a regular interval. Red-rumped Swallow arrived a century ago, but the pace has recently quickened with White-rumped Swift arriving in the 1960s, Trumpeter Finch in the 1970s, Black-winged Kite in the 1980s (albeit via Portugal and Extremadura), Little Swift in the 1990s with Common Bulbul seemingly trying to follow in this century. Quite spectacular too is the spread of dragonflies. Since old records are scarce for this species group, the recorded changes are more recent, but perhaps even more remarkable. Violet Dropwing was recorded in the 19th century but numbers only really took off in the 1950s and it has now spread into France, Italy and southern Greece. Long Skimmer was first discovered in 1980 and has spread to lowland Central Spain (the coast, Extremadura). Orange-winged Dropwing was first recorded only in 2007(!) and has now spread over most of Andalucía.

Climate change is likely to be a driver behind these new colonisations (see conservation chapter). Even though it is hard (or impossible) to tell how it prompts individual species to 'take the flight north', there is a clear increase in colonisations largely by southern species expanding north and not vice versa. A few Andalucían species are human introductions, either accidental or deliberate. The small butterfly Geranium Bronze is the most conspicuous example.

Main biogeographical regions in eastern Andalucía

(West)-Mediterranean region
e.g. Subalpine Warbler
(Sylvia cantillans)

Ibero-African region
e.g. Caralluma
(Caralluma europaea)

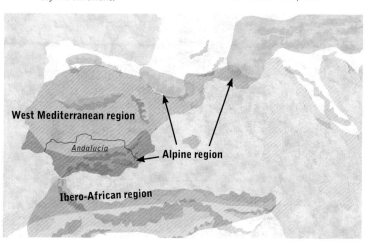

West Mediterranean region

Andalucia

Alpine region

Ibero-African region

Relict species or recent colonists from other biogeographical regions

Alpine region
e.g. Alpine accentor
(Prunella collaris)

Local endemics
e.g. Spanish Brassy Ringlet
(Erebia hispania)

Recent colonists
e.g. Violet Dropwing
(Trithemis annulata)

FLORA AND FAUNA

Flora

The most attractive semi-desert flora is seen on routes 1, 2, 3 and site A, B and C on page 130-131. Botanically rich limestone routes are 8, 9,10, 15 and site A on page 167 and site A on page 212. The flora of the hedgehog zone is present on routes 5, 6, 7 and 10. The unique flora of the Sierra Nevada can be explored on routes 17, 18, 19 and site A on page 204. Orchid aficionados should focus on routes 8, 15, 20 site A and C on page 212-213.

Andalucía is one of the richest botanical regions of Spain, only rivalled by the Pyrenees and their foothills. A good deal of the region's richness is found in the east, where wildflowers of semi-deserts can be found in close vicinity to Alpine species.

As is to be expected with such a wide range of environmental conditions, wildflowers in each area flower at different times in the year. Eastern Andalucía is one of the very few areas in Europe that have wildflowers in bloom throughout the year, with sand-crocuses *(Androcymbium)* and White Hoop-petticoat Daffodils* *(Narcissus cantabricus)* flowering at the coast in January and the peaks of the Sierra Nevada coming in bloom in late June.

Botanical islands

The concept of 'biological islands', as outlined in the introduction (page 63), is particularly applicable to the flora. The main botanical hotspots are the isolated peaks of the Sierra Nevada, the Sierras of Huétor, María and Cazorla plus the desert basin of Cabo de Gata and Desierto de Tabernas. The metaphorical 'sea' between these islands of endemism has much less to offer.

The radically different combinations of soil type, temperature and rainfall give each of these areas a distinctive plant life.

For the visiting naturalist, the flora of eastern Andalucia flora has two sides. On the one hand there are the endemic species – localised, highly specialised plants, much celebrated by local conservationists. This element of the Andalucían flora is for the *connoisseurs* – its rareness is not, as you may perhaps expect, readily apparent. Many of the local endemics are variants of familiar species of brooms and members of the cress-family *(Brassicacea)* – not easily distinguished from the familiar species. They are not plants whose unique beauty or odd appearance will bowl you over, not least because without specialised (Spanish) identification keys,

you simply won't recognise many of them.

Yet there are also many flowers that are immediately attractive, like the masses of flashy rockroses, the drifts of daffodils, the heavily scented brooms, and of course the orchids. Although the bulk of these flowers is not unique to this region, they will still be the great draw for many visitors. Only a few wildflowers score in both categories, being both rare regional specialities and highly attractive, easily distinguished species. Eight of these we have paid particular attention to in the pages that follow.

In spite of its barren appearance, the desert is actually a superb wildflower habitat, with species such as Sea Heath and Almería Sea-lavender (top) and Almería Rockrose (bottom).

In this chapter, we will focus on each of these botanical 'islands', first describing the common and conspicuous wildflowers and end with a brief description of the local endemics that are the prize draws.

8 plant species to look out for

< Caralluma

Caralluma europaea
This curious plant is native to North Africa and the Middle East and has its only European sites in the semi-deserts of Almería and in southern Sicily. It is the only native plant in Europe with a cactus-like growth form – no leaves and a suc- culent stem. Rare on dry, volcanic rock in Cabo de Gata (route 2; site A and B on page 130). The closely related *Caralluma munbyana* is found in northern Murcia.

Maltese Fungus >

Cynomorium coccineum
The Maltese Fungus is another strange plant with- out leaves. The dark, dense-flowered parasitic spe- cies is more reminiscent of a fungus than a plant. It is widespread in the southern Mediterranean but usually absent or very rare. In eastern Andalucía it is locally common in sandy areas (route 1 and 5).

< Almeria Sea-lavender*

Limonium insigne
One of several sea-lavenders in the region. Almeria Sea-lavender is endemic to south-east Spain, grow- ing in dry barrancos (route 1, 2, 5).

< Cistanche

Cistanche pelyphea
Another parasitic plant, stout and with bright yellow flowers. It is quite common in saline soils along the Andalucían coast (route 4, 5).

< Hedgehog Broom
Erinacea anthyllis
A rounded, spiny bush of the broom family, flowering spectacularly in May-June. It is confined to the east and south of Spain and is very typical of the hedgehog broom zone (see page 41). Dry, limestone mountain slopes above 1,000 metres (routes 5, 6, 7, 10 and 11).

Cazorla orchid >
Orchis cazorlensis
A robust orchid, closely related to Spitzel's Orchid of the mountains of central Europe, but this species is restricted to the Sierra Cazorla and a few other sites in Spain with snow cover in winter. Open mountain woodlands (route 8).

< Eelgrass-leaved Butterwort*
Pinguicula vallisneriifolia
A pretty butterwort species, endemic to the Cazorla mountains, where it grows on permanently wet limestone cliffs (route 9).

< Cazorla Violet
Viola cazorlensis
An atypical-looking but pretty pink violet that forms (in contrast to other violets) a small bush. It is confined to the mountains of south-east Spain where it grows on dry limestone cliffs (route 8; site A on page 167).

Limestone supports a lot of drought-adapted plants that are unique to south-east Spain and nearby Morocco. Two conspicuous ones are Boissier's Bindweed (top) and Woolly Viper's-Bugloss (bottom) both covered in long white hairs to reflect the bright sunlight.

Flora of the Limestone Sierras

The most exuberant and eye-pleasing flora is probably found in the limestone mountains of the Sierra de Cazorla, Segura y las Villas, the Sierra de Huétor, Magína and María-Vélez. Although each of these areas have some characteristics unique to that specific spot, what they share is a showy, Mediterranean flora – one found too in the Sierra Baetica in western Andalucía and the limestone mountains in eastern Spain, up into Catalonia.

The scrublands up to roughly 1,300 metres are a burst of colour in spring. The large, pink flowers of the Grey-leaved Cistus compete with the deep green leaves of the Dwarf Fan Palm, purple-pink spikes of Wild Rosemary bushes and the bright blue of Blue Aphyllanthes and Beautiful Flax. Not infrequently, these scrublands are the haunts of attractive orchids with Dull Bee, Yellow Bee and Mirror Orchids growing in profusion, joined locally

by Southern Early-purple, Giant and Man Orchids. We found the richest orchid sites in the Sierra de Huétor, where Sawfly, Spanish Omega, Naked-man, Fan-lipped and Pink Butterfly Orchids can also be found.

Shadier places frequently have swathes of wild daffodils (in particular Rush-leaved Jonquil and Pallid Narcissus), White Asphodel and, locally, Western Peony, Violet Bird's-nest and Dense-flowered Orchids. Narrow-leaved and Red Helleborines brighten the undergrowth of the more open forests.

When exploring the limestone sierras, always check valley bottoms, riverbanks and other wet places. In spring, these are excellent places for narcissi and (in Cazorla) for two of the rarest orchids: the Cazorla Orchid (*Orchis cazorlensis*) and the Algerian Butterfly Orchid (*Platanthera algeriensis*). Much more common and widespread, yet very attractive, is the Robust Marsh-orchid, whose tall pink spikes grace the wetter spots.

Above the tree limit (1,200 – 2,000 m) the hedgehog vegetation (page 41) replaces the woodlands. It sports a unique flora of tussock-forming, ground-hugging species adapted to harsh environmental conditions. The domed, dense bushes are frequently spiny to ward off herbivores. Many of these 'hedgehog' species are restricted to the mountains of the east and south-east part of the peninsula. Some are also found in the mountains of the Maghreb. The blue-flowering Hedgehog Broom (p. 69) is the dominant plant, locally joined by Spiny Vella* (*Vella spinosa*), Spiny Alison* (*Hormatophylla spinosa*) and Evergreen Milkvetch* (*Astragalus giennensis*), all of which have a similar form. Between the bushes, there are other typical wildflowers of the habitat, often in good numbers, such as the beautifully painted Cazorla Stork's-bill* (*Erodium cazorlanum*), Stinking Hellebore and Rush-leaved Jonquil. In the higher reaches of the Sierra de Cazorla, the ground-hugging, Silver-leaved Bindweed* (*Convolvulus boisierii*) is a local speciality. Orchids are less common here, but widespread species like Mirror and Dull Bee Orchid may still be found.

The cliffs and gorges are another wildflower haunt. Again, the Sierras de Cazorla and nearby Sierra de Segura are the most attractive spots, where attractions such as Cazorla Violet and Eelgrass-leaved Butterwort* (*Pinguicula vallesneriifolia*; p. 69) can be found.

The best season to explore the limestone mountains is between March and June. The lower areas, in particular those exposed, southern slopes come into flower early, peaking in March and April. The hedgehog broom zone starts flowering in early May and continues to be of interest well into June.

The vegetation above roughly 1200 metres (depending somewhat on the particular sierra) is covered with a vegetation of spherical, spiny bushes, adapted to drought, high grazing pressure and solar radiation. Most shrubs are unique to this vegetation zone, such as *Vella spinosa* (top) and *Hormatophylla spinosa* (bottom).

Frequent wildflowers of the limestone mountains

Scrublands Dwarf Fan Palm (*Chamaerops humilis*), Wild Rosemary (*Rosmarinus officinalis*), Rosemary Broomrape (*Orobanche latisquama*), Grey-leaved Cistus (*Cistus albidus*), Sage-leaved Cistus (*Cistus salvifolius*), Lavender-leaved Sage (*Salvia lavandulifolia*), Blue Aphyllanthes (*Aphyllanthes monspeliensis*), Rusty Toadflax (*Linaria aeruginea*), Beautiful Flax (*Linum narbonense*), asphodels (*Asphodelus spp.*), Dull Bee Orchid (*Ophrys fusca*), Spanish Omega Orchid (*Ophrys dyris*), Yellow Bee Orchid (*Ophrys lutea*), Mirror Orchid (*Ophrys speculum*), Pink Butterfly Orchid (*Anacamptis papilionacea*)

Pine woods Liverleaf (*Hepatica nobilis*), Stinking Hellebore (*Helleboris foetidus*), Western Peony (*Paeonia broteroi*), Spurge-laurel (*Daphne laureola*), Box (*Buxus sempervirens*), Rush-leaved Jonquil (*Narcissus assoanus*), Pallid Narcissus (*Narcissus pallidulus*), Red Helleborine (*Cephalanthera rubra*), Narrow-leaved Helleborine (*Cephalanthera longifolium*), Cazorla Orchid (*Orchis cazorlensis*), Southern Early-purple Orchid (*Orchis olbiensis*), Man Orchid (*Orchis anthropophora*), Dense-flowered Orchid (*Neotinea maculata*), Naked-man Orchid (*Orchis italica*)

Hedgehog zone Hedgehog Broom (*Erinacea anthyllis*), Spiny Vella* (*Vella spinosa*), Spiny Alison* (*Hormatophylla spinosa*), Andalucian Alison* (*Hormatophylla baetica*), Boissier's Milkwort (*Polygala boissieri*), Silver-leaved Bindweed (*Convolvulus boissieri*), Genista longipes, Genista pseudopilosa, Evergreen Milkvetch* (*Astragalus giennensis*), Erodium cazorlanum, Aragon Restharrow (*Ononis aragonensis*), Olive-leaved Daphne (*Daphne oleoides*)

Cliffs Snapdragon (*Antirrhinum majus*), Cazorla Violet (*Viola cazorlensis*), Fairy Foxglove (*Erinus alpinus*), Saxifraga carpetana, Southern Polypody (*Polypodium cambricum*), Scilla cazorlensis, Saxifraga rigoi, Saxifraga camposii, Antequera Toadflax* (*Linaria anticaria*), Campanula velutina, Maidenhair Fern (*Adiantum capillus-veneris*), Rustyback Fern (*Asplenium ceterach*), Eelgrass-leaved Butterwort* (*Pinguicula vallesneriifolia*; wet cliffs), Sarcocapnos baetica, Pyrenean Columbine (*Aquilegia pyrenaica*)

Flora of the Sierra Nevada

With peaks of well over 3,000 m, the Sierra Nevada has an Alpine flora on its peaks while its lower flanks are covered in a Mediterranean vegetation. As a rule of thumb, the flora gets more exciting as you gain altitude, thus reflecting the idea that the Alpine environments on the Sierra Neveda form an ecological 'island'.

The peak flora consists for the larger part of familiar Arctic-Alpine groups like saxifrages, rock-jasmines and gentians, which evolved into species unique to the Nevada.

Before climbing to the botanical treasure trove of the high Nevada, it is worth spending some time on the lower slopes. Roughly between the altitudes of 1,300 to 1,600 m the natural vegetation consists of Holm and Portuguese Oaks, but they are largely replaced by conifer plantations (of limited interest) and a rockrose dominated scrubland. The rockrose scrub is rather different from that of the limestone soils. Instead of Grey-leaved Cistus, it is Gum, Sage-leaved, Laurel-leaved and Narrow-leaved Cistus that dominate the slopes. When these all flower in mid-April and May, they are a feast for the eye. What is noteworthy here is that this vegetation is uncommon in these parts of Spain. Rather, it is similar to that of the Sierra Morena and parts of central Iberia.

Moving up to an altitude of 1,600 – 2,500 m, the natural woodland is dominated by Pyrenean Oak with Scots Pine on limestone outcrops. Where woodland peters out, hedgehog scrub takes over with a wide variety of shrubs, including Hedgehog Broom, Evergreen Milkvetch (*Astragalus giennensis*), *Genista versicolor*, Granada Cotoneaster* (*Cotoneaster granatensis*) and Spanish Barberry* (*Berberis hispanica*). On limestone soils, look for the beautiful Woolly Viper's-bugloss* (*Echium albicans*). Wet grasslands are the haunt of Nevada Daffodil and Spanish St Bernard's Lily* (*Anthericum baeticum*).

Above 2,500 metres, the botanical highlights of the Nevada flora are to be found. Between the rocks there is Nevada Saxifrage, Spiny Alison* (*Hormatophylla spinosa*), Nevada Houseleek* (*Sempervivum minutum*) and Nevada Violet* (*Viola crassiuscula*). Some of these grow on acidic soils, found around the Mulhacén massif (see route 19), whilst others prefer the limestone pockets beneath the Pico Véleta.

In depressions in the landscape the high altitude peatlands or *borreguiles* (see page 32), form another wildflower haunt. This is where you'll find Spanish Gentian* (*Gentiana boryi*), Nevada Speedwell* (*Veronica turbicola*) and Nevada Butter-wort* (*Pinguicula nevadensis*).

The highest zone of the Sierra Nevada boasts a curious mix of endemic species (the vast majority) and those that also occur in the Arctic and Alps. Glacier Buttercup (top) belongs to the latter, whilst Cold Fleabane (centre) and Nevada Toadflax (bottom) are endemics.

Flora of the Sierra Nevada
Mediterranean flora (up to 1,600m) Gum Cistus (*Cistus ladenifer*), Cistus clusii, Grey-leaved Cistus (*C. albidus*), Sage-leaved Cistus (*C. salvifolius*), Andalucían Birthwort* (*Aristolochia baetica*), Yellow Hypocist (*Cytinus hypocistus*), Sunset Foxglove (*Digitalis obscura*)
Hedgehog and upper pine forest flora (1,600-2,500m) Nevada Cinquefoil* (*Potentilla nevadensis*), Spiny Alison* (*Hormatophylla spinosa*), Spiny Vella* (*Vella spinosa*), Hedgehog Broom (*Erinacea anthyllis*; limestone), Evergreen Milkvetch (*Astragalus giennensis*), Genista versicolor, Granada Cotoneaster (*Cotoneaster granatensis*), Spanish Barberry (*Berberis hispanica*), Bearberry (*Arctostaphyllos uva-ursi*), Woolly Viper's-bugloss (*Echium albicans*; limestone), Nevada Daffodil (*Narcissus nevadensis*), Spanish St Bernard's Lily (*Anthericum baeticum*).
Peak flora (above 2,500m) Purple Alison* (*Hormatophylla purpureum*), Glacial Eryngo* (*Eryngium glaciale*), Nevada Saxifrage (*Saxifraga nevadensis*), Nevada Violet (*Viola crassiucula*), Nevada Toadflax (*Chaenorhinum glareosum*), Glacial Toadflax (*Linaria glacialis*), Glacier Buttercup (*Ranunculus glacialis*), Pyrenean Poppy (*Papaver lapeyrousianum*), Erodium cheilanthifolium, Vandelli's Rock-jasmine* (*Androsace vandellii*), Wilkomm's Bellflower* (*Campanula wilkommii*), Vitaliana (*Androsace vitaliana*), Cold Fleabane (*Erigeron frigidus*)
Borreguiles: Snowy Plantain* (*Plantago nivalis*), Nevada Thrift* (*Armeria splendens*), Nevada Butterwort* (*Pinguicula nevadensis*), Starry Saxifrage (*Saxifraga stellaris*), Nevada Speedwell* (*Veronica turbicola*), Sorrel-leaved Buttercup (*Ranunculus acetosellifolius*), Narrow-leaved Buttercup* (*Ranunculus angustifolius*), Marsh Gentian* (*Gentiana pneumonanthe*), Sierra Gentian* (*Gentiana sierrae*)

The south-Spanish Thymelea is often called by its Spanish name *Probayernos*, literally the son-in-law test. The roots and branches are so tough that it takes a huge effort to pull the plant out of the ground – an ideal test for whether a man was worthy of your daughter's hand.

Flora of the Semi-deserts

If you thought desert-like areas are poor in wildflowers, a visit to the Almería province will set you straight. To fully appreciate this region, you need to be there in winter or spring (January to May), when you'll encounter a dazzling number of wildflowers, many of which you won't find elsewhere in Spain or even the world.

The diversity in soil types is in no small part responsible for this richness. The volcanic rocks of Cabo de Gata, the Gypsum soils of Yesos de Sorbas (*Yesos* is Spanish for Gypsum), the sands and saline soils of the coasts and the sandstones of the Desierto de Tabernas each have a slightly different flora. Cabo de Gata Snapdragon* (*Antirrhinum charidemi*) grows only in Cabo de Gata, Tabernas Sea-lavender* (*Limonium tabernense*) is endemic to the Desierto, while the splendid Whorl-leaved Narcissus* (*Narcissus tortifolius*) is a typical gypsum plant.

Most of the dry semi-desert hillsides are covered in low bushes, usually known by their Spanish names *tomillar* and *espartal*, after the plants that dominate the vegetation – *tomillo* (thyme and closely related labiates) and esparto grass. The *tomillares* appear dusty, scorched wastelands, but at closer inspection, they have a high diversity of dwarf shrubs, particularly members of the labiate (mint) family, like horehounds (*Marrubium, Balota*), lavenders (*Lavandula*), thymes (*Thymus*), germanders (*Teucrium*), ironworts (*Sidiritis*) and Jerusalem-sages (*Phlomis*). Another typical species of these slopes is Almería Rockrose, a dwarf bush, much lower than the rockroses in the mountains. It grows together with various yellow-flowered rockrose species of the genus *Fumana*.

There are also Carob Trees, Dwarf Fan Palms and the tough Esparto Grasses. Don't confuse them with the False Esparto grass, which' nodding spike and white, papery leaves are a sight on the dry slopes. They make a very scenic image against the low rays of the setting sun. Your appreciation for this grass will soon fade when you walk through an area with False

Some plants will stop you in your tracks due to their bright flowers. The sand-crocus *Romulea bulbocodium* is definitely among them – all the more so because it grows in otherwise rather colourless semi-deserts.

76

The Small-leaved Iceplant is the only member of this largely South-African plant group that is native to Europe. It is common in the salt flats of Cabo de Gata, where it grows together with other introduced iceplants.

Cabo de Gata Snapdragon* is one of the endemic plants of Cabo de Gata.

Esparto and notice that the sharp, screw-shaped needles drill themselves into your socks and flesh. A very effective way to learn that not all grasses disperse via the wind – some have other means of transportation: you. Both Esparto and False Esparto were used for decades to weave baskets – it was already one of the main natural resources of the region in Roman times (see box on page 52).

In the Cabo de Gata area, the hillsides support some other attractive shrubs and herbs, unique to the south-east of Spain and North-Africa. Look for the odd flowers and strange, two-horned fruits of the Spanish Silk-vine (*Periploca angustifolia*), Bean-caper and Aizoon.

Notwithstanding the attractive shrubs on these slopes, it is the dry ravines, (the *ramblas* and *barrancos*) where wild-flower lovers will want to spend most of their time. Between the pretty bushes of Wild Oleander you'll find some endemic beauties like Almería Sea-lavender (*Limonium insigne*), the pink cabbage *Moricandia moricandioides*, Almería Rockrose, and Sea Mallow. Two curious parasitic plants are true eyecatchers: one is the flashy yellow Cistanche, a relative of broom-rapes and the other is Maltese Fungus (p. 68). The latter is a dark reddish, sometimes almost black, phallic in shape. By the doctrine of signatures (the idea that a plant's shape hints to the bodypart it is a cure for) the

Tomillares (and roadsides in semi-deserts) Purple Poppy (*Roemeria hybrida*), Esparto Grass (*Stipa tenacissima*), False Esparto Grass (*Lygeum spartum*), Iberian Jerusalem Sage (*Phlomis lychnitis*), Purple Jerusalem Sage (*Phlomis purpurea*), *Satureja obovata, Teucrium capitatum, Teucrium compactum,* Hairy Ironwort (*Sideritis hirsuta*), Hairy Horehound (*Ballota hirsuta*), *Marrubium alysson,* Thyme-leaved Rockrose (*Fumana thymifolia*), Fumana ericoides, Fumana laevipes, Narrow-leaved Cistus (*Cistus monspelliensis*), *Helianthemum syriacum, Helianthemum violaceum, Ulex canescens,* Bolina Greenweed* (Genista spartioides), *Lapiedra fontanesii,* Spanish Coris* (*Coris hispanica*)

Sandy and saline areas (dunes and ramblas) Wild Oleander (*Nerium oleander*), Maltese Fungus (*Cynomorium coccineum*), Yellow Cistanche (*Cistanche pelyphea*), Almería Toadflax (*Helianthemum almeriense*), Linaria nigricans, Sea-heath (*Frankenia corymbosa*), Curry Plant (*Helichrysum stoechas*), Canary Boxthorn (*Lycium intricatum*), *Silene secundiflora, Silene litorrea,* Opposite-leaved Saltwort (*Salsola oppositifolia*), Andalucian Saltwort* (*Salsola papillosa*), Lobe-leaved Sea-lavender* (*Limonium lobatum*), Almeria Sea-lavender (*Limonium insigne*), Winged Sea-lavender (*Limonium sinuatum*), Iceplant (*Mesembryanthemum crystallinum*), Small-leaved Iceplant* (*Mesembryanthemum nodiflorum*), Almeria Sand-crocus (*Androcymbium europeum*), Yellow Horned-poppy (*Glaucium flavum*), Sea Daffodil (*Pancratium maritimum*), Coris (*Coris monspelliensis*)

Cabo de Gata region Wild Jujube Bush* (*Ziziphus lotus*), Caralluma (*Caralluma europaea*), Maytenus senagelensis, Cut-leaved Lavender (*Lavandula multifida*), Probayernos (*Thymelaea hirsuta*), Gold-coin (*Pallenis maritima*), Cabo de Gata Snapdragon (*Antirrhinum charidemi*), Charidem's Pink (*Dianthus charidemi*)

Maltese Fungus was considered a cure for erectile dysfunction in folk medicine.

The final plant-hunting area is the coastal strip of Cabo de Gata and Cañada de las Norias– both the rocky coast and the dunes. In particular the short coastal stretch between the Rambla Morales and San José (routes 1 and 2) is a botanical heaven. The sandy and saline parts are alive with various sea-lavenders (in particular Winged – Limonium sinuatum), Sea-heath, Wild Jujube Bush* (Ziziphus lotus), Branched Restharrow* (Ononis ramosissima), Gold-coin, and Curry Plant. In saline wastelands, you'll find masses of the curious Iceplants, which appear to be covered in dew, but the 'droplets' are in fact glands that prevent evaporation. There are also various endemic wildflowers here, such as Cabo de Gata Snapdragon* (Antirrhinum charidemi) and Charidem's Pink* (Dianthus charidemi).

Mammals

Spanish Ibex are quite common and often seen on routes 3, 8, 9, 10, 11, 12, 15, 19 and site C on page 179. Red Deer are common on route 5, 8, 13 and site C on page 179, while Wild Boar and Mouflon are often seen on routes 8 and 13. Smaller animals occur throughout. Route 8 is particularly rewarding for Red Fox, Red Squirrel and other small animals. Route 13 is entirely devoted to tracking down Iberian Lynx, but Egyptian Mongoose is also frequently seen here.

Mammals, usually so secretive, are quite in evidence in many parts of eastern Andalucía. Bigger grazing animals like Wild Boar and Red and Fallow Deer, are in some places, common and tame. Herds of Wild Ibex are a frequent sight high up in the Nevada, while a glimpse of the very rare and sought-after Iberian Lynx is, though not easy, a distinct possibility if you make a determined effort in those few areas where it's found (see page 170).

The Spanish Ibex is a remarkable animal. In contrast to its Alpine cousin, it occurs in mountains from sea level to the highest peaks of the Sierra Nevada.

Herbivores

There are six hooved herbivores (ungulates) in eastern Andalucía: Spanish Ibex, Red Deer, Fallow Deer, Roe Deer, Mouflon and Wild Boar. The Spanish Ibex is endemic to the Iberian Peninsula. With flexible

hooves and short legs it can run smoothly over rocky slopes. The males have horns that sweep backwards and to the side in an impressive arc, making them fancy hunting trophies, something that almost caused their extinction. Fortunately, hunting is now restricted and Spanish Ibex has become a fairly commonplace sight in many areas in the south and east of Andalucía.

Unlike its Alpine cousin, the Spanish Ibex is not restricted to the high mountains. Any quiet, mountainous terrain, from sea-level up to 3400 m, may harbour Ibex. We even found them in the Desierto de Tabernas!

Red Deer are native to the region, but numbers are often unnaturally high as they are a prized hunting trophy (and therefore released to boost the numbers and maximize the hunting success). They can be numerous in fenced hunting areas as well as in protected areas such as the Sierra de Cazorla. The smaller Fallow Deer inhabit major parts of Sierra de Andújar, Despeñaperros and Cazorla. They generally occur in scrubland, woodland edges or near rivers. The Roe Deer that is so common in temperate Europe, is still rare in eastern Andalucía, but numbers are increasing rapidly.

Andalucía's first Mouflons were introduced from Corsica (where they themselves were introduced in Neolithic times) for hunting in the Sierra de Cazorla in 1954. Ever since, more herds dwell in vast fenced areas intended for hunting. Lastly, the Wild Boar is abundant and widespread, particularly in places with underbrush to hide in. They are largely nocturnal. In places, it crossbreeds with free-roaming pigs. These 'wild pigs' (*cerdo asilvestrado*) can be more numerous than 'pure' Wild Boar.

Carnivores

Eastern Andalucía harbours a whole array of small carnivorous animals, plus two very rare top predators: the Iberian Lynx and the Wolf.

The Iberian Lynx is smaller and more tawny coloured than the European Lynx, and has a beautiful 'leopard pattern' coat. These are adaptations to a different habitat (open scrubland and parkland instead of forests) and a different prey. Iberian lynxes are Rabbit hunters. They are endemic to the peninsula and critically endangered. Only two natural populations persist, although an extensive recovery programme has boosted numbers somewhat and recently, Lynxes have been reintroduced in other places in Spain and Portugal. The Sierra de Andújar (route 13) is the best place on earth to observe this unique animal.

The Wolves are virtually never seen and sources are conflicting: some claim it is extinct, but according to others, a small population persists in

80

Iberian Lynx

The history of Iberian Lynx is a dramatic one, but nevertheless one with a hopeful ending. At the end of the 19th century it was widespread on the Iberian Peninsula. Today, Andalucía is its only stronghold. How could things have come to such a pass?

The Iberian Lynx habitat is one of Holm Oak forests with dense undergrowth, alternated with open areas. Lynx require large territories with a healthy Rabbit population. A single animal may explore over 10 km a day and will defend a large territory of up to 20 km². It uses a variety of hunting techniques, all based on ambushing the prey from dense vegetation.

Well into the 20th century, all carnivores were considered a pest and could freely be hunted, causing, as the human population rose, a steady decline of the Lynx. In the 1950s, the disease myxomatosis, caused the population of Rabbits to collapse, and with it that of the Lynx. Parallel to this, the creation of reservoirs, eucalyptus and pine plantations both destroyed and fragmented the natural habitat of both. In search of prey, Lynxes had to cover greater distances,

Iberian Lynx, reputed to be the world's rarest and most threatened feline.

the remoter parts of the Sierra. Lynx researchers in Sierra de Andújar recently caught female Wolves with their cubs on camera (meant for monitoring the Iberian Lynx). Nobody knows whether these animals were just passing through, are recolonising or represent a relict population.

In contrast, the Red Fox is almost everywhere, reaching even the 3,000m mark in the Sierra Nevada! It is often seen and sometimes even tame. Of the smaller predators, Weasel, Polecat, Beech Marten, Badger, Otter, Egyptian Mongoose, Genet and Wild Cat are all present. Many of them are widespread, mostly in the mountains. The Otter is restricted to the rivers of the Sierra Tejeda and the Sierra Morena. The sleek, diurnal Egyptian Mongoose was introduced from North Africa by the Moors. It thrives in scrublands, with the highest numbers in Sierra Morena and Cazorla. Seeing it remains a matter of luck – occasionally it chooses to cross a road or track just when you happen to be there. The Genet also originates from Africa. This handsome feline with its black spots and lines on a grey coat is fairly common in the wooded parts of our sierras. It shares its habitat with the Wild Cat.

which, due to road and railway construction, became an increasingly dangerous undertaking.

In 1970s the alarm was raised: the Iberian Lynx had disappeared completely from the north and east of the country and the populations that remained were isolated and separated. Only 1100 lynxes were left in 1988, the majority in two large populations: Coto Doñana in western Andalucía in the Sierra de Andújar in northern Andalucía. In the same year came another hammer blow in the form of a second disease, the Rabbit Haemorrhagic Disease, which reduced the rabbit population still further.

In 1996 a large-scale conservation project was started to restore habitat, create ecological corridors between existing populations, prevent poaching and reduce traffic casualties. Only in 2006 did the tide start to turn. With EU-funding, public campaigns, speed reductions on minor roads, construction of wildlife crossings, an increase in Rabbit populations and, above all, captive breeding programs have boosted the numbers of Lynx. Recently, individuals were reintroduced to bolster the existing populations and establish new ones in Castilla – La Mancha, Extremadura and in Portugal. The current population has doubled since 2006 to more than 300 individuals, while the breeding centres hold a good genetic stock.

The Lynx is not out of the woods yet, though. Roads keep taking their toll and habitat fragmentation has not been halted. You can follow the fortunes of the Iberian Lynx on **www.lifelince.org** and **www.iberlince.eu**.

Smaller mammals

Shrews, voles and mice live everywhere in eastern Andalucía. Among the many species, we should mention the Snow Vole that lives in rocky areas high up in the Sierra Nevada (over 2,000m) . It is a relict species of the high mountains of Europe that was stranded here on this 'cold island' after the ice ages (see page 63). Climate change is currently threatening its existence (see page 59).

Most mice and shrews live in the woodlands, scrub and arable lands, but a few have a more peculiar choice of habitat. The Mediterranean Water Shrew and Southern Water Vole live on riverbanks and hunt in the rivers that flow from Sierra Nevada, Cazorla and Despeñaperros. The Garden Dormouse prefers shrubs and low trees in the lowlands, where it runs agilely over branches. Red Squirrels are restricted to the woodlands of the Sierra Nevada, Despeñaperros, Sierra de Tejeda and Cazorla, where it can be numerous. It was reintroduced in the Sierra de Baza.

The ranges of two species of hedgehog meet in eastern Andalucía. The Common Hedgehog is quite rare except for humid riverine and mountain forests, while the Algerian Hedgehog prefers dry places below 600 m, both cultivated and natural.

Both Rabbit and Iberian Hare are quite common. Rabbits occur up to 1,500m. The highest densities are found in relatively flat lands with scrub and grasslands. The Rabbit population has seen enormous fluctuations in recent years due to the outbreak of a series of rabbit diseases (see text box on Lynx). As it is such an important prey species for vulnerable predators like Iberian Lynx, Spanish Imperial and Bonelli's Eagles, conservationists follow the fortunes of the Rabbit population carefully. Finally, the Iberian Hare, an inhabitant of open country, is endemic to Spain and Portugal.

Due to mild winters, bats are active almost throughout the year. There are many species, of which Lesser and Greater Horse-shoe Bats, Grey Long-eared and Lesser-mouse-eared Bat and Schreiber´s Bat are most numerous. The small bats that flutter around in villages are most likely Soprano Pipistrelles, a species that is smaller than the Common Pipistrelle that takes its place in temperate Europe.

The Brown Hare of northern Europe is replaced here by a different species, the Iberian Hare, which is smaller and has a white belly.
Wild Boar is common in some mountain ranges such as Cazorla. It is a much appreciated game animal.

Birds

Birds of semi-deserts, steppes and arid plains are found on routes 1, 2, 3, 5, 6, and sites A and B on page 130. Birds of limestone mountains and cliffs are best tracked down on routes 7, 8, 10, 11, 14 and site A on page 167 and site A on page 212. These are generally also good for raptors, as are the dehesa routes (13, 14 and site A and B on page 178), which are very rewarding for finding Mediterranean birds in general. The numerous birds of marshes are found scattered throughout the region. The best routes 1 and 4, and site D and E on page 132-134, site D, E and F on page 180-182, sites B and C on page 205-206 and site C on page 213. The area's limited number of seabirds are best viewed around the cape of Cabo de Gata (routes 1 and 2) and los Escullos (site B on page 130). The Acantilados de Maro Cerro (page 212) also offers chances on viewing seabirds. Birds of high altitudes should be looked for in routes 17 and 19, and site A on page 204.

The where-to-watch-birds-list with locations for each species is given on page 229.

Andalucía was amongst the first European destinations to become famous among birdwatchers. From the mid-19th century onwards British ornithologists explored Coto Doñana, Grazalema, Cádiz and Gibraltar, all in western Andalucía. In the east Córdoba, Granada, the Sierra Nevada and Alpujarras were favourite tourist destinations, but mostly for their architecture, scenic beauty and walking. The full potential of birding sites like the Almería saltpans and Desierto de Tabernas was only realised in the 1970s and 1980s. The descriptions of the British birdwatcher Andy Paterson who is based in the Costa del Sol, kindled the interest for these areas, while the birdlife of Cazorla, Laguna de Zoñar, Andújar and Despeñaperros was discovered even later.

This difference in popularity between western and eastern Andalucía continues to this day, yet is not entirely justified. Eastern Andalucía has a number of brilliant sites (with species that are absent from or very scarce in the west!) that deserve a greater interest than they receive today.

Eastern Andalucía as a birdwatching destination typically has a high diversity of breeding birds, but many of the 'goodies' are restricted to specific areas. For Azure-winged Magpies, the north-western sierras and Sierra de Huétor are the places to be, while Roller and Great Spotted Cuckoo are more numerous in the Hoyas. A steppe bird like Little Bustard is found in the Hoyas, but is absent or scarce in Almería, where Trumpeter Finches are found and for which you'll search in vain elsewhere. All in all, you have to do a bit of travelling to 'bag' the sought-after species.

Therefore, in this chapter we describe the most remarkable birdlife by area, with reference to the habitats in which the birds are found.

Two birds that are confined to areas with distinct environmental conditions. The Alpine Accentor (left) only breeds in the highest parts of the Sierra Nevada, whereas the Trumpeter Finch (right) is exclusive to the dry ramblas in the south-eastern semi-desert.

Raptors

In many parts of eastern Andalucía, raptors are rather scarce. Only in the northern sierras is the density and diversity of birds of prey high. The eastern Sierra Morena (Andújar and Despeñaperros) is perhaps the richest area. It is the only part of the region with breeding Spanish Imperial Eagle and Black Vulture. The Imperial Eagle is increasing. There are now around 30 breeding pairs in the area. Of the Black Vulture, there are about 100 pairs. The Griffon Vulture, so common in many parts of Spain, is numerous only in the Sierra Morena, Cazorla and María-los Vélez, where in total approximately 900 pairs live. It is surprisingly absent elsewhere, although there are a few small colonies scattered in the region and non-breeding birds do venture down to, for example Sierra de Almijara. Egyptian Vulture, a summer visitor, is decreasing and only found in the Sierra Morena and Cazorla where, with about 15 pairs, it is a fairly rare bird. The re-introduced Lammergeier is exclusive to the Sierra de Cazorla although as the population grows, birds may wander further afield (see box on page 86).

Much more widespread are Buzzard, Kestrel and Short-toed Eagle, which are found pretty much throughout eastern Andalucía. Booted Eagle is present all over but largely missing in the semi-deserts. Eastern Andalucía is the major stronghold in Europe for the threatened Bonelli´s Eagle. It occurs in the Sierra Baetica, Cazorla and above all in the Almería desert. The numbers are fairly low, though, and as this eagle spends much of its time perched on a cliff, it remains a difficult bird to find. Finally, the Golden Eagle is, in this region, a true Sierra eagle. Only in winter do they venture down to the lowlands. Both Sparrowhawk and Goshawk are found largely in the sierras as well.

In summer, Lesser Kestrel is found nesting in remote abandoned sheds, villages and towns in the lowlands while the resident Peregrine, in contrast, is very much a bird of the mountains. It is found in low numbers throughout the Sierras.

Montagu's Harrier is quite common in the Guadalquivir basin but becomes increasingly scarce as you travel towards the south-east corner of Andalucía. The same goes for Marsh Harrier and Black Kite. In fact, the whole of Almería province is comparatively poor in breeding raptors, as it almost entirely lacks vultures, harriers, kites, Booted and Short-toed Eagles.

The spectacular Griffon Vulture is a frequent sight across the sierras of much of Spain. In eastern Andalucía it is rather local, but should be easy to track down in the Sierra de Andújar, Cazorla, María, Almijara and a few other places.

Lammergeier

The Lammergeier has an odd diet that consists almost exclusively of the bones scavenged from carcasses. It is capable of swallowing whole bones up to the size of a sheep's vertebrae. When bones are too big, they are dropped from a great height onto favoured 'anvil' rocks to shatter them. The Spanish name *Quebrantahuesos* (the Bone Breaker) suits it well.

In the 1880s Lammergeier was described as "decidedly common in the Sierra Nevada, and all the region between Granada and Jaen". But the Lammergeier (like nearly all raptors) was regarded as a harmful predator. By the 1950s only a handful remained in the sierras of eastern Andalucía. A combination of shooting, poisoning and egg collecting (the latter mostly by the British) was the final nail in the Lammergeier's coffin. The last confirmed breeding was in 1983 in the Sierra de Cazorla and when the last individual, called *El Solitario*, finally died around 1987, the Lammergeier was officially extirpated in Andalucía.

Scarcely had it disappeared before plans were in hand to bring it back. The regional Government started a reintroduction programme in collaboration with the International Vulture Foundation (**www.4vultures.org**), who had a captive population of Lammergeier and experience in reintroducing them to the Alps. As a result, in 1996 the Lammergeier breeding centre *Guadalentín* was opened in the Sierra de Cazorla, the second biggest in Europe after the centre in Vienna. In 2006 the first Lammergeier was set free in Cazorla. As the birds are slow to reach maturity, the team behind the reintroduction knew that they were playing a long game. Some birds have crossed all over Spain to the Picos de Europa and the Pyrenees and later returned to Cazorla. In 2015, the team's patience was rewarded when *Tono*, a male released in 2006, and *Blimunda*, a female released in 2010, not only nested, but raised a young bird, aptly named *Esperanza* (Hope). By this time a total of 39 birds had been released, of which at least 22 survive. The programme is ongoing with five more birds released in 2016 and more planned in subsequent years.

An intensive publicity campaign is ongoing to educate the public, especially hunters, of the dangers of laying out poison aiming to kill stray dogs and foxes. The campaign is direly needed – within a single year, four of the introduced Lammergeiers had died from poisoning and another one was shot. Thanks to its transmitter the culprit was identified, found guilty, heavily fined and jailed for several months. Clearly the government is taking its reintroduction task serious and the long-term prospects are positive. The project developments can be followed on **www.gypaetus.org**.

Lammergeier

Birds of steppes and desert

The birdlife of the Hoyas de Guadix and Baza overlaps, at least in part, with that of the semi-deserts of Almería.

The semi-deserts are one of the few regions in eastern Andalucía that have firmly established a name for themselves among birdwatchers. A mixture of wetland and seabirds as well as desert birds make for a high diversity of birds in a small area. As this habitat with its dry gullies and Esparto steppes is absent from other regions in Spain, its birdlife supports species that are uncommon or even absent elsewhere. The greatest draw is undoubtedly the Trumpeter Finch – a desert bird that has its only mainland population in Europe here, with its dual core in Cabo de Gata and Desierto de Tabernas. Their numbers are increasing –an estimated 800 pairs nest in Almería alone with more colonies now being established in suitable habitat in Murcia, Alicante, the Guadix-Baza depression and even in Valencia. Even in their main range they are not always easy to find, but a walk near San José (route 2) is often productive – they fly around rocky *ramblas*.

Much more numerous is the Black Wheatear that usually perches conspicuously on prominent rocks. This bird has a small world range, covering northwest Africa and Spain, where it is declining in many areas (the tiny French population now seems to be extinct). Nowhere else on the Peninsula will you find this beautiful bird in such high densities as in the semi-deserts of Almería.

Other rambla birds are Sardinian and Spectacled Warblers, Rock Sparrow and cliff dwellers like Blue Rock Thrush, Alpine and Pallid Swift, Crag Martin and Red-rumped Swallow.

Different birds inhabit the plains, where, camouflaged and pressed against the ground, they merge with their surroundings and are hard to find except in the morning and evening when they sing and are more active. Short-toed Larks are most numerous and easy to find, but the dedicated birder may also track down at least a selection of the sought-after birdlife.

Among them is the now very rare and cryptic Dupont´s Lark. In striking contrast to other larks, the Dupont's hardly ever flies. Instead it runs from patch to patch in tussocky semi-deserts and is very hard to find. Its song is conspicuous though, and this is how to locate them in spring. (Note that the use of recordings to attract this bird is both illegal and a serious problem in some well known locations). The Dupont's Lark was only recognised as a breeding species in Spain in 1967, but is now in serious decline. The core population is found further north in the Ebro basin

(Aragón and Navarra) and in the Páramos between Teruel and Soria, but it has scattered small populations across Spain including in south-east Andalucía.

The Thekla, Short-toed and Lesser Short-toed Larks are much more common and widespread. They breed in natural steppes (Thekla and Short-toed) and saline semi-desert plains with glassworts and other succulent bushes (Lesser Short-toed Lark). The latter is most common close to the coast, but in the Desierto de Tabernas and even in the Hoya de Baza it is found too.

Black-bellied Sandgrouse, Iberian Grey Shrike and Stone Curlew breed in the fields and semi-desert of Almería (routes 1, 5, 6). Small sheds are often rewarding spots, with common or Lesser Kestrel, Little and Barn Owl, Hoopoe and Rock Sparrow among the birds to look out for.

The Hoyas de Guadix and Baza are covered in steppe-like grasslands and fields rather than semi-deserts. The birdlife overlaps in part with that of Cabo de Gata and the Desierto: Black-bellied Sandgrouse, Hoopoe, Lesser Kestrel, Iberian Grey Shrike, Blue Rock Thrush, Black Wheatear, Stone Curlew, Spectacled Warbler, Rock Sparrow and Chough are present in both. Other birds show a clear preference for the arable land and steppes of the *hoyas*. Among them are Montagu's Harrier, Little Bustard, Tawny Pipit, Crested, Short-toed Lark and Calandra Lark. The colourful Roller and Great Spotted Cuckoo occur in the hoyas in densities rarely seen elsewhere in Spain.

Two common dryland birds: Calandra Lark prefers grassy steppes and cereal fields (top), while Spectacled Warbler breeds in low bushes and shrubby saltflats (bottom).

In the Guadalquivir basin (in the provinces of Córdoba, Jaén and Granada) there are low numbers of Little and Great Bustards. The Great Bustard is the only steppe bird that occurs only west of the Sierra Baetica. Some 200 birds survive on the Córdoba and Jaén plains around Baena.

Birds of the wetlands

Wetlands in eastern Andalucía are small and few so it is all the more re-markable that they have such an extraordinary rich birdlife. They concentrate around two areas – the coast of Almería, with both fresh and saltwater lagoons, and the endorheic lagoons and riparian marsh in Córdoba province in the Guadalquivir basin.

Near Almería, the saltpans of Cabo de Gata (east of the town) and brackish lagoons of Punta Entinas–Sabinar (west of Almería) are a magnet for waders, gulls and other aquatic birds. The Flamingo is the most obvious bird, numbering up to several thousands. They don't breed here. Most come from the colony of Laguna de Fuente de Piedra in central Andalucía – Europe's second largest flamingo colony. The flamingos share their habitat with an ever changing palette of waders. During migration and in winter (basically from August to May) Dunlin, Little Stint, Curlew Sandpiper, Ruff, Ringed Plover, Black-tailed Godwit, Whimbrel and Green Sandpiper are frequent visitors with many others turning up regularly. They join the resident breeding Kentish Plover, Avocet and Black-winged Stilt.

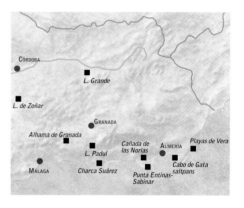

The location of the most important wetland sites in eastern Andalucía.

Top birds of the semi-deserts of Almería
Cabo de Gata and Desierto de Tabernas Bonelli's Eagle, Black-bellied Sandgrouse, Stone Curlew, Dupont's Lark (rare), Lesser Short-toed Lark, Short-toed Lark, Thekla Lark, Black Wheatear, Black-eared Wheatear, Spectacled Warbler, Iberian Grey Shrike, Trumpeter Finch, lots of wetland and sea birds (see below).
Top birds of the Hoyas de Guadix and Baza Stone Curlew, Little Bustard, Black Wheatear, Black-eared Wheatear, Montagu's Harrier, Black-bellied Sandgrouse, Calandra Lark, Short-toed Lark, Tawny Pipit, Hoopoe, Roller, Great Spotted Cuckoo, Iberian Grey Shrike

On the beach and in the saltpans, Audouin's, Black-headed and, on passage, Slender-billed Gulls occur among the more frequent Yellow-leggeds. Their numbers fluctuate but there are usually some resting on dams or beaches. Little and Common Tern are also about, and Caspian and Whiskered Tern occur on passage. Towards the drier parts of the saltmarsh, Avocet and Collared Pratincole nest in small numbers together with the numerous Kentish Plover, Black-winged Stilt, Yellow Wagtail and Lesser Short-toed Lark. Both lagoons are great for wildfowl in winter, while in spring, Osprey, Purple Heron, Night Heron and groups of Whiskered Terns may show up. The freshwater lagoons at the Almería coast (Punta Entinas Sabinar, Cañada de las Norias, Playas de Vera – route 4; sites on page 132-134) offer a different set of birds, which are more reminiscent of the endorheic lakes in the Guadalquivir basin (such as Laguna Grande, Laguna de Zoñar – page 181-182). The great attractions here are White-headed Duck (most common in Punta Entinas Sabinar, Laguna de Zoñar) and Marbled

Little Egrets breed on the coastal marshes, the inland endorheic lagoons and along the Guadalquivir river. Consequently, together with Grey Heron, it is the most widespread heron species.

Duck (Punta Entinas Sabinar) – two very rare and endangered birds which occur only in a few coastal lagoons and temporary lakes in Spain and Morocco in the west, and Turkey and nearby areas in the eastern Mediterranean.

The Crested Coot is similarly endangered in Spain (but widespread in tropical Africa) and has been reintroduced in Punta Entinas-Sabinar, Charca de Súarez and Alhama de Granada (sites B on page 205 and C on page 213). They are frequently joined by Red-crested Pochard, and Squacco Heron.

Some of these sites have extensive reedbeds and tamarisk thickets that are habitat for Marsh Harrier, Little Egret, Little Bittern, Night Heron, Purple Heron and Purple Gallinule. Such sites have often high densities of Cetti's Warbler, Zitting Cisticola, Great Reed, Melodious and Olivaceous Warbler, while the surrounding dry lands are not infrequently the haunts of Rufous Bush Robin, Stone Curlew, Short-toed Lark and Montagu's Harrier.

Top birds of the wetlands
Saltpans of Almería (summer / year-round) Stone Curlew, Little Ringed Plover, Avocet, Black-winged Stilt, Kentish Plover, Collared Pratincole (rare), Shelduck, Little Tern, Audouin's Gull, Yellow-legged Gull, Greater Flamingo
Passage / winter: Osprey, Dunlin, Curlew Sandpiper, Black-tailed Godwit and other waders, Slender-billed Gull, Whiskered Tern, Sandwich Tern, Caspian Tern
Freshwater lagoons and surroundings (summer / year-round) Stone Curlew, Little Bittern, Little Egret, Purple Heron, Squacco Heron, Great Crested Grebe (local), Little Grebe, Black-necked Grebe (rare), Marsh Harrier, Montagu's Harrier, Marbled Duck (local), White-headed Duck, Red-crested Pochard, Crested Coot (local), Purple Gallinule, Greater Flamingo (local), Bee-eater, Zitting Cisticola, Great Reed Warbler, Short-toed Lark, Rufous Bush Robin, Olivaceous Warbler.
Winter Black-necked Grebe, Teal, Shoveler, Wigeon
Riverine marsh (summer / year-round) Night Heron, Cattle Egret (rare), Grey Heron, Golden Oriole, Turtle Dove, Iberian Woodpecker, Little Egret, Reed Warbler, Great Reed Warbler, Nightingale, Cetti's Warbler, Melodious Warbler

Visit the salt pans or Punta Entinas-Sabinar (route 1 and 4) in the evening and you can make your own postcard image.

Locally, the riparian (river-fringing) habitat offers rich birdlife as well. The attractiveness and species composition greatly depends on the size of the site and the type of vegetation. Reedbeds, willow and tamarisk thickets attract Reed, Great Reed, Cetti's and Melodious Warblers, Nightingales and herons. The largest heronries are found at riverine sites and often support Little and Cattle Egret (the latter is surprisingly rare in east Andalucía) and Grey and Night Heron, with little Bittern and Purple Heron breeding in the reeds. If there is open water, ducks and grebes are present (though sought-after species like White-headed Duck are lacking). The gallery forest attracts Golden Oriole, Iberian Green Woodpecker, Penduline Tit, Turtle Dove, White Stork and Black Kite.

Seabirds

Eastern Andalucía is not a great place for seabirds, but there are a few interesting species you might see, especially around Cabo de Gata. Apart from the widespread Yellow-legged Gull, the Shag should be mentioned as it has one of its few Mediterranean breeding sites on islets and inaccessible cliffs of Cabo de Gata. Seawatching from any viewpoint can be interesting, especially with onshore winds during migration. Cabo de Gata (in this case the we mean the cape itself rather than the entire area) is an excellent seawatching site. The movements of shearwaters are complex, but large numbers of Cory's (now increasingly referred to as Scopoli's) and Balearic Shearwater can be seen (except in mid-winter).
In winter, birds at sea include Mediterranean Gull, Gannet, Cormorant, Sandwich Tern, Razorbill and Great Skua. – usually in low numbers.

Seabirds
Shag (breeding), Balearic Shearwater, Cory's Shearwater, Yellow-legged Gull, Mediterranen Gull, Sandwich Tern, Gannet (winter), Razorbill (winter), Great Skua (winter)

Cliffs, karst and pinewoods – birdlife of the limestone sierras

With Griffon, Egyptian Vultures, Lammergeier, Golden, Bonelli's, Booted and Short-toed Eagles, Peregrines and Kestrels, raptors form the most visible and iconic birds of the limestone Sierras. With cliffs and extensive woodlands in remote sites, breeding spots are plenty, while the valleys, plateaux and surrounding lowlands provide good hunting grounds.

To see Cory's
Shearwater head for
the cliffs of Cabo de
Gata and scan the sea.
These birds are of
the Mediterranean
race, which is
increasingly 'split'
and called Scopoli's
Shearwater).

The raptors share the precipitous cliffs with a set of attractive birds. Eagle Owls, Ravens and Red-billed Choughs are invariably cliff dwellers. Colonies of the latter, breeding on ledges and in cavities, are found in all mountainous areas. They feed on natural grasslands and farmland.

Crag and House Martins and Alpine Swift are also common, breeding in holes and cracks up to altitudes of 2,500 m. The flight of the Alpine Swift is spectacular as it flies low and with incredible speed over the rocky crests. This is mostly seen in the morning and evening – at midday they climb to great heights and can be very hard or even impossible to spot.

In areas with rocky slopes, rather than cliffs, the birdlife changes, especially where there is a scatter of shrubs and trees. The more barren rock slopes are ideal sites for the two rock thrushes. The Common (or Rufous-tailed) Rock Thrush is migratory and breeds on the higher slopes and upland karst plateaux. The Blue Rock Thrush is sedentary and prefers the warm, Mediterranean slopes, nesting from sea level to roughly 1,800 metres. They share their habitat with Rock Bunting, Thekla Lark, Black-eared and Black Wheatears, Black Redstart and Rock Sparrow. The latter two use (derelict) buildings just as comfortably as natural rocky habitats. The same applies to Rock Dove whose semi-domesticated cousins, Feral Pigeons, are found in urbanised areas.

An attractive birding habitat is the transition zone between coniferous forest and rocky plateaux. The dense stands of forest hold but few bird species – Crested Tit, Firecrest, Bonelli's Warbler, Nuthatch, Short-toed Treecreeper and Crossbill being the most noteworthy. However, in the open parkland sites with tall, isolated trees, rocky slopes and grassy patches, all sorts of

Top birds of the sierras

Cliffs, karst and hedgehog vegetation: Golden Eagle, Bonelli's Eagle, Booted Eagle, Short-toed Eagle, Griffon Vulture (only S. Morena, Cazorla, María), Egyptian Vulture (only S. Cazorla and Morena), Lammergeier (only S. Cazorla), Eagle Owl, Kestrel, Peregrine, Alpine Swift, White-rumped Swift, Crag Martin, Thekla Lark, Short-toed Lark, Black-eared Wheatear, Black Wheatear, Northern Wheatear (only S. Nevada), Alpine Accentor (only S. Nevada), Rock Thrush (high up), Blue Rock Thrush, Red-billed Chough, Raven, Rock Sparrow, Spectacled Warbler, Rock Bunting, Ortolan Bunting

Pinewoods and pinewood parkland: Cirl Bunting, Crossbill, Firecrest, Short-toed Treecreeper, Citril Finch (only S. Cazorla, Nevada), Azure-winged Magpie (only S. Cazorla, Huétor).

Rivers: Dipper (only S. Cazorla, Nevada), Kingfisher (rare), Grey Wagtail

They never cease to puzzle the birdwatcher: the widespread Crested Lark (left) and the near identical Thekla Lark, a North African-Iberian endemic (right). Both are common in the region, with Crested typically found on flatter arable land and Thekla preferring Mediterranean scrub with scattered trees, typically on hillsides and at greater elevations.

combinations of birds appear: Rock Buntings may use the same singing post as Crossbill, Crested Tit may share a branch with Black Redstart and so on. In addition, there are a few birds that prefer this open woodland over other habitats. These are Cirl Bunting, Woodlark, Mistle Thrush and – cherry on the cake – the Citril Finch. The Citril Finch is a rare and localised bird, endemic to the high mountains of western Europe. It has its southernmost populations in the Sierra Cazorla and Sierra Nevada. It is quite rare but increasing and can be found in open park-like coniferous forest close to the treeline.

Climbing above the treeline, the birdlife drops drastically in number and diversity. On Spain's highest mountain, birds are scarce. Apart from the

The Sierra Morena has a fabulous range of raptors. The Sierra de Andújar, the only part of the Sierra Morena that lies within the area of this book, is the only place in the region where Black Vulture (in photo) and Spanish Imperial Eagle can be seen consistently.

occasional Rock Thrush, Chough or Black Redstart, there are two birds of note – Northern Wheatear and Alpine Accentor. The latter nests above 2,500 m where it inhabits rocky areas and often visits snowfields which attract insects.

Birds of Sierra Morena – dehesas and scrublands

We describe the Sierra Morena (Andújar, Despeñaperros) separately as the birdlife is quite distinct from the other sierras. The great difference lies in the open habitat of holm oak dehesa, which is home to sought-after species like Spanish Imperial Eagle, Black Vulture and Black Stork. These three occur, within the range of this guidebook, only in the Sierra Morena. Raptors are common in the region anyway – there are good populations of Griffon Vulture, Black Kite, Booted and Short-toed Eagle and smaller numbers of Golden and Bonelli's Eagle and Egyptian Vulture. In general, the tree-breeding raptors do well in these wooded, remote hills and low mountains, while the relatively low number of cliffs limit the species that prefer this breeding habitat (except Griffon Vulture, which is well represented).

The dehesa has much more to offer than raptors alone. Apart from the many widespread Mediterranean birds (see next page), Azure-winged Magpie, Rock Sparrow, Woodlark, Iberian Grey and Woodchat Shrikes are common in the dehesas. Within the area of this guidebook, the Sierra Morena is the principal area for Spanish Sparrow (which is now expanding its range). Even though cliffs are less in evidence than in the limestone sierras, there

Top birds of the Sierra Morena
Black Stork, Golden Eagle (scarce), Bonelli's Eagle (scarce), Spanish Imperial Eagle, Booted Eagle, Short-toed Eagle, Griffon Vulture, Egyptian Vulture, Black Vulture, Black Kite, Black-winged Kite, Alpine Swift, Pallid Swift, White-rumped Swift (scarce), Iberian Green Woodpecker, Turtle Dove, Crag Martin, Thekla Lark, Woodlark, Black-eared Wheatear, Blue Rock Thrush, Red-billed Chough, Raven, Rock Sparrow, Rock Bunting, Cirl Bunting, Azure-winged Magpie, Golden Oriole, Spanish Sparrow, Rufous Bush Robin, Cirl Bunting, Rock Bunting

are sufficient to support healthy populations of Blue Rock Thrush, Black-eared Wheatear, Crag Martin, Red-rumped Swallow and White-rumped Swift (which breeds in abandoned Red-rumped Swallow nests). Add to this the rivers and the apron of farmlands below the hills and the picture of a birdwatching paradise is complete. The riparian woodlands and thickets (though few) support Golden Oriole, Iberian Green Woodpecker and various herons. Olive groves and hedgerows are home to, among others, Rufous Bush Robin and Olivaceous Warbler.

Widespread Mediterranean birds
One of Andalucía's attractions is the presence of a large number of often colourful birds that are widespread in the Mediterranean basin but little seen in the north. Eastern Andalucía is a delight for *Sylvia*-warblers, the hidden gems amongst songbirds. Except when in song (usually early in the morning), they all conceal themselves deep in bushes so patience is required to spot them as they emerge for just a few seconds. Subalpine Warbler prefers mountain slopes with Holm Oak and scrub while Dartford Warbler is a bird of lower altitudes and denser scrub. Sardinian Warbler is abundant in almost any dense scrub, although it becomes scarce at higher altitudes. The highest densities of Spectacled Warbler are found in the arid areas with few bushes in Almería (where some may winter), but the bird is also found in low scrub up to 2,000 m in the Baetic Sierras. The Orphean Warbler favours open dry woodland with small well-spaced trees usually below 1300m. It is often hard to find as it occurs in low densities. The Whitethroat is associated with mountainous and hilly areas being absent from lowland valleys. The well-known Blackcap nests in the mountains of Andalucía while scores of wintering birds from the north feed in the olive orchards from October to March.
'Leaf warblers' (*Phyllo-scopus*) are represented by Bonelli's Warbler which summers in the woodlands across the region, but Iberian Chiffchaff does

so only in the mountains of Jáen and Córdoba. In winter both are replaced by Common Chiffchaff (although the Sierra Nevada has an isolated breeding population of this species). Willow Warbler, and more rarely Wood Warbler, pass through on migration. Red-rumped Swallow is generally common in dehesas and agricultural areas, where Hoopoe, Little Owl, Bee-eater and Lesser Kestrel are also widespread. Both Iberian Grey Shrike and Woodchat Shrike are widely distributed in open woodlands, orchards and agricultural fields – the first always scarcer than the latter, except in semi-desert and steppe habitat. The Red-necked Nightjar is common in dehesas and steppes and easily distinguished by its song. The European Nightjar occupies the upland plateaux and mountain slopes. The Red-legged Partridge is ubiquitous as is Scops Owl. Towns and villages are usually home to a Barn Owl or two, a few Hoopoes and masses of Spotless Starling, House Martin and Swallow. The massive morning and evening flights of swifts over the villages gives you the grand start and finale of a day's birding in eastern Andalucía. There are two species that breed in houses. The familiar Common Swift dominates towns and villages in the interior, while Pallid Swift prefers the settlements on the coast.

How wonderful it is that Spain's brightest, most colourful and cheerful bird, the Bee-eater, is so common in Andalucía (top). In the villages close to the coast, the Pallid Swift is much more common than the Common Swift (bottom).

Reptiles and amphibians

Routes 8, 9, 13 and 14 and sites A and B on pages 178 - 181 are good for finding amphibians. Reptiles are present in a wide variety of routes – for most species it is a matter of how rather than where to search (see page 228 for tips). Of the localised species, the Spur-thighed Tortoise is best sought on route 6. Chameleons should be looked for on route 1 and 4. The same, plus routes 2, 3 and sites A to E on page 130-134, are good for Mediterranean House Gecko. Spanish Algyroides is numerous on route 9.

Eastern Andalucía is home to no less than 15 species of amphibian and 30 species of reptiles (counting according to the new taxonomy; see page 102), several of which are endemic to the Iberian peninsula or even to Andalucía. The key to this herpetological wealth is, at least in part, historical. After the last ice age, populations of a single species got divided as one part moved north and the other up into the mountains. This process is most dramatically shown by the Fire Salamander. Of all 14 currently recognised subspecies, no less than 9 are endemic to the Iberian peninsula. Two of these can be found in eastern Andalucía: the subspecies *longirostris* and *morenica*. *Longisrostris* reaches the eastern edge of its distribution range in the Sierra de Almijara while *Morenica*, also on the eastern edge of its distribution range, can be found from the Sierra de Andújar to the Sierra de Cazorla. The great diversity of habitats is another ground for the great diversity of species.

As is often the case with reptiles and amphibians, finding them is a matter of perseverance, luck and thorough preparation. This section will help you with the latter, leaving the perseverance up to you and luck in the lap of the gods.

Amphibians

All young amphibians and a good few of the adults too, depend on water. The region's many rivers, (episodic) streams, lakes, reservoirs and ponds are the places to head for when looking for newts, toads and frogs. As opposed to temperate Europe, amphibians in the Mediterranean tend to *aestivate* (oversummer) rather than *hibernate* (overwinter). They are active in autumn, winter and spring, but dormant in summer.

The largest and perhaps most impressive amphibian is the Sharp-ribbed Newt. This bulky animal, endemic to the Iberian Peninsula and Morocco, occurs up to 1,500 metres in a broad range of habitats from riverine wetlands to reservoirs and drinking troughs. Within the area described in this

book, its most healthy populations can be found in the Sierra
de Andújar, the Sierra de Loja
and around the Guadalquivir
and Genil rivers. The Southern
Marbled Newt occurs in roughly the same habitats, but is a little more picky about the water
quality. The best populations
can be found in the Depression
of Granada (especially the
Zafarraya plain) and the Sierra
de Almijara. The Bosca's Newt
occurs in western Iberia. In our
region, it is only found in the
Sierra Morena.

The common frog in this part of the
world is the Iberian Water Frog – a close
relative of the green frogs in northern
Europe. It is found in all sorts of standing waters. More exciting is an encounter
with an East Iberian Painted Frog – only
distinguished from its close relative in
1986, it is endemic to the peninsula and
also occurs in a broad spectrum of wet-
lands, mostly in the hills and mountains. In the Sierra de Cazorla it lives
alongside the very similar West Iberian Painted Frog (another Iberian
endemic), which can also be found in the Sierra Morena. Both species live
a more hidden live than the Iberian Water Frog, from which they differ by
their inconspicuous eardrums and round pupils.

The Parsley Frog and Iberian Parsley Frog are much smaller than the
other frogs. Both occur in the area described by this guidebook and, like
the painted frogs, are very hard to tell apart. Their ranges meet near the
Sierra de Cazorla. Parsley Frogs occur in fairly dry habitats and can reproduce in unlikely places like flooded car tracks.

Two species of tree frog occur in East Andalucía. The most common is
the Stripeless Tree Frog that is found in two separate areas – a broad
strip along the Mediterranean coast from Granada province to Rio Adra
in Almeria and in the north, in the Sierra Morena. It primarily inhabits
the lowland habitats with a lush riparian growth. In the Laguna Grande

Of all the Andalucían frogs, the Iberian Water Frog (top) is most strongly tied to permanent fresh water. Nevertheless, even in this dry region they are common and easily seen in the right habitat. This is in sharp contrast to the small Parsley Frog (bottom), which occurs in all sorts of tempo-rary waters, yet is very hard to find.

(page 181) it occurs alongside its northern cousin, the European Tree Frog, which reaches the southern edge of its range here.

The Southern Midwife Toad is one of the highlights of the region. It is endemic to south-eastern Spain. It occurs in most of the mountain ranges and locally in the lowlands. In the Sierra Morena, the Iberian Midwife Toad replaces the Southern Midwife Toad.

The Western Spadefoot occurs in aquatic habitats with sandy soils. This bulky amphibian lives a mostly hidden life but its enormous tadpoles usually give its presence away. It occurs mostly in the lowlands of Jaen and Granada provinces.

The huge Western or Spiny Toad, until recently regarded as a subspecies of Common Toad, is widespread in the region. It requires clean waters of some depth. Its size (large specimens can reach a length of over 20 cm), its often blotched or striped skin differentiate it from the Common Toad. Last but not least, the small Natterjack Toad is widespread and numerous. Its ability to swiftly reproduce in temporary pools enables it to occur even in the most arid parts of Almería.

Reptiles

The reptile life of eastern Andalucía encompasses tortoises, terrapins, turtles, chameleons, geckos, lizards, skinks, worm lizards and snakes.

The Spur-thighed Tortoise is one of the region's highlights. There are only two populations on the Spanish mainland. One is in Coto Doñana (western Andalucía) and the other roughly in the triangle Sorbas – Mazarron – Sierra de María. It is rare and not easily seen. The Spanish Terrapin, an aquatic species, is far more common. It occupies fresh and brackish, clean

Chameleons prefer sandy areas in the dry lowlands with tamarisks and brooms.

and polluted waters alike.

In recent years an attempt has been made to reintroduce the marine Loggerhead Turtle to the region, which has abandoned the beaches of the Western Mediterranean as a breeding site. When mature, turtles return to the beaches they came from to lay eggs. In 2007, young animals were released on the beaches of Cabo de Gata and hopefully they'll return. As it takes a

Loggerhead at least 17 years to reach sexual maturity, the result of the reintroduction will only become apparent in the 2020s.

The Common Chameleon is another one of Andalucia's gems. Like the tortoise, it is believed to have been introduced at some point by the Moors. Chameleons prefer sandy soils and a well-developed vegetation of scrubs. Broom and tamarisk appear to be favourite, especially those along the coast. Two geckos can be found in the region. The Moorish and the Turkish or Mediterranean House Gecko. Both occur in roughly the same habitats, but the latter is more restricted to the coastal zone. Although they live in a wide range of habitats, they are most easily seen in or near human settlements. A warm summer evening spent on the terrace of a restaurant may very well yield a sighting of one or more geckos hunting on a wall or a roof for all the insects that are attracted to the light.

The Iberian Wall Lizard and Large Psammodromus (also a lizard) are both in the competition for title of the most frequently seen reptile. Both are good climbers and frequently found on rocks, boulders, walls and tree trunks, with the Wall Lizard having a preference for rocky terrain and Large Psammodromus for scrubland and leaf litter, but there is a considerable overlap in habitat. The species are easy to tell apart – the Large Psammodromus is, as its name suggests, rather large and has an olive back with two cream stripes on either side. Its small cousin, the Spanish Psammodomus is rarer and tied to more sparsely vegetated areas. It has a series of small, light spots on its back, rather than stripes. The Spiny-footed Lizard is another frequently seen lizard in sparsely vegetated, sandy or loamy habitats. Where it occurs, it often does so in high numbers.

The Ocellated Lizard is one of Andalucía's most spectacular lizards due to its size. Exceptional specimens of over 80 centimetres long have been recorded. It occurs in a wide variety of habitats and is frequently seen. The population in the Sierra Nevada and Almería province are now considered to belong to a separate species (see page 102).

The small Spanish Algyroides with its typically keeled scales, is the region's only endemic lizard. It occurs in the Sierra de Cazorla and adjoining mountain ranges.

The region also has two skinks. Bedriaga's Skink prefers sandy soils and some vegetation. It is a secretive animal which is rarely seen. Western Three-toed Skink is even more snake-like and looks somewhat comical with its impractically diminutive limbs. It is more restricted to cool and damp habitats and is therefore absent in most of the province of Almería. The Iberian Worm Lizard, as its name suggests, is completely legless. It resembles an oversized earthworm but careful inspection will reveal a

The Ladder Snake (a juvenile here) is probably the most common snake of the region.

mouth, a nose and two strongly degenerated eyes. It is found throughout the region and is surprisingly common, if rarely seen. Like the earthworm, it leads a largely subterranean life.

The Montpellier Snake is the region's largest snake. Adults can measure up to 240 centimetres in length. It is a typical Mediterranean species and occurs in fair numbers in dry and warm habitats throughout the region. The Horseshoe Whip Snake seeks out comparable habitats, but is far less numerous. The Ladder Snake is common in sunny, stony habitats with at least some vegetation. It is the most frequently encountered snake in Almería. Grass and Viperine Snake are both aquatic, occurring in and along streams and other bodies of water. The Viperine Snake is especially common and can be found in most waters in the lowlands and mountains up to 2000 m. Isolated populations of Smooth Snake occur in the Sierra Nevada and the Sierra de Cazorla where they occupy rocky terrain with a sparse vegetation of pine or oak trees. The very similar Southern Smooth Snake and False Smooth Snake occur throughout the region in a much broader range of habitats. Finally, Lataste's Viper, Andalucia's only snake with a truly venomous bite, occurs primarily in open terrain, both above the tree line on karst plateaux and in sandy coastal areas and semi-desert.

The Nevada Ocellated Lizard has only recently been considered a separate species. It occurs in the Sierra Nevada as well as in Almería and is much paler than the widespread form that is found in the rest of the Iberian Peninsula.

Splitting Reptiles

Reptile and amphibian taxonomy is currently in a state of flux with several newly described species and DNA studies suggesting 'splitting' some diverse groups. Amongst the groups most affected are wall lizards, psammodromuses and Worm Lizard. Most are defined by range and all are very difficult to distinguish (if at all) in the field, so we have retained the old terminology. The Ocellated Lizard has also been split into two species – the familiar form across most of Spain and a distinctively greyer, paler species, the Sierra Nevada Ocellated Lizard.

Insects and other invertebrates

Butterflies of coastal and desert regions are best sought on routes 1, 2, 3, the Hoya de Baza (page 147) and sites B and C on page 205-206. Butterflies of limestone mountains should be looked for on routes 6, 7, 8, 9, 10, 15 and site A on page 212. The specialities of the Sierra Nevada are found on routes 17, 18, 19 and site A on page 204. Attractive dragonfly routes with specialities as Ringed Cascader, Splendid Cruiser, Epaulet Skimmer, Banded Groundling and Orange-winged Dropwing are routes 1, 4, 8, 9, 14 and 20 and sites A, D and E on page 178-180 and sites B and C on page 205-206.

The diversity in habitat ranging from arid desert to estuaries and Alpine meadows, offers a dazzling wealth of insects. The following chapter is inevitably too short to do this amazing diversity justice, so we'll focus on the conspicuous and most easily encountered species, with special emphasis on butterflies and dragonflies.

Butterflies in Eastern Andalucía

Andalucía hosts approximately 150 different species of butterflies, of which the vast majority (about 148) have populations in the area of this guidebook. Key players here are definitely the blues (*lycaenids*) and satyrs (*satyrids*) which contain an attractive mix of widespread Mediterranean and localised Iberian species. Many of the widespread European species don't make it down to east Andalucía, or are very rare and localised (e.g. Silver-washed Fritillary). So from the perspective of a British, Dutch or German visitor, most of the 148 species are exotic.

The butterfly diversity peaks in early July and a trip combining the Sierra Nevada, Sierra de Huétor and the Alpujarras could, with dedication and good identification skills, yield no less than 120 species.

Of the east Andalucían regions, the Sierra Nevada is doubtlessly the most exciting. Nowhere else in Spain are there so many endemic species concentrated in a small area, namely the zone around the upper tree limit (roughly 1,800 metres) and higher. Other butterfly hotspots are Sierra de Cazorla, Sierra de María-Vélez and Sierra de Huétor. Within these nature parks, woodland glades, karstic grasslands, rocky outcrops and flowery roadsides push numbers to such an abundance that, at times, grasslands appear enveloped by a whirling cloud of butterflies. Butterflies are on the wing in different generations from March until October. Although spring and autumn offer striking species, most can be expected from early June to the beginning of August. Spring – the season most naturalists visit the region – yields much lower numbers and less variety, but a different set of species, including attractions like Provence Hairstreak, Common Tiger Blue and the conspicuous Spanish Festoon.

In summer, many butterflies shelter from the heat around mid-day, but you can still find them in fair numbers on flowering bushes like brambles, or near puddles, drinking troughs and sandy edges of streams. Here they gather by the hundreds or sometimes even thousands to drink. Staking out such sites offers excellent opportunities to compare species and hone your ID-skills.

Two southern orange-tips. The Provence Orange-tip (left) has yellow wings (male) and is common in open woodlands and scrub. The Desert Orange-tip (right) is, as the name suggests, restricted to the dry badlands of the Hoya de Baza, Desierto de Tabernas and Cabo de Gata.

Butterflies of the Sierra Nevada

From June onwards, alpine grasslands (over 1,800 m) turn into a butterfly hotspot. The rocky grasslands near the summits of the Sierra Nevada (Route 17, 19) are highly recommended as the patches of vegetation, *borreguiles* and rocky areas above 2,500 m is where you'll find local endemic species like Nevada and Zullich's Blues and Spanish Brassy Ringlet. Two other high mountain species, the Nevada Grayling and Southern Hermit, occur both here and in the Sierra de la Sagra and Sierra de María.

A little further down, but still around or above the tree level, flowery gullies are the haunts of seven endemic Nevada subspecies of more widespread butterflies: Safflower Skipper, Apollo, Purple-shot Copper, Idas Blue, Heath Fritillary, Andalusian False Grayling and Black Satyr. Peacock, Iolas and Amanda's Blue have relict populations in the Sierra Nevada, being absent from the central Iberian Peninsula. The Sierra

Extraordinary butterflies of Eastern Andalucía

Spanish Festoon	*Zerynthia rumina*	Conspicuous and common
Apollo	*Parnassius apollo*	Endemic subspecies in S. Nevada and S. de María
Desert Orange-tip	*Colotis evagore*	Rare and local species in hot areas
Sooty Orange-tip	*Zegris eupheme*	Local and hard to find, spring
Spanish Greenish Black-tip	*Euchloe bazae*	Spanish endemic, local in Hoya de Baza in spring
Common Tiger Blue	*Tarucus theophrastus*	Local, only around Wild Jujube Bushes
Provence Hairstreak	*Tomarus ballus*	Rare in eastern Andalucía, conspicuous, early spring
Spanish Purple Hairstreak	*Laeosopis roboris*	Local species, usual along streams
Chapman's Green Hairstreak	*Callophrys avis*	Very rare in S. Nevada, since 2012 in S. de Cazorla
Geranium Bronze	*Cacyreus marshalli*	Invasive species, getting more abundant
African Grass Blue	*Zizeeria knysna*	Rare species, arable coastal areas, very small
Lorquin's Blue	*Cupido lorquinii*	Rare species
Carswell's Blue	*Cupido carswelli*	Endemic for southern Spain
Iolas Blue	*Iolana iolas*	Rare species restricted to S. Nevada
Zullich's Blue	*Plebejus zullichi*	Endemic for S. Nevada, high mountains
Idas Blue	*Plebejus idas*	Endemic subspecies in S. Nevada
Spanish Zephyr Blue	*Plebejus hespericus*	Endemic for southern Spain, rare
Mother-of-Pearl Blue	*Polyommatus nivescens*	Endemic for Spain, local, almost white
Nevada Blue	*Polyommatus golgus*	Endemic in S. Nevada and S. de la Sagra
Andalusian Anomalous Blue	*Polyommatus violetae*	Endemic for southern Spain, rare
Panoptes Blue	*Pseudophilotes panoptes*	Endemic for Spain
Mountain Argus	*Aricia montensis*	Endemic subspecies in Sa Nevada
Spanish Argus	*Aricia morronensis*	Endemic for Spain, rare, high mountains
Two-tailed Pasha	*Charaxes jasius*	Beautiful and conspicuous Med. species
Monarch	*Danaus plexippus*	Vagrant, local resident
Plain Tiger	*Danaus chrysippus*	Vagrant, local resident
Heath fritillary	*Melitaea athalia*	Endemic subspecies in Nevada
Aetherie Fritillary	*Melitaea aetherie*	Very rare in Jaen province
Spanish Fritillary	*Euphydryas desfontainii*	Rare, beautiful species
Spanish Marbled White	*Melanargia ines*	Common, endemic for southern Iberian Peninsula
Andalusian False Grayling	*Arethusana Boabdil*	Endemic subspecies
Southern Hermit	*Chazara prieuri*	Endemic in S. Nevada and S. de María
Nevada Grayling	*Pseudochazara hippolyte*	Endemic in S. Nevada
Spanish Brassy Ringlet	*Erebia hispania*	Endemic and only ringlet in S. Nevada
Cinquefoil Skipper	*Pyrgus cirsii*	Local, typical low, fast flight

Nevada is also home to other interesting, more widespread butterflies, such as Spanish Argus, Escher's Blue, Silver-spotted Skipper, Black-veined White, Lorquin's and Mother-of-Pearl Blue.

The tiny Common Tiger Blue is a north-African species that in Europe only occurs in the Cabo de Gata region (top). Spanish Festoon (bottom) is more widespread in open woodlands and scrubland – anywhere where its host plant Birthwort grows. Both are spring species.

Butterflies of the limestone mountains – Sierra de Huétor and Cazorla

In the limestone mountains, woodland clearings, particularly those that are sheltered and rich in flowers, are the places to be for butterflies. These are, on average, probably even richer in number of species than the Sierra Nevada. Such patches at modest elevation (roughly up to 1,000 m) mostly have species with a Mediterranean distribution. In spring, you'd typically find Black-eyed Blue, Spanish Festoon, Provence Orange-tip and Scarce Swallowtail, while in summer (June – August), now oppressively hot, these places attract Sage Skipper, Idas, Silver-studded and Escher's Blues, Rock Grayling and Hermit.

Higher up, the woodland clearings are the realm of the Orange-tip, Common and Chapman's Blue and Marsh Fritillary. In any type of limestone grassland you can find Panoptes, Adonis, Green-underside, Osiris and Spanish Chalkhill Blues, Spotted and Knapweed Fritillaries, Hermit and Striped Grayling.

When shrubby areas are nearby the butterfly diversity reaches a climax and species like Blue-spot Hairstreak, Black-eyed Blue, Twin-spot Fritillary, Southern Marbled Skipper, Sage Skipper and Dusky Meadow Brown can be added to the list. Forested streams in limestone mountains attract Cardinal, Large Tortoiseshell, Spanish Purple Hairstreak, Wood White and Speckled Wood.

Butterflies of the coastal region

The coastal strip of eastern Andalucía is worth visiting for a small collection of butterflies, that is, with the likes of Monarch, Plain Tiger and Common Tiger Blue, highly attractive. Due to the climate, butterflies are on the wing almost throughout the year. Spring is a rewarding period, offering Green-underside Blue, Spanish Marbled White and Green-striped White (which are also common deeper inland).

Spanish Gatekeeper, Clouded Yellow, Bath White, Mallow Skipper and Mediterranean Skipper share the same habitat of coastal scrublands, but are uncommon in spring. Their numbers build up as the season progresses. Summer in Cabo de Gata is challenging, yet prime-time for the beautiful and unmistakable Desert Orange-tip. It is found near the rocky slopes on the coast from March to August, with numbers peaking in July. Arable lands close to the coast are favoured by the tiny African Grass Blue which lays its eggs on Medick species. The exotic species like Monarch and Plain Tiger (or African Monarch) require non-native milkweeds which grow in some urban parks (e.g. Motril and the Alhambra). They can be seen almost throughout the year, with highest numbers in autumn.

The tiny Geranium Bronze, member of the blues family and native to South Africa, invaded Europe via the Balaeric Islands in 1988 and has spread over most of Spain and is now colonising the rest of Europe. Its larval food is the Garden Geranium, which also originates from South Africa. The Geranium Bronze is widespread but particularly common in city parks as its food plant is also found here.

Butterflies of grasslands

The diversity in grasslands is enormous and discontinuously appears through the Andalucían regions. In the steppe grassland of the Hoya Guadix and Hoya de Baza in spring you are most likely to see Clouded Yellow, Western- Green-striped- and Portuguese Dappled White. The star species here is the endemic Spanish Greenish Black-tip, which is restricted to Hoya de Baza where it is found in fertile spots between the sandy dunes. In early spring the Provence Hairstreak is attracted to the short and overgrazed grasslands here. Later in summer these arid locations become suitable for Sooty and Desert Orange-tip.

Fields and nutrient-rich grassland such as those found in the Guadalquivir basin and around so many towns and villages in the rest of east Andalucía, host a score of widespread and often common species, such as Common Blue, Small White, Small Copper, Grayling, Spanish Marbled White, Dusky Heath, Great Banded Grayling and Meadow Brown.

108

Dragonflies and damselflies

Andalucía is, with approximately 56 species of dragonflies and damselflies, one of the European hotspots for this group. Even though the best sites are in the western part of the region, there are several superb dragonfly wetlands within our region. Combined, they play host to at least 49 species.

The great attraction of the Andalucían odonate fauna (dragonflies and damselflies combined) is the presence of several essentially African species, some of which are currently expanding their ranges northwards. To this group belong Purple and Orange-winged Dropwing, Northern Banded Groundling and Desert Darter. A second set of sought-after species consists of (west) Mediterranean species with a very patchy distribution. Splendid Cruiser, Orange-spotted Emerald and Yellow and Pronged Clubtail fit this profile. Both these groups are well represented in eastern Andalucía, although most of them occur only in very distinct hotspots.

The fresh and brackish lowland marshes that stretch along the Mediterranean coast are like a precious string of dragonfly-friendly pearls. These are the places to go to find Long Skimmer, Northern Banded Groundling, Black Pennant and Black Percher and, occasionally, Vagrant Emperor – all of them species that occur widely in Africa and are very rare elsewhere. The brackish environment of Entinas-Sabinar (route 4) is worth looking out for the nomadic Dark Spreadwing.

Shady streams in the mountains are hotspots for dragonflies in the region (top). One of the rarities to look for here is the Pronged Clubtail (bottom).

Special dragonflies of Eastern Andalucía

Copper Demoiselle	*Calopteryx haemorrhoidalis*	Locally abundant on shady streams
Iberian Bluetail	*Ishnura graellsii*	Widespread on most waters in Andalucía
Mercury Bluet	*Coenagrion mercuriale*	Very rare, marshes and streams with vegetation
Mediterranean Bluet	*Coenagrion caerulescens*	Marshes and slow streams, very rare
Vagrant Emperor	*Anax ephippiger*	Impressive migrant from Africa
Western Spectre	*Boyeria irene*	Rare, along small shady streams
Splendid cruiser	*Macromia splendens*	Impressive species, very rare in S. Cazorla
Orange-spotted Emerald	*Oxygastra curtisii*	Very rare on streams in S. Cazorla
Large Pincertail	*Onychogomphus uncatus*	More on shaded streams
Yellow Clubtail	*Gomphus simillimus*	Small rivers, local in S. Cazorla and S. Morena
Pronged Clubtail	*Gomphus graslinii*	Small rivers, local in S. Cazorla
Yellow-veined Skimmer	*Orthetrum nitidinerve*	Very rare and hard to find
Epaulet skimmer	*Orthetrum chrysostigma*	Locally abundant on streams
Long Skimmer	*Orthetrum trinacria*	Freshwaters, elongated and slender for a Skimmer
Desert Darter	*Sympetrum sinaiticum*	Rare African species, small waters in arid areas
Violet Dropwing	*Trithemis annulata*	Beautiful African species, now common
Orange-winged Dropwing	*Trithemis kirbyii*	Beautiful African species, frequent in the south
Banded Groundling	*Brachythemis impartita*	Rare, clear bands, usually on the ground
Black Percher	*Diplacodes lefebvrii*	Rare African species, usually near the coast
Black Pennant	*Selysiothemis nigra*	Rare African species, usually near the coast
Ringed Cascader	*Zygonyx torridus*	Rare African species, very local on Río Chillar

Another dragonfly hotspot is the Sierra de Cazorla. Dainty and Mediterranean Bluets, Splendid Cruiser, Orange-spotted Emerald and Yellow and Pronged Clubtail have their strongholds in Andalucía here. They all belong to a group of dragonflies with a restricted (west) Mediterranean distribution. They fly together with the more widespread White Featherleg and Copper Demoiselle (both common) and Beautiful Demoiselle, Western Spectre, Large Pincertail and Common Goldenring (uncommon and largely restricted to well-wooded rivers).

Outside these two hotspots, there is still plenty to discover.

The Long Skimmer is one of several African dragonflies that has recently crossed the Straits and established populations in Andalucía. It is found in just a few wetlands in the south, such as Charca de Suárez.

Depending on the type of wetland (typically ranging from large puddles to lakes fringed by vegetation), the common species are Iberian Bluetail, Southern Skimmer, Blue and Lesser Emperor, Broad Scarlet, Violet Dropwing, Red-veined Darter and sometimes also Common Winter Damsel. Small rivers are excellent places to look for attractive species like the Epaulet Skimmer, Desert Darter, Orange and Violet Dropwing and Small Pincertail.

Other invertebrates

There are thousands of 'other invertebrates' most of which are only on the radar of the most dedicated specialists. We mention just a few here, which are either very common or conspicuous, or are for other reasons of interest for naturalists.

Andalucía hosts at least 140 species of field crickets and grasshoppers, which amounts to half of the Iberian species. Perhaps the most conspicuous is the large Egyptian Locust which is a regular invader from Africa and one of the few large grasshoppers in spring.

In keeping with the flora and butterfly fauna, the Sierra Nevada hosts many endemic grasshoppers, including *Chortippus nevadensis, Phyllodromica baetica, Pycnogaster inermis, Omocestus bolivari* and the wingless *Eumigus rubioi* (p. 202), which occurs in the *borreguiles*. The odd and endemic *Baetica ustulata* has a distinctive black back and is indigenous to the summits of the Sierra Nevada. It belongs to a genus that is purely Iberian.

The arid parts of southeast Spain offer more endemics. *Steropleurus squamiferus* is only known from arid soils with brooms in the Sierra de María-Velez (Route 7). *Dericorys carthagonovae* which occupies brackish and saline environments in the Rambla de Tabernas and the marshes of Sabinar (route 3, 4).

The conspicuous Long-nosed Grasshopper (*Truxalis nasuta*; p. 131) is common around Cabo de Gata (route 1, 2, 4). The related praying mantises are more difficult to find, except in summer when the adults are around. Various species occur in the region, including *Mantis religiosa, Empusa pennata* and *Ameles spallanzania*.

Scorpions and Megarian Banded Centipedes hide underneath rocks during the day and come out to hunt at night. A careful lifting of a flat rock might reveal them, but be careful for their sting/bite is painful! Remember to replace the rock in the same way to avoid damaging their hideout.

Here and there you'll find small holes lined with webbing in rocky grasslands – they are home to the fearsome-looking but fairly harmless

European Tarantula or Wolf Spider. Much more dangerous is the small, glossy black-with-red-spots Black Widow (*Latrodectus tredecimguttatus*). It has a painful (though not fatal) bite. Black Widows cause problems in the greenhouse complexes of Almería as they hide among the vegetables and bite the people that harvest the fruits.

Another step down into the world of obscure and complex animals groups brings us to the moths. The conspicuous diurnal Provence Burnet (*Zygaena occitanica*) with ringed red spots belongs to a wide group that includes also some rare endemics like the Nevada Burnet (*Zygaena nevadensis*). Other eye-catching diurnal species are Humming-bird Hawk-moth, Silver-striped Hawk-moth, Cream-spot Tiger Moth and Crimson Speckled Moth. Keep distance of the distinctive knotted nests in Pine trees belonging to the Pine Processionary caterpillars as their hairs provoke a nasty allergic skin reaction!

Another dazzling insect on flowery grasslands is the fast-flying owlfly or ascalaphid. These colourful insects are related to the ant-lions. *Libelloides longicornis* and *L. baeticus* are widespread and frequent in the Alpujarras and Sierra Nevada, while *L. ictericus* and *L. cunii* are more occasional. Another member of the ant-lions in flowery grasslands is the majestic and conspicuous Thread-winged Lacewing (*Nemoptera bipennis*) with its royal veils.

Dry grasslands are home to several strange creatures, such as owlflies (right) and Thread-winged Lacewing (left).

PRACTICAL PART

Eastern Andalucía is unique in Europe. First and foremost, it has Europe's only semi-desert. Cabo de Gata, Desierto the Tabernas and their surroundings are the only places on the continent where annual precipitation, sun hours and vegetation fulfil the criteria for this status (routes 1-4 and sites on page 130-134). Consequently, these impressive, barren landscapes have attracted naturalists for ages. The ambience of these deserts so resembled the 'Wild West' that many Hollywood directors decided to shoot their Western movies here. The flora and fauna is also unique, with many endemics or African species which find the edge of their range in southeast Andalucía.

Then there are the high mountain ranges of Eastern Andalucía, each of which is an ecological gem of its own. Dramatic landscapes coupled with high levels of endemism make these sierras superb destinations for wildlife-minded travellers.

The Sierra Nevada cannot be overlooked and towers high above Granada (routes 15-19). This massive mountain, the highest of mainland Spain, is home to many endemic insects and plants. A lot of them can be found on the *borreguiles*, unique mountain peatlands found only around the Sierra's highest peaks. Flanked by the gentle Alpujarras to the south and Sierra de Huétor to the North, the Sierra Nevada forms a special, isolated, biogeographical system.

The summits of the Sierra María-Vélez (routes 6-7) rise above 2000 m and include, in addition to many endemics, some relict species of the ice ages, some of which are also known from the Sierra Nevada.

The grassland and steppes of in the interior of east Andalucía are rewarding too. These *hoyas* (routes 5, 7 and Hoya de Baza on page 147) offer impressive desolate landscapes and a rich birdlife of the steppes. From here it is easy to access Sierra de Cazorla y Segura; several adjoining nature parks that, combined, form Spain's largest protected area (routes 8-10). The Sierra de Cazorla has not only impressive mountain landscapes and streams (including the source of the Río Guadalquivir), but also a rich flora, Spain's only endemic lizard (the Spanish Algyroides) and (reintroduced) Bearded Vultures. Finally, the Sierra de Andújar, part of the Sierra Morena (routes 13-14), is best known for harbouring one of two surviving populations of Iberian Lynx, the rarest feline in the world.

These and many other splendid natural areas make Eastern Andalucía one of Europe's finest ecotourism destinations. This guidebook aims to show you how and where to best experience it yourself.

Walking in the Alpujarras. From early spring to early summer and later again in autumn, this part of Andalucía offers the perfect conditions for hiking.

The badlands of Almería

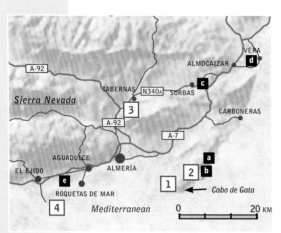

Overview of the Almería region. The letters refer to the sites on page 130-134.

Being in the rainshadow of the Sierra Nevada, the province of Almería is extremely dry. Consequently, the routes and sites in this area all explore the unique semi-desert area of this part of Spain.

The harsh environment left the area underdeveloped until a few decades ago when modern irrigation techniques suddenly made the unrelenting sunshine an asset. Large areas of excellent habitat are now covered by the unattractive white plastic 'poly-tunnels' which are the depressing hallmark of the Almería greenhouse agriculture. There is not much to attract the naturalist here, except for a small gem: the Punta Entinas-Sabinar nature reserve (route 4), located southwest of the crowded Roquetas del Mar. In this 15 km-long strip of protected coastline you will find a wildlife paradise despite being bookended at either end by holiday resorts and hemmed in by a sea of agricultural poly-tunnels to the north. East of the sea of plastic lies one of Spain's most special nature reserves, the Natural Park of Cabo de Gata-Nijar, a protected biosphere (route 1 and 2 and site A and B on page 130-131). It is a volcanic region, extremely arid and virtually treeless, characterised by rolling mountain ranges separated by wide valleys, and, at the coast, spectacular cliffs and virtually deserted beaches. Mountains are covered with clumps of Esparto and False Esparto Grass interspersed with Carob Trees, Dwarf Fan Palm and a score of shrubs, many of which are uniquely adapted to this dry environment. Cabo de Gata has some extraordinary wildlife, offers superb birding and is of great botanical interest. Just a few of its star species are Trumpeter Finch, Dupont's Lark, Black Wheatear (common), the odd plants of Maltese Fungus and Caralluma, and the pretty and localised butterfly, the Common Tiger Blue.

Further inland lies the desolate Desierto de Tabernas (route 3), in which a person can feel very small. It offers a desert atmosphere you will find nowhere else in Europe.

Ecologically, the desierto has a lot to offer. The particularly harsh climate and distinct geological conditions produced a unique area with many endemics. Here it is the dry riverbeds (barrancos or ramblas) and their rocky valleys that are the rich pickings. They do not only hold a breeding population of Trumpeter Finch (restricted to south-east Spain in mainland Europe), but also harbour a rich invertebrate and reptile life. If you crave for still more desert, you can extend your visit to include the largely barren and rugged mountain range of Sierra de Alhamilla. It rises to its maximum height at Pico Colativí (1,387m). Above 800 m, where it is a little less hot and dry, there are some outstanding holm oak woodlands. A bit east of the Desierto de Tabernas lies a final gem – the gypsum massif of Yesos de Sorbas (site C on page 132). Here the drought combined with a special, ultra-basic soil create a different environment again. This area is especially attractive for wildflowers, adapted to this odd soil type. Last, but not least, the natural attractions of the southeast extend beyond the shores of this region. Especially off the coast of Cabo de Gata lies a submarine reserve (part of the Parque Natural Sierra de Gata) which holds one of the most biodiverse and unscathed submarine ecosystems of the Mediterranean Sea. There are dive and snorkel sites from where you can discover this unexpected submarine environment.

Clear skies, a blue sea, dry hills and perfect tranquillity – those are the ingredients for a spring visit to the dry Almeria province. This is the trail near Los Escullos (site B on page 130).

Route 1: Cabo de Gata

Best season
Feb-May
Of interest
Year-round

6 HOURS, 25 KM
EASY

The essential Cabo de Gata route.
Wonderful landscape, superb birdlife and
rich flora.

Habitats semi-deserts, salt pans, saltwater marsh, dunes, sea cliffs
Selected species Maltese Fungus, Almería Rockrose*, Small-leaved Iceplant,
Greater Flamingo, White-headed Duck, Trumpeter Finch, Black-bellied
Sandgrouse, Black Wheatear, Dupont's Lark, Rufous Bush Robin, Spanish
Terrapin, Chameleon, Common Tiger Blue, Black Pennant, Black Percher

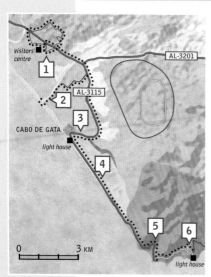

Of the many routes you can take in the Cabo de Gata, this one is the absolute must. It takes you through the various habitat types Cabo de Gata has to offer. From the salt pans, dunes and lagoons to the impressive volcanic basalt formations of the Sierra de Cabo de Gata, it offers good chances of observing the most sought-after birdlife of the region like Trumpeter Finch, White-headed Duck and Black Wheatear. Apart from birds, the scenery is wonderful and there is a very good range of reptiles, insects and wildflowers to be found.

Starting point Los Amoladeras visitors' centre (on the AL-3115 between Retamar and Cabo de Gata).

A signposted trail called *Los Amoladeras* departs behind the visitors' centre. Bear in mind that when the centre is closed, so too are the gates to the car park so park just outside the gates if you want to avoid the risk of your car being locked in.

1 This trail takes you through an abandoned sisal plantation and a fairly intact stretch of semi-desert habitat. It is the best spot along

the route for Black-bellied Sandgrouse, which is most easily found in the early morning. Iberian Grey Shrikes and Little Owls use the tall stems of the sisal flower as perches. All of the region's larks may be found here, including the rare, declining and highly elusive Dupont's Lark. The best way to locate the latter is by its peculiar song. Thymelaea is the most characteristic native plant of this landscape. Wild Jujube bush* (*Ziziphus lotus*) can also be found. This is a good example of an African plant that also occurs in the southeast corner of Spain. Butterfly enthusiasts will want to scan these bushes carefully as they are home to the diminutive Common Tiger Blue, which has its European stronghold here on the Almería coast. Long-nosed Grasshopper is fairly common, as is the graceful Thread-winged Lacewing. Small-leaved Iceplant grows on the dry dunes along with its larger cousin, the Common Iceplant (native to South-Africa).

The dunes of Cabo de Gata support a great flora (top), with masses of Gold-coin and Winged Sea-lavender in spring and in late winter the pearly-white flowers of Sea Daffodil (the leaves in the foreground). This is also a great site for Common Tiger Blue, one of the butterflies that are restricted to the arid south-east of Spain.

Take the car and follow the AL-3115 towards Cabo the Gata. Some 500 metres beyond the roundabout, go right (signposted *camping Cabo de Gata*). At the camp site, the tarmac ends. Proceed along the dirt track and take the first track on the left, which skirts the bank of a dry river bed. Find a suitable place to park the car and explore the riverbed.

2 This is the Rambla Morales, an atypical rambla in the sense that its river mouth never dries up completely, making this a very attractive site for aquatic species in the midst of all this drought. The star species here is without a doubt the White-headed Duck, which occurs in good numbers and is not hard to see. Marbled Duck and Purple Gallinule also occur, but are more elusive. Other birds to be seen here include Black-winged Stilt, Kentish Plover, Little Tern, Gull-billed Tern, Slender-billed Gull and

PRACTICAL PART

Black-necked Grebe whilst on passage, almost anything can turn up! The Maltese Fungus, a strange parasitic plant (page 68), can be found along the edges of the rambla and Yellow Horned-poppy grows in the dunes. Spanish Terrapins can be seen basking on the banks or peeking out of the water. The tamarisk bushes support a good population of Common Chameleon. In summer near the water, Lesser Emperor and Black-tailed Skimmer are easy to spot. Black Pennant and Black Percher are occasional visitors. A typical butterfly of this area is the Mediterranean Skipper, a truly coastal species.

Return to the AL-3115 and turn right towards Cabo de Gata village. Before the road enters the village, visit the bird hide on the left hand side.

3 This hide overlooks the north-western corner of the famous *Salinas de Cabo de Gata*. This is a good spot for waders like Avocet, Kentish Plover and Black-winged Stilt. Many others are possible during migration, as are many species of tern. Slender-billed Gull is also frequent on the *salinas*. Zitting Cisticola frequents grassy terrain.

The Rambla Morales is among of the best places in the whole of Spain to see the endangered White-headed Duck.

Continue into the village of Cabo de Gata and go left on the first roundabout. This road leads to the lighthouse of Cabo de Gata with the beach on your right and the *salinas* on your left.

4 Three more bird hides can be found on the edge of the Salinas along this road. All offer more or less the same species, yet we recommend visiting all three. In addition to the birds that may also be seen at the first hide, Flamingos are the most obvious attraction, with dozens or at times even hundreds of birds present. The strip of low dunes between the beach and the salt pans is of great botanical interest, with both iceplants, masses of Winged Sea-lavender, Sea-heath, the catch-flies *Silene litorrea* and *S. ramosissima*, Dune Galingale and Pedunculate Toadflax* (*Linaria pedunculata*), all putting on a great show in spring. The 'dandelion' with the black centre of the flowerhead is Coastal Reichardia* (*Reichardia gaditana*), another African-Iberian species. Birds include large numbers of Thekla and the occasional Short-toed,

View over the cliffs of
Cabo de Gata.

Lesser Short-toed and Calandra Larks. Trumpeter Finch is also seen here fairly regularly and Spectacled Warbler frequents the scrub, along with the more common Sardinian Warbler. Spiny-footed Lizard is easily observed on and around the sandy trails. At the coast, Sea Daffodil flowers in August to October, while in mid-winter, this is the location of the rare Almeria Sand-crocus* (*Androcymbium europeum*).

5 The road climbs up towards the Sierra de Cabo de Gata, where Dwarf Fan Palm dominates the vegetation. Black Wheatear is frequent and Dartford Warbler is also possible. This is also one of the best places for Trumpeter Finch, although this highly mobile species is hard to pin down to a specific location. Butterflies you may encounter include Green-striped White, Spanish Marbled White, Bath White, Mallow Skipper, Long-tailed Blue and Spanish Gatekeeper. The endemic flora of Cabo de Gata is represented by *Sideritis osteoxylla* and Almería Rockrose* (*Helianthemum almeriense*). The large, yellow flowers of Goldcoin are conspicuous.

6 The main road leads to the lighthouse, while a tarmac road branches off to the left some 500 m before the cape (signposted *Aula del Mar*) leads to an ancient watch tower. The viewpoint near the lighthouse provides views over the famous *Arrecife de las Sirenas* (Siren's Reef). This is an excellent spot for watching seabirds like Shag, Cory's and Yelkouan Shearwaters and Audouin's Gull.
The road to the guard tower crosses more likely Black Wheatear and Trumpeter Finch territory.

Return via the same way.

PRACTICAL PART

Route 2: San José

!

No shade
on this route

Best season
February-May
Of interest
Year-round

FULL DAY
EASY

Another splendid walk along the coastal cliffs.
A favoured haunt of Trumpeter Finch and one of Spain's two Shag colonies.
Rich desert flora.

Habitats semi-desert, beaches, coastal cliffs and barrancos
Selected species Trumpeter Finch, Black Wheatear, Shag, Audouin's Gull,
Rock Sparrow, Stone Curlew, Cabo de Gata Snapdragon*, Cabo de Gata Pink*,
Yellow Horned-poppy, Sea Daffodil, Common Tiger Blue

This route takes you from San José to the lighthouse (*faro*) of Cabo de Gata (the end point of the previous route) along one of Spain's most pristine coastal strips. Arid plains and mountains are fringed by scenic bays with golden beaches and splendid granite coastal cliffs. This is one of the best wildflower walks of Cabo de Gata, but birdwatchers will enjoy it too, as there is a great mixture of desert species and seabirds.

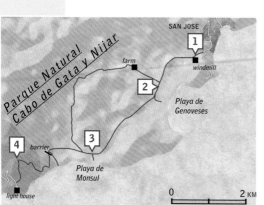

Note that the playas de Monsúl and Genovese are popular beaches so beat the crowds and start this route early. The first stretch of this route can be driven by car.

Starting point San José.
In the village, keep right and follow the signs *Playa Mónsul* and *Playa Genovese*. Park near the Andalucían windmill.

1 The scrubland around the windmill is covered in masses of Almería Rockrose* (*Helianthemum almeriense*). Take care to distinguish it from the similar-looking *Helianthemum violaceum*, which has oblong, rather than linear, leaves. Various asphodels, Hairy Horehound* (*Ballota hirsuta*) and the sea-lavenders *Limonium sinuatum* and *L. lobatum* and Iberian and Purple Jerusalem-sages make for a great bouquet. A scatter

of Dwarf Fan Palm adds a green tone. In the shelter of the gully there are butterflies like Green-underside Blue and Spanish Gatekeeper.
Sardinian Warbler and Spotless Starling take shelter in the small bushes and Eucalyptus trees.

The main road continues and cuts through a small steppe-like depression.

The unspoilt beach of Playa Monsúl (top). The cliffs here are home to the endemic Charidem's Pink (bottom).

2 The dry and flowery grassland gives way to more fertile soil. In spring the pink Mallow-leaved Bindweed flowers in profusion. Thekla Lark and Woodchat Shrike are easily seen, but keep your eyes open for Stone Curlew as well. A small Prickly Pear plantation is situated in the middle of the depression. A short hike to the left (signposted *Playa Genovese*) leads to the beach and adjacent dunes where a glasswort of the African deserts, *Anabasis articulata*, grows, together with Yellow Horned-poppy.

Continue the road to Playa Mónsul. For the next kilometre you pass an abandoned Sisal plantation. Beyond it, you'll see the sea, just behind the dunes.

3 Check the Wild Jujube Bush* (*Ziziphus lotus*) around the building and close to the road for Common Tiger Blue. Follow the trail down to the beach. Here you find some impressive rock formations and it is a good place to look for Sandwich Tern, Audouin's Gull and Gannets. In this area you find typical flowers of the coastal areas like Sea Daffodil, Ice Plant and Goldcoin. Black Wheatears are common on rocky slopes while its relative, the Black-eared Wheatear, favours more level terrain.

Continue on the main track that leads through scrubland and across the dry *Barranco del Mónsul*. The barrier is as far as you can go by car. The final section that connects with the Faro de Cabo de Gata must be covered on foot.

4 Beyond the barrier there is a clear shift in landscape and vegetation. On your left, there are well-preserved sections of coastal cliffs and on your right rocky slopes. Scan the sea for gulls, terns and the occasional Gannet, Yelkouan and Cory's Shearwaters. Peregrine nest on the cliffs and may be seen hunting in the area. On the cliff below Shag (of the Mediterranean race *desmrestii*) has one of its last colonies on the Spanish Mediterranean coast. Along the track, look for butterflies like Green-striped White, Portuguese Dappled White, Blue-spot Hairstreak, Southern Brown Argus and Spanish Gatekeeper. The best place for insects and flowers is the large valley about half way to the lighthouse.

Trumpeter Finch (top) and Black Wheatear (bottom) are two sought-after birds of rocky habitats that can be found in the barrancos on this route.

The diverse vegetation here includes some interesting species like Boccone's Sea-spurrey* (*Spergularia bocconei*), the local endemic Cabo de Gata Snapdragon* (*Antirrhinum charidemi*) and Cabo de Gata Pink* (*Dianthus charidemi*), Sea Mallow, more Almería Rockrose and the curious Virgin's Mantle (*Fagonia cretica*).

The rocky slopes are a favourite haunt of the Trumpeter Finch, which can best be located by the calls that gives it its name. In the same area Subalpine Warbler, Blue Rock Thrush, Black Wheatear, Rock Bunting, Raven, Alpine and Pallid Swifts and are frequently seen.

You can walk all the way up to the lighthouse. Return via the same way.

Route 3: Desierto de Tabernas

6 HOURS
EASY

Europe's only inland semi-desert.
A unique flora and fauna, set in an extraordinary landscape.

Best season
February-May
Of interest
October-June

Habitats semi-desert, ramblas, mountains
Selected species Trumpeter Finch, Black Wheatear, Bonelli's Eagle, Rufous
Bush Robin, Back-bellied Sandgrouse, Wild Oleander, Ladder Snake, Spanish
Ibex, Maltese Fungus, Almería Sea-lavender, Yellow Cistanche, Desert Orange-tip

This route takes you through the splendid semi-desert landscapes of the Desierto de Tabernas, with *ramblas*, steppes and mountains. It is home to many typical desert birds like Trumpeter Finch and Black Wheatear, and a good number of attractive wildflowers that include plants of dry cliffs as well as a number of salt-tolerant plants like Cistanche, Maltese Fungus and sea-lavenders. The region is famous for serving as background to many clas-

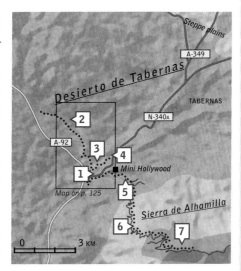

sic Hollywood movies (see textbox on page 24). A fact to which the many Western-themed recreational parks bear testimony.

Starting point The A92 exit to the N340a Tabernas/Sorbas.
Immediately after the exit, the N340a takes you across the *Rambla de Tabernas*. After the bridge, turn right onto a dirt track and park. Follow the dirt track on foot as it descends into the rambla. Follow the streambed to the right.

The Yellow Cistanche (top) and Maltese Fungus (bottom) are two odd-looking, parasitical plants that grow on saline vegetation in the Rambla of Tabernas.

1 A hike through this dry riverbed is the best way to explore the semi-desert. The arid soil, the abandoned farmhouses and fields make for an impressive, if somewhat unsettling landscape. It is particularly interesting from an ecological point of view. Although the riverbed is (usually) dry, the ground is more damp here than outside the rambla, which attracts all manner of plants and animals. It is one of the best spots in mainland Europe to find Trumpeter Finch. Black Wheatear, Rock Sparrow and Rock Bunting are common. Alpine Swift hunts in the gorge and Lesser Kestrel is also present. The Tamarisk and Oleander thickets are favoured by warblers. Of the attractive flora, Maltese Fungus can be found in the sand beneath the Tamarisks, while the endemic Euzomodendron prefers more rocky substrate. The latter is a bushy species of Mustard, one of the few with woody stems. Conspicuous patches of the pink flowering Almería Sealavender* (*Limonium insigne*) form a bright contrast to the pale carpets of False Esparto Grass.

Ahead, the rambla splits in two. One trail goes left (northwest along the A92) and the other turns right (east along the N340a towards the town of Tabernas). Both are worth exploring.

2 The branch that follows the A92 provides more of the habitat and species described at the previous point. The ramblas are also excellent spots to look for snakes. On our own exploration of the area, we found an enormous Ladder Snake here.

3 In the gorge that leads to Tabernas, you'll see a conspicuous line of holes in the cliff face to the right. This is an odd geological phenomenon typical of silty arid badlands, called 'piping' – the natural formation of drainage tubes, which gradually collapse. Look in the dry sand in these pipes for the funnel-shaped traps of Antlions. In spring, botanists will be pleased to find the stout, yellow Cistanche broomrape, while in summer, the Desert Orange-tip flies in this area.

4 Some 900 metres after the trail to Tabernas branches off to the right, a narrow gorge empties into the Rambla de Tabernas from the right. This gorge is wetter than the surrounding land and an exploration of this small 'oasis' may very well be rewarded with sightings of some interesting butterflies, dragonflies and birds.

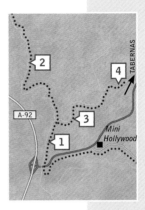

Retrace your steps back to the car and continue along the N340a in the direction of Tabernas. After 700 m you will find the 'Mini Hollywood' theme park on your right. Turn right here towards the entrance and, keeping the theme park on your right, follow the road that leads into the mountains. This hardly used service road leads all the way to a radio tower on the summit of the Sierra Alhamilla. Note that the road can be in a very bad condition and is in times impossible to navigate with a normal rental car! The Sierra Alhamilla is Europe's most arid mountain range. This road allows you to explore it from its base all the way to the summit.

Rambla de Tabernas in the evening light.

5 In the lower ranges, just beyond mini-Hollywood, the steppe terrain hosts Calandra Lark, Stone Curlew, Black-eared Wheatear and Woodchat Shrike plus small numbers of Black-bellied Sandgrouse. The flora in spring is splendid too, with Caralluma, Broom-like Kidney-vetch* (*Anthyllis cytisoides*), beautiful stands of Purple Jerusalem-sage, Red Horned-poppy, the African-Iberian endemic *Maytenus senegalensis* and more Almería Sea-lavender* (*Limonium insigne*).

6 Ascending in more mountainous terrain, check the gorges for Black Wheatear and Trumpeter Finch. The wheatear is quite common, but for the finch you'll need to search a little harder.
Very typical of this part is the colourful scrub of Bolina Greenweed* (*Genista spartioides*).

The Bolina Green-weed* (*Genista spartioides*) is a conspicuous plant in the Sierra de Alhamilla – it flowers in April and May.

7 The highest zones in this part of the sierra are covered with Aleppo Pines. Here you can find species which are adapted to life in coniferous forests like Common Crossbill, Firecrest, Coal and Crested Tits.

Time permitting, visit the semi-desert plains just northeast of Tabernas – a good area for steppe birds that also sports an interesting flora. Explore the minor roads that depart from the A349.

Route 4: The salt pans and dunes of Punta Entinas-Sabinar

6 HOURS
EASY

Of interest
Year-round

A natural oasis between the endless greenhouses.
Prime birdwatching spot; best place to find Marbled Duck.

Habitats dunes, salt pans, saltmarsh
Selected species Phoenician Juniper, Marbled Duck, White-headed Duck, Crested Coot, Collared Pratincole, Gull-billed Tern, Greater Flamingo, Slender-billed Gull, Common Chameleon, Bedriaga's Skink, Spiny-footed Lizard, Black Percher

Punta Entinas-Sabinar is, with Cabo de Gata, among the very few spots that escaped the monstrous urban development which has scarred most of Almería's coast. Don't be put off by the approach through the unrelenting kilometres of plastic greenhouses that enshroud Las Norias de Daza (which is rightly described as

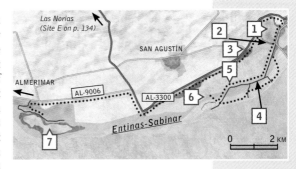

one of Europe's most hideous landscapes) as this natural park remains an ecological gem which absolutely merits a visit.
Although primarily known as a birding site, Punta Entinas is also an important enclave for several species of reptiles and insects.

Starting point Playa Serena

Getting there : On the A7 between Almería and El Ejido, take exit 420 and follow *La Mojanera*. In this village, follow signs for Roquetas de Mar. After a short while, Parque Natural Sabinar is signposted. When you arrive at the reedy fringe of a lake, turn left (signposted *Roquetas de Mar*). At the next roundabout, take the exit signposted *Urbanización Playa Serena*. Beyond the football field on the right, turn right onto the *Avenida de Cerrillos*.

PRACTICAL PART

The wetlands and dunes of Punta Entinas-Sabinar (top) are primarily known as a birdwatching site, but there are some rare, southern dragonflies too, such as this Black Percher (bottom).

1 Before you arrive at the reserve gate, you have some clear views over a lake on the right. This lake has a good number of White-headed ducks which are usually easy to spot (albeit distant). Red-crested Pochard and other waterfowl are also possible.

Park your car at the entrance gate and proceed into the park on foot.

2 The Tamarisk scrub on the dunes near the gate is home to a small population of Chameleon. At times, masses of Clouded Yellow and Painted Lady look for nectar in the low vegetation. The Black Percher (a dragonfly) honours its name by perching up on the vegetation while Iberian Bluetail prefers to remain hidden within.

3 After 500 m, the *Salinas Viejas* (old salt pans) become visible. The abandoned salt pans, transformed into splendid saltwater marshes, are the main attraction of the reserve. This is where the rare and otherwise elusive Marbled Duck is relatively easy to find. Other species you may see here are White-headed Duck, Common Shelduck, Purple Gallinule, Slender-billed Gull, Gull-billed Tern, Little Tern, Collared Pratincole, Kentish Plover, Black-winged Stilt, Avocet and Marsh Harrier. Some of the old banks that used to separate the salt pans are still accessible. You may use them to take a closer look at the salt marshes.

4 Left of the track the terrain is drier with patches of sandy dunes, scrublands and shallow or dried-up pools. Spiny-footed Lizard is frequent

along the track. With some luck you may also come across a Stone Curlew or a Hoopoe. The scrub is home to Sardinian, Spectacled and Dartford Warblers. Lesser Kestrel sometimes drifts over to hunt. One strange creature that is endemic to the Iberian peninsula occurs here: the Bedriaga's Skink. This buffy lizard with its minuscule limbs is shy and not easy to find. It is able to burrow quickly in loose sand and does so when alarmed.

5 Further ahead, the *Salinas Viejas* make way for the *Salinas de Cerrillos*. These saltpans are far less overgrown and therefore harbour less wildlife. Flamingo, however, is very common.

6 The trail ends at an abandoned pumping station where once the water flow into and out of the saltpans was managed. It is a nice, shady spot for a picnic with views over the *salinas*.

You may choose to return to the car the way you came, but it is also possible to walk along the beach back to Playa Serena or by the myriad of trails through the dunes that all lead back to the gate. The ruin of an old watch tower may be worth a visit to those interested in the history of the region (see also page 54).

While you are in the area, visit the westernmost lake of the reserve near Almerimar. To get there, return to the AL-3300 and follow it towards Almerimar (via AL-9006). Where the greenhouses on the right end, take the first dirt track left. Park near the cliff and proceed on foot along the trail that descends from the cliff to the lake.

The marshes of Punta Entinas-Sabinar are home to the rare Marbled Duck.

7 This lake has a lot of waterfowl and many flamingos but its main claim to fame is a reintroduced population of Crested Coot. You'll need a telescope to distinguish them from the numerous Common Coots, particularly in winter when the red-knobs that give the bird its alternative name, Red-knobbed Coot, have shrunk into insignificance. An additional attraction here is the chance of coming across a Roller.

130

Additional sites in and around Cabo de Gata

A – Rodalquilar and Ruta de Minería

Best season
February-May

We highly recommend a visit to the botanical garden in Rodalquilar, where you get an excellent overview of the peculiar semi-desert flora of the Almería province. The botanical garden is also the starting point for an attractive historical walk to and through the ruins of a large, 19th century mining complex.

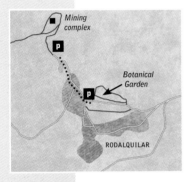

Mining was (and to a degree still is) an important industry in eastern Andalucía. This complex dates from 1504 when it was built to extract alum. In the 19th century, gold was an important ore. The site was closed in the 1960's when the gold was nearly depleted. These facilities, now deserted, were scenes for famous movies like Indiana Jones and the Last Crusade and some 'Spaghetti' Westerns.

The route through the mining complex follows a dirt road above the old factory and crosses an attractive semi-desert landscape dominated by a Phoenician Juniper scrub. Particularly attractive are the hues of colour in the rocks, which are best appreciated in the mornings and evenings. The many mine shaft entrances are important breeding sites for birds and bats. Lesser Kestrel, Black Redstart and Blue Rock Thrush are frequent birds.

The scrubland around Rodalquilar is dominated by Phoenician Junipers.

The second part of the route is rather different. It leads through flat agricultural land. Dwarf Fan Palms grow in the rocky grasslands and numerous flowers colour the thin turf. Rock Sparrow and Common Linnet are attracted to spilt seeds, while Woodchat and Iberian Grey Shrikes hunt for insects from shrubs and poles. Near a distinctive water storage hut, shaped like an igloo, is the start of the walking route *Sendero Cortijo del Fraile* that takes you 1.4 km into the stony grassland.

Moorish Geckos are common in the coastal region of Almería.

B – Walk from San José to Fondeadero de los Escullos

Best season
February-May

The Loma Pelada trail leads along the coast at the foot of the volcanic domes from San José to Fondeadero de los Escullos. It is an easy linear route of approximately 6.5 km length that offers a stunning scenery of cliffs, ravines, small beaches, all of volcanic origin. The vegetation varies from fairly lush, grassy places to dry scrubland. This route is superb for finding the characteristic flora and fauna of Cabo de Gata. Among the birds, Trumpeter Finch and Black Wheatear are star species. Out at sea, there are Audouin's Gull, Shag, Gannet and Sandwich Tern and shearwaters. On your quest for flora, check the gullies that run down to the sea for Thymelea, Caralluma and Spanish Silkvine.

Long-nosed Grasshopper (left) is a frequent sight in the dunes. Spanish Silkvine (right) is one of the odd plants typical of Cabo de Gata.

Find the start of the walk by turning left at the roundabout at the entrance of San José. Pass the camp site and continue on the dirt track. Go straight at the three-way fork and park near the information panel, from where the trail starts (green markings). Alternatively, start on the north side where you can park near the Higuera creek south of Los Escullos.

C – Karst en Yesos de Sorbas

Best season
January-May
Of interest
October - June

This eroded landscape is composed of gypsum (*Yeso*) and is one of the most spectacular of its kind in the world. The karstified gypsum plain is bone-dry and forms a stark contrast with the Río Aguas that has cut through the uplands. Being fed by ground water from deep within the gypsum soils, it is one of the few rivers in the area that maintains a constant flow year-round. Encased by sheer-sided ravines, the natural springs have created a mini-oasis of great ecological importance in the midst of the desert.

In places, the river is lined with dense vegetation, such as reeds, rushes and bulrushes, with oleanders, willows, poplars and ash trees growing along its banks. There are masses of Nightingales, Cetti's Warblers and Great Reed Warblers. Golden Oriole also breeds. The cliffs and the plain sport impressive gypsum formations. Crag Martin and Black Wheatear, Bonelli's Eagles and Common Kestrels inhabit the rocky cliffs. Spectacled Warblers prefer the arid, upland steppe.

The Yesos de Sorbas is one of Spain's few remaining refuges of the highly endangered Spur-thighed Tortoise, while Spanish Terrapin, Moorish and Turkish Geckos, Ladder and Horseshoe Whip Snakes are other noteworthy reptiles. The gypsum soil is a rare, alkaline kind of substrate that supports a number of rare plants, some of which are endemic. True stars of Yesos de Sorbas are Spanish Coris (*Coris hispanicus*), Whorl-leaved Narcissus* (*Narcissus tortifolius*), Cartagena Toadflax* (*Chaenorhinum grandiflorum*), the yellow rockrose *Helianthemun alypoides* and the tall, white-flowered germander *Teucrium*

The gypsum bedrock has an odd structure (bottom). This ultra-basic rock type supports many rare orchids, such as this Fan-lipped Orchid (top).

turredanum, all of which are endemic to Sorbas and surroundings. Of the latter, only 6 populations are known. Fan-lipped and Mirror Orchids are fairly frequent.

There is a well-marked trail of 2 km through the reserve – the PR-A97 *Sendero de Los Molinos de Río Aguas*, which starts 7 km east of Sorbas. Turn off the right side of the N-340 onto the A-1102 local road that leads to a small group of scattered farmhouses known as *Los Molinos del Río Aguas*. Park just beyond the km 5 post from where the PR-A97 is signposted, which brings you by the Río Aguas up to Nacimiento.

At Nacimiento you can wander round a bit. From Los Molinos del Río Aguas in opposite direction, you enter the gorge *Barranco del Tesoro*, which is the principal botanical site.

D – The marshes and river mouths of Playas de Vera

The tourist resort Playas de Vera is located east of Vera on the coast. There is a marsh and there are three small estuaries which are all worth a visit for their birdlife.

Of interest
Year-round

The marshes are easy to find along the ALP 118 coastal road, opposite the *Consum* supermarket. It is possible to walk around the edge of the marsh. The quiet north side offers the best view over the laguna during the morning. Slender-billed Gull, waders and waterfowl like Teal, Red-crested Pochard, Common Pochard and White-headed Duck are often present. The marsh houses Purple Gallinule, Little Bittern and Marsh Harrier, while Cetti's Warbler can often be heard. Bonelli's and Booted Eagle frequently soar overhead. Spring and autumn are interesting for migrating songbirds. Note that Playas de Vera is a naturist beach and binoculars and telephoto lenses are not appreciated.

Both north and south of Playas are the river mouths of the Río Almanzora, Río Antas and Río Aguas, all of which are worth visiting.

Slender-billed Gulls in the evening light, at the river mouth of Playas de Vera.

They are important gull roosts with Audouin's, Mediterranean, Black-headed, Yellow-legged and Slender-billed Gull. These sites are best approached from the beach and are good for waders as well.

Reedbeds and marshy spots are good for finding Purple Gallinule, White-headed Duck, Glossy Ibis, Cattle Egret, Little Bittern, and Great Reed, Savi's, and Moustached Warblers.

The Río Almanzora lies approximately 3 km north of Playas de Vera, where access is easy from either embankment.

The estuary of the Río Antas is just south of Playas and best visited by taking the roundabout before (north) of the river in the village of Puerto de la Rey. You exit onto the Av. Puerto Rey and go right at the Y-junction (Av. la Laguna) to arrive at the estuary.

The Río Aguas flows approximately 2 km south of Garrucha and north of Vista de los Ángeles-Rumina. Park before the bridge on the beach.

E – Cañada de Las Norias

Of interest
Year-round

The two lakes of Cañada de las Norias are located north of the village of Las Norias. and are nowadays designated as Ornithological Reserve. Despite the alienating and depressing environment with shimmering plastic as far as the eye can see, the area holds a superb selection of waterfowl and passerines.

Amongst the residents are Purple Gallinule, Penduline Tit, Whiskered Tern, Red-Crested Pochard, White-headed and Marbled Ducks, Lesser Short-toed Lark, a large Squacco Heron colony and lots of waders.

Dragonflies include beauties like Lesser Emperor, Violet Dropwing and Green-eyed Hawker.

To get to Cañada, take the *Las Norias / La Mojonera* exit from the E15 and follow *Las Norias*. The most eastern part of the lake (turn left just after the school zone sign) offers the best birding.

The Cañada de las Norias has a large colony of Squacco Herons.

The central plains of East Andalucía

As you travel from Granada to the coasts of Almería, you cross an empty land – bleak, featureless plains and arid sierras exude a forlorn atmosphere. Most travellers see little more of the central plains than the views from the A92N motorway and that is a shame. Although perhaps not as rich as the Cabo de Gata, Sierra de Nevada or Cazorla, the plains (*hoyas*) are interesting enough to spend some time exploring them. As they are located in

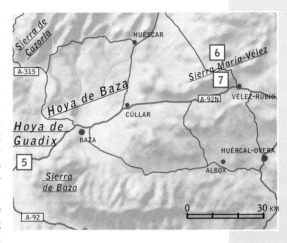

the centre of eastern Andalucía, other great sites are never far away.

Steppe-like fields and grasslands dominate the Hoyas de Guadix and Baza – both are of great value for steppe birds. The plains are dissected by mountain ranges, a few rivers and areas of sand dunes. Guadix is the central town of the area.

Despite being sedimentation plains, the hoyas are far from flat. Encircled by higher mountains and creviced by deep gorges, the hoyas display some of the most breath-taking scenery in the region and are a superb location for landscape photographers. At an altitude of between 800 and 1,000 metres, the climate on the plateaux is harsh, which is reflected in the landscape.

The *hoyas* boast a rich flora and fauna, of which the birds form the greatest draw (route 5 and Hoya de Baza; page 147). The surrounding sierras are superb as well. The desolate Sierra de Baza rises up to 2,270 m and is a wonderful area, but with a very poor infrastructure, hence hard to explore. The area is best accessed from Gor in the west or from the northeast via Caniles. The Sierra María is more easily explored (route 6 and 7). Attractive areas of inland sand dunes are found in the Hoya de Baza (site on page 147).

The Greenish Black-tip, a butterfly of deserts, has one of its few populations in Spain in the Sierra de Baza.

136

Route 5: Hoya de Guadix

6 HOURS, 50 KM
EASY

Best season
February-June

Of interest
Year-round

Steppes, badlands and dehesas with a rich birdlife.

Habitats steppe, dehesa, limestone mountains, hedgehog scrub, rivers
Selected species Mirror Orchid, Wild Tulip, Red Deer, Black-bellied Sandgrouse, Little Bustard, Great Spotted Cuckoo, Roller, Griffon Vulture, Calandra Lark, Portuguese Dappled White

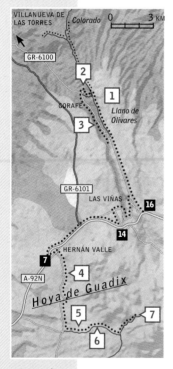

Black numbers refer to motorway exits.

The ancient seafloor that now constitutes the Hoya de Guadix (plain of Guadix) is one of Andalucía's finest steppe areas. Where water has carved into the friable sediments, the steppe gives way to deep gorges and impressive badlands. The lush gorge of Gorafe and the badlands of *El Colorado* are two splendid examples. This route visits both the badlands and the plains. Scenically it is beautiful and the birdlife is rich, although some species are fairly difficult to track down. Historically, the region is of interest as well. Spain's most extensive Dolmen field and the Moorish cave dwellings bear witness to the rich history of the region.

Starting point Exit 16 to Gorafe.
Where the road to Gorafe turns left into the gorge, turn right onto a dirt track signposted Parque *Megalítico*.

1 This dirt track takes you through some splendid dehesas and steppes. Calandra Lark and Rock Sparrow are common. It is also possible, though with a bit more luck and perseverance, to see Black-bellied Sandgrouse, Tawny Pipit, Black-eared Wheatear and Little Bustard. Griffon Vultures can be seen soaring overhead. You will also see several stone tombs (dolmen). These are remnants of an ancient civilization that existed on the banks of the Río Gor. Some 5000 years ago, this valley was at an important crossroads of trade routes.

Shortly after the track enters an almond grove. A track to the left descends into the gorge towards Gorafe.
Beyond this point a network of tracks
continues all the way to Villanueva
de las Torres. If you want to see more
steppe and the beautiful Colorado badlands it is well worth exploring. Follow
Campillo for a scenic little steppe
area and *Colorado* for some splendid
badlands. Be aware though that the
quality of the tracks can be very bad
in places or even impassable without
4x4. Return if you feel the track is not
safe to drive! The route described here
turns left to Gorafe.

2 This road snakes into the gorge.
You have excellent views along
the valley and the cliffs, where Black
Wheatear, Rock Bunting and Red-
billed Chough breed. Here you can
also admire some typical *cuevas trog-
loditas* or cave houses.

In Gorafe, follow the GR-6100 back to the A92N.

3 This green gorge offers some scenic views. A high
number of magpies makes it an excellent spot to
look for its parasite, the Great Spotted Cuckoo, which
reaches its highest density in Spain in this region.
There are various side tracks where you can stop and
explore.

Follow the A92N to Guadix and take the Hernán Valle exit (exit 7). Turn left
into the village, proceed all the way to the other side and take a sharp right
at a small roundabout with a large boulder.

4 This road leads into the steppes of Hernán Valle where you have another shot at Little Bustard, Stone Curlew, Black-bellied Sandgrouse,

The maze of gorges
and table mountains
of *El Colorado* is
superb (top). Little
Owls breed in the open
plains of the Hoya de
Guadix (bottom).

Little Owl and Thekla, Short-toed, Lesser Short-toed and Calandra Larks. Black Wheatear and Great Spotted Cuckoo also occur. The Roller, a scarce bird in much of Europe, is surprisingly common.

After 6.5 km on this road, turn left on a crossing onto a dirt track (the tarmac road ahead leads into a valley).

5 This dirt track brings you towards the foothills of the Sierra de Baza. It crosses some more steppe, groves and dehesa before reaching a farm. Keep an eye out for all the aforementioned species en route.

At the farm, turn left. After 140 metres, the track forks. Turn right.

The plains of the Hoya de Guadix are a great place to see Rollers (top). Red Deer frequently descend from the nearby sierras to graze on the steppes (bottom).

6 You then arrive at the first rocky outcrops of the Sierra de Baza. Explore this area at will. Red Deer are common in the area. You are now high enough to have entered the hedgehog vegetation zone (see page 41) and you will see by the many spiny cushions of the blue Hedgehog Broom (p. 69), flowering in May. On rocky slopes, look for Wild Tulips.

When this track ends at a T-junction, turn left towards the hills.

7 This track (and the route) ends at a quarry. Black-eared Wheatear and Iberian Grey Shrike breed in the area and Mirror Orchid grows abundantly near the quarry in late April – May. The valley left of the track is also worth exploring for wildflowers.

Route 6: Steppes and Mountains of Sierra de María de los Vélez

FULL DAY
EASY

Surprising day trip in a theatre of steppe, mountains and little visited places.

Best season
February-June
Of interest
Year-round

Habitats steppe, scrubland, forest
Selected species Spanish Fritillary, Lesser Kestrel, Little Bustard, Black-bellied Sandgrouse, Stone Curlew, Tawny Pipit, Black Wheatear, Rock Bunting, Rock Thrush, Provence Hairstreak, Mother-of-Pearl Blue, Lorquin's Blue, Provence Hairstreak, Mediterranean Bluet

This route provides a complete overview of the Sierra María- los Veléz – a little visited limestone mountain range with a fine mixture of Mediterranean and hedgehog scrubland, pine and oak woodland, temporary streams and a large area of steppes. This route visits all these habitats and offers good birdwatching (particularly steppe birds), while several strolls into the countryside should yield an attractive flora, butterfly and reptile fauna.

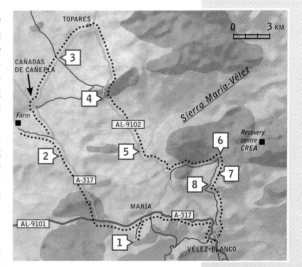

Starting point Vélez-Blanco
Follow the A-317 out of the village in the direction of María to the A-317. Turn right to María and just beyond this village turn left to *Umbría de la Virgin* and the Botanical Garden.

1 Before entering the botanical garden look for the rare Provence Hairstreak in the adjacent grassland. The large botanical garden of Umbría de la Virgen shows many habitats that naturally occur in the

region. As it not grazed like most of the Sierra, the wildflowers of the region occur in higher than usual numbers. Among them are various flax and toadflax species, Spanish Fritillary and Sunset Foxglove. In September the Saffron Crocus is abundant.

Within the garden you have the option to walk a 1.5 or a 3.2 km loop. The latter climbs up to an altitude of 1,600 metres, homeland of many botanical specialities and of the Apollo butterfly. Throughout the site, butterflies like Mother-of-Pearl Blue, Comma and Oriental Meadow Brown can be found, the latter preferring the rocks to warm up. The birdlife includes Rock Bunting, Bonelli's Warbler, Subalpine Warbler and Short-toed Treecreeper. The garden's opening times are Tue-Sun from 10:00 to 14:00 and 18:00 to 20:00 (May – September) and 10:00 to 16:00 (October – April).

By car, return to the A-317 and turn left. The first stretch is dominated by almond groves that give way to pine forest further on. After 4.3 km, turn right to la Cañada on a road that crawls up through the pinewoods and later enters a wide area of steppe.

2 Explore the steppe for Black-bellied Sandgrouse, Little Bustard, Tawny Pipit and Calandra Lark. We recommend checking the first dirt track to the left to the old *Cortijo del Pozo Gallardo*. Rock Sparrows, Black-eared Wheatear and Tawny Pipit can be found, while Lesser Kestrel breeds at the *Cortijo*.

The Jardín botánico: for a 'garden' the landscape is rather wild.

Leave the A-317 beyond la Cañada and turn right after this farming village to Topares.

3 This stretch of steppe is again interesting for birds. Lesser Kestrel, Red-billed Chough and Iberian Grey Shrike can turn up any-where, while near farms and ruins, you might encounter Rock Bunting, Hoopoe and Woodchat Shrike.

In the small village of Topares keep right and follow the sign to Vélez-Blanco. You pass

through a rolling countryside of fields with scattered solitary oaks. Listen here for Quail – a bird of fields that has become rare in many places as a result of changing agricultural practices.

4 At *Km 19* you reach an excellent limestone area with pines and oaks. Park and stroll around in search of wildflowers and butterflies. The entire area is a hotspot for rare 'weeds' of arable fields, which are presented here by the pretty Purple Poppy* (*Roemeria hybrida*) and its relative, the odd, yellow Hypecoum. In addition, there are Yellow Bee Orchid, the small, yellow rockrose *Fumana ericoides* and its white, bushy cousin *Helianthemum violaceum*. Several hedgehog species, like Spiny Vella* (*Vella spinosa*) and Spiny Alison* (*Hormatophylla spinosa*) grow here too, together with Iberian Jerusalem-sage and Blue Aphyllanthes. Among the butterflies, Green-underside and Lorquin's Blue are species to look out for. The latter is endemic to Andalucía and southern Portugal.

Continue downhill through the salmon-and-cream coloured limestone hills, with Mount Gabar as a conspicuous rock in the background. At *Km 11*, park on the dirt track at your left. Walk down to the small river.

Although they're not easy to find, Stone Curlews are not at all rare in the steppes and arid fields around the Sierra María (top). The Spur-thighed Tortoise (bottom) in contrast, is a rare and secretive creature. It is thought to have been introduced by the Greeks or Moors and has its main Spanish stronghold in these mountains.

PRACTICAL PART

142

5 Two water sources attract a lot of wildlife. The air is full with sounds of frogs and crickets. Shallow pools, fringed with Water Parsnip are suitable habitat for dragonflies like Mediterranean Bluet, Iberian Bluetail and Southern Skimmer. Small wasps of the subfamily *Vespinae*, (the 'yellowjackets'), make conspicuous nests in the sedges. You may find Red-rumped Swallow and Hoopoe, while the reedbed may host Water Rail.

The road continues through scrubland and later almond groves. Where you re-enter the Nature Park of María-Vélez, turn left in the direction of Gabar. After 4.5 km, the road forks. Turn right. You enter pinewoods again. Stop at the intersection just beyond a small white house.

Two special species that you may find in spring in the open pinewoods of the Sierra de María: Blue-spot Hairstreak (top) and Spanish Fritillary – the flower, not the butterfly (bottom).

6 A belt of grasses indicates a dry river bed, which Red Deer and Wild Boar use to rest and forage. Thyme, Rosemary and other herbs attract butterflies. Crossbill and Crested Tit occur in the pine forest. A specialty of the woods here is the impressive Southern Pine Hawk-moth – look for it on the tree trunks.

From here you can make a detour (4.5 km) to the campsite and the Recovery Centre in Endangered Species (CREA) ,which has a breeding program running for the Spur-thighed Tortoise, that occurs in Las Almohallas, part of the Sierra de María. Our route goes right on the tarmac in the direction of Vélez-Blanco.

7 This is a section of terraced agricultural land mixed with Juniper scrubland. Woodlark, Hoopoe, Bee-eater and Black-eared Wheatear are widespread in this area.

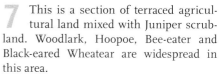

8 After approximately 5 km you cross a small river (dry in summer). Rosemary and other herbs attract butterflies like Adonis Blue, Red-underwing Skipper and Great Banded Grayling. Golden Oriole, Bee-eater and Red-rumped Swallow are frequent and Ocellated Lizard is easily found.

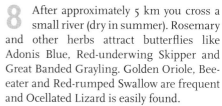

The route continues and brings you back to the village of Vélez-Blanco.

Route 7: Circling around the Maimón mountain

FULL DAY, 18 KM
MODERATE

Day trip around the Maimón massive with rich wildlife and prehistoric caves in the Sierra María-Vélez.

Best season
February-June
Of interest
Year-round

Habitats mountain, grassland, scrubland, forest
Selected species Griffon Vulture, Booted Eagle, Black Wheatear, Rock Bunting, Rock Trush, Apollo, Ladder Snake, Montpellier Snake

The circular walk around Mount Maimón is perhaps the most attractive walk in the Sierra de María – Los Vélez. It leads through a diverse landscape of scrub and pine forest to the foot of the steep cliffs of Maimón where raptors leisurely glide overhead. This circuit is of interest to all naturalists whether they like birds, butterflies or wildflowers. When time is short, this route is also possible (though bumpy!) with a car.

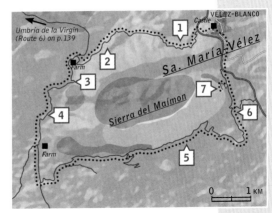

Starting point Los Fajardo castle of Vélez-Blanco

Leave the village down to the A-317 and turn right. About 200 metres, in the curve of the road, go left onto the dirt track where the walking route *La Umbría del Maimón* leads up the hill (well-marked with white arrows). Continue on foot.

After 800 metres you have a splendid panorama from the pass *Collado de Las Arenas*, which overlooks the Los Fajardo castle and behind it, the table mountain of *La Muela Grande*, a conspicuous landmark. Continue along this dirt track and further up into an open pine forest.

View over Velez-Blanco and the Maimon mountain in the background (top). The Ladder Snake is the most frequently encountered snake on the route around Maimon (bottom).

1 On the first stretch of 1.2 km, before the first almond grove, you cross a dry riverbed, where butterflies and other insects take advantage of the nectar-rich Lavender, Thyme and Rosemary. Dusky Meadow Brown, Panoptes Blue and Blue-spot Hairstreak amongst others, are drawn to the flowers. Bonelli's Warbler is singing from the trees and Hawfinch is sometimes present too. Check the sky for the raptors, like Booted Eagle and Griffon Vulture.

The pines give way to rocky scrub, almond groves, oak scrub and gullies. After a few km, the *Fuente del Peral* appears on your right side.

2 *Fuente* means water source and this humid area has a taller vegetation. A small water trough suits the needs of Western and Natterjack Toads. Butterflies are drawn to the water as well. Spanish Marbled White, White Banded Grayling, False Ilex Hairstreak and Rock Grayling are common. Ladder and Montpellier Snakes and Ocellated Lizards occur in the surrounding dry scrub.

You bypass a farm, beyond which the *Umbría del Maimón* track goes straight towards María. Our route goes left towards *Puerto del Peral*, which is about 1 km ahead. Stop at the panoramic viewpoint on the pass.

3 Both sides of the mountain pass offer great views over the surrounding landscape. The area around the pass is worth examining a bit more thoroughly. It has the interesting flora of the hedgehog zone and of Juniper grasslands, with species like Hedgehog Broom, Spiny Vella* (*Vella spinosa*), Spiny Alison* (*Hormatophylla spinosa*) and Iberian Jerusalem-sage. Subalpine Warbler, Black Redstart, Rock Bunting and Black-eared Wheatear are noteworthy birds. It is also a good stretch to see the Apollo butterfly, particularly on wind-free days.

4 The track leads down along a gully. The scrubland hosts shrikes, warblers, Black-eared Wheatear and Hoopoe.

About 1 km beyond the pass, just outside the boundaries of the Parque Natural, you arrive at a junction. Turn left here. A short climb through a stony grassland and an open pine forest brings you beneath the steep slopes of mount Maimón.

The nevada subspecies of Apollo has orange rather than red spots.

5 The giant, beautiful but very rare Spanish Moon Moth has a population here. The south-facing slopes provide excellent breeding habitat for raptors, which use the warm, rising air to take off. Many Griffon Vultures breed on the steep slopes, while Golden, Booted and Short-toed Eagle frequently soar by. From the cliffs, the subtle songs of Black Wheatear, both Rock Thrushes and Rock Bunting can be heard. Look

An Ocellated Lizard, basking in the sun.

for Iberian Grey Shrike on suitable perches, while parties of Red-legged Partridge wander underneath the pine trees.

When the conspicuous *Muela Grande* table mountain is back in view, you start your descent back to Vélez-Blanco.

6 The next stretch runs through irrigated agricultural land where familiar birds like Greenfinch, Goldfinch and House Sparrow are abundant. Woodlark may be singing while Woodchat Shrike hunt insects from bushes and fences. The water troughs attracts amphibians and dragonflies.

Griffon Vultures are rather uncommon in this part of Spain, but there is a sizable colony on the south flank of the mountain.

The track splits several times. Keep choosing the lefthand option and the Maimón on your left.

7 A track branches off to the left, leading you, after a 700 m walk, to the *Cueva de los Letreros*. This is a national monument, preserving a cave with sketches of prehistoric rock paintings of human figures, birds, animals and astronomical signs dating back to 4-5000 BC). Note that entry to the cave is only possible as part of an organised visit. Ask for details in the visitors' centre in Vélez-Blanco.

The bright, purple-blue Hedgehog Brooms are in full bloom near the pass (point 4) in May.

The route ends on the A 317 just south of Vélez-Blanco near a petrol station and the *Pinar del Rey* campsite.

Other sites in the area - Hoya de Baza

The relatively flat Hoya de Baza lies between the towns of Baza and Benamaurel and comprises various types of steppe grassland, home to Black-bellied Sandgrouse, Little Bustard, Stone Curlew, Roller and Great Spotted Cuckoo. There are also a few Dupont's Lark and Lesser Short-toed Larks.

Best season
February-June
Of interest
Year-round

The Hoya is cut into two by the Río Baza. The western part has a more agricultural character. Farmland and natural steppes form a mosaic, dotted with a few steppe lagoons, such as the *Humedál del Baíco*. This saline lake is superb for waterfowl, waders, herons and flamingos, while steppe birds occur in the surrounding grasslands. Other birds of interest are Olivaceous Warbler, Spectacled Warbler, Red-billed Chough and Montagu's and Marsh Harriers. Among the reptiles, Spiny-footed Lizard, Horseshoe Whip, Montpellier, Ladder and False Smooth Snake are most numerous.

The eastern part of the hoya consists of a superb area of inland dunes, that stretches out from the Río de Baza to Venta del Peral). It can best be explored from the dirt road on the north side of the A 92 motorway between La Jámula (exit 50) to Venta del Peral (exit 58). The dry and sandy rolling Esparto grasslands here are surprisingly rich in butterflies! Among the more attractive species are – in spring – Provence Hairstreak, Portuguese Dappled White and the very rare Spanish Greenish Black-tip. Sooty and Desert Orange-tip take their place in summer.

Black numbers refer to motorway exits.

Small cereal fields in between these dunes are of vital importance to birds, including Short-toed Eagle, Great Spotted Cuckoo, Roller, Iberian Grey Shrike and Tawny Pipit. Among the wildflowers, the parasitic are conspicuous, with eye-catching species like Yellow Cistanche, Maltese Fungus and various broomrapes. Other interesting wildflowers include Large Sea-lavender* (*Limonium majus*), Clusius' Milkvetch* (*Astragalus clusii*), Sad Stock and Wild Caper.

The Sierra Cazorla and Sierra Mágina

The Parque Natural de Cazorla, Segura y Las Villas covers 200,000 hectares and is the largest protected area in Spain. Two major rivers of southern and eastern Spain have their source here: the Guadalquivir (the largest river in Andalucía) and the Segura (which feeds many reservoirs and reaches the Mediterranean east of Murcia).

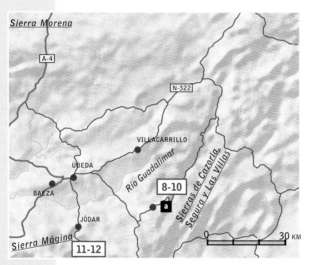

The limestone soils of Sierra Cazorla, Segura y Las Villas is extensively covered with pine woods and is home to a unique flora and fauna. The verdant scenery is laced with streams and rivers that are interrupted by magnificent waterfalls and divided by peaks of over 2,000 metres.

Overview of the Sierra Cazorla and Mágina. The letter refers to the site described on page 167.

Species like Cazorla Violet, Spanish Algyroides lizard and Lammergeier (reintroduced) are regional specialities, while the rivers are home to a rich dragonfly fauna. Above the tree line and on rocky slopes are rock thrushes, Red-billed Choughs and Rock Sparrows. Also, you are probably more likely to encounter Red Deer, Wild Boar, Mouflon and Spanish Ibex here than anywhere else in Andalucía.

Not far from Cazorla, between the towns of Jaén and Jódar, lies the isolated Sierra Mágina amidst the olive, almond and cherry groves. Like Cazorla and María – los Veléz, the summits of Mágina rise well over 2,000 m. The flora and fauna is rich, and consist of species similar to those in the Sierra de Cazorla. In spring, orchids abound. At least eighteen species are known from the Sierra de Mágina.

Routes 8 – 10 and the site on page 167 cover different aspects of the the Sierra Cazorla, while routes 11 and 12 are devoted to the Sierra Mágina.

Route 8: Discovering the Sierra de Cazorla

FULL DAY
EASY

Best season
March-July
Of interest
Year-round

Great introduction to the natural wonders of Sierra de Cazorla.
Highly diverse flora and fauna, including many endemics.

Habitats river, cliffs, pine forest, forest glades
Selected species Spanish Ibex, Mouflon, Red Deer, Wild Boar, Red Fox,
Lammergeier, Dipper, Bonelli's Eagle, Citril Finch, Cazorla Violet, Cazorla
Orchid, Algerian Butterfly Orchid, Fragrant Orchid, Southern Midwife Toad,
Lorquin's Blue, Spanish Fritillary, Pronged Clubtail, Orange-spotted Emerald,
Splendid Cruiser

The Sierra de Cazorla is Spain's largest natural park and the options for walks and car routes are virtually endless. Whichever way you choose to explore the region, this is the route to start with. In a series of stops and strolls, you'll get acquainted with the diversity of Cazorla's habitats and you have a great chance of finding a good selection of its unique flora and fauna, especially butterflies, dragonflies, wildflowers and wildlife.

Starting point visitors' centre *Torre del Vinagre* on the A-319, next to the Guadalquivir in the heart of the Nature Park.

1 The more attractive native flora of Cazorla is conveniently displayed in the botanical garden. Some of the species you'll be able to see in the wild further on this route. If you happen to be here in spring, bear in mind that some of the high altitude species already in bloom in this garden will not yet be flowering in their wild environment. The garden attracts some native fauna as well. Nightingale, Golden Oriole, Serin and Nuthatch are often present, while butterflies such as Spanish Festoon and Green Hairstreak forage on flowers.

A tarmac road descends from the visitors' centre to the river Borosa (see route 9).

2 A short stop at the river may offer a glimpse of Dipper or Kingfisher, but the real attraction of this site is the rich dragonfly fauna. The first 200 metres of the riverbank is very rewarding. Behind the old warden's house, there are Mercury Bluet, Small Red Damsel and Keeled Skimmer, while on the river itself, some very special species can be found: Pronged Clubtail, Orange-spotted Emerald, Splendid Cruiser, White Featherleg and Western Demoiselle. Early summer is the best season for them, and at this time you may also see the splendid butterfly Two-tailed Pasha (a second brood of which flies in August-October).

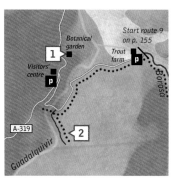

Take the car and drive towards Cazorla, passing the touristy village of Arroyo Frío. About 1.7 km further south you cross the Guadalquivir at an old electricity station. Park here.

3 Stroll along the river and look around in the fields. Along the river and behind the ruins of the electricity station, an Ash wood indicates a small floodplain with Pendulous Sedges that forms the optimal habitat for Common Goldenring and Spanish Purple Hairstreak.
On foot, follow the A-319 road between here and the luxury hotel 1 km ahead. The moist woodlands are home to some rare orchids, like Cazorla Orchid (endemic to East Andalucía), Algerian Butterfly Orchid (generally rare and largely restricted to Cazorla and north-Africa), and Fragrant and Bird's-nest Orchid, both of which are rare in the Mediterranean. The forest edges attract good numbers of butterflies including High Brown Fritillary, Lulworth Skipper, Mother-of-Pearl Blue and Large Tortoiseshell.

Continue by car and turn left at the junction to Nava de San Pedro. In Vadillo Castril, cross the bridge and park 140 metres further on. Return on foot to the bridge for a short walk in the gorge.

4   This 1.6 km walk (*Cerrada de Utrero*) is attractive because of the steep gorge composed of limestone. There is a colony of Griffon Vulture on the cliffs and Red-billed Chough, Crag Martin, Alpine Swift and Raven also breed in the area. Here we saw a young Lammergeier from the reintroduction program (see page 86). There are a number of cliff-dwelling wildflowers, such as Rustyback Fern, Grass-leaved Buttercup, the toadflax *Linaria verticillata* and Rocket Larkspur* (*Consolida ajacis*). Iberian Wall Lizard is frequent and highly visible, but you need to search much harder for the Southern Midwife Toad. On the river, Beautiful Demoiselle and Large Pincertail are common, while the butterflies Southern White Admiral, Cardinal, Large Tortoiseshell and Rock Grayling gather near the river.

By car, continue in the direction of Nava de San Pedro.

5   The road crosses stands of pine and mixed forest. Pay attention in the clearings as Red Deer, Fallow Deer and Wild Boar are frequently seen and can be quite tame. Red Squirrels jump across the road and

The spectacular short walk to the Cerrada de Utrero (left). On the rocks, you may find the toadflax *Linaria verticillata* (right).

even Foxes seem undisturbed in this area. A trained eye discovers more Cazorla Orchids (look for the moist patches) between the drifts of delicate Pallid Narcisses and Cuatrecasas Jonquils* (*Narcissus cuatrecasasii*) – the latter endemic to the southeastern Spain.

As you pass a small house with a helicopter platform, you enter a restricted area that is only open to the public between 9.00 and 21.00. The road continues as a dirt track. After 3.5 km, you pass a forester's house. A bit further on you can park behind a small bridge with large concrete blocks. On foot, walk back some hundred metres and explore the roadside and grassy patches in the forest.

The Sierra de Cazorla is a treasure trove of rare flora and some of the rarities, such as the Jonquil Narcissus cuatrecassasii (top) and the Cazorla Orchid (bottom), can be found with relative ease.

6 In late spring, Robust Marsh Orchid, Common Gladiole and various other wildflowers are found near the small springs. Twin-spot Fritillary and Cardinal are around, while Small Skipper, Silver-studded Blue and Wood White congregate near muddy patches. Small streams along the road verges are suitable habitat for Common Goldenring.

Continue the main track and pass Nava de San Pedro.

7 The next stop is at a wide valley with a clear mountain stream, flanked by lush meadows and a plantation of poplars – the kind of landscape that makes you feel you are somewhere in temperate Europe rather than deep down in the south of Spain. This is a good area to look and listen for Golden Oriole, Mistle Thrush, Grey Wagtail and Iberian Green Woodpecker. In spring, the cheerful tufts of daffodils and Cowslip are all too familiar. But look carefully and you find drifts of Yellow Bee Orchids and the daffodil *Narcissus longispathus*, which is endemic to Cazorla and a few nearby ranges. Towards the summer, look for Sunset Foxglove.

Continue along the track.

8 Stop at the 'Mirador Estrecho de los Perales' to view the limestone pillars where Spanish Ibex is frequently seen. Griffon Vultures and various kinds of eagles may soar over. Walk a few hundred metres further up to a small plateau that offers another opportunity to see deer, Ibex and Wild Boar. Check the woodland edges for Citril Finch and, within the pine forests, look and listen for Crossbill and Coal and Crested Tits. Note the first Hedgehog Brooms start to appear, indicating you are at an altitude of 1,400 m and on the edge of a new vegetation zone.

Return to point 4 of this route and turn left before the bridge of Vadillo Castril and head to the source of the Guadalquivir river (indicated as being 13 km further ahead). The tarmac runs out behind the camp site but the route continues as a well-maintained dirt track. After 10 km you reach the turning to the official source of the Guadalquivir source which is signposted as being another 220 m ahead.

9 On foot, follow the short trail to the source of the mighty Guadalquivir that runs all the way across Andalucía, through the cities of Córdoba and Sevilla, feeding the marshes of Coto Doñana National Park before pouring into the Atlantic Ocean.

Interesting habitat is to be found about 300 metres further along the track – a recreation area which is an excellent spot for butterflies. Wild Boar uprooted the soil and as a result the grassland is filled with Spanish Lemon Thyme* (*Thymus baeticus*) and thistles – great nectar plants for butterflies. In June, we have encountered over 30 species within an hour, including Mother-of-Pearl Blue, Provence Orange-tip, Black-veined White, Spanish Fritillary, Adonis Blue and Lorquin's Blue. Scan the rock formations in the distance for Raven, Short-toed Eagle and Peregrine Falcon, while Iberian

The Spanish Purple Hairstreak is always found around streambeds. It has the fascinating habit of laying its eggs in river beds that are dry in summer and submerged in winter. The eggs spend the winter season under water, safe from predators.

Green Woodpecker, Golden Oriole, Mistle Thrush and Hawfinch can be found closer by, in the woodlands.

Return to the junction. Here you're faced with a choice – either consider this the end of the excursion, or continue the route to La Iruela. In the latter case you follow a stony but otherwise perfectly drivable track (at the time of writing), but one that is, at 24 km, rather long.

10 Following the track to La Iruela, it won't be long before you pass the small fountain *Prado de las Ubillas*. Mouflon are frequently seen in this area. Also look and listen for noisy flocks of Azure-winged Magpie. A bit further on, at the *refugio de Collado Zamora* you are treated to a scenic view.

The track forks here – follow the left branch. Where the rocky grasslands give way to pine forest, turn right to El Chorro (1.2 km). To your left you have, through the forest, a sneak preview of the vulture colony of the next stop. Park at the house of El Chorro and walk down to the viewpoint.

It doesn' t matter whether you take the road to Vadillo-Castril or to Cazorla, wildlife is easy to find in these sierras along either route.

11 This gives you the ideal position to observe Griffon and Egyptian Vulture as they glide by at eye level. Deep cracks in the limestone walls of this spectacular gorge are used as nest sites by Alpine Swift, Blue Rock Thrush, Kestrel, Red-billed Chough and Peregrine Falcon. In the scrub, look for Mirron and Southern Early Purple Orchids, Western Peony, Yellow Pheasant's-eye in spring, while the colourful Jerusalem Sage attracts butterflies like Cleopatra, Meadow Brown and Swallowtail in July.

The track eventually brings you on the western slopes of the range, with scenic views over the badlands, with Quesada and eventually Cazorla on your left. After 7.5 km you will leave the restricted area and you will reach tarmac once again. It is another 4 km to La Iruela, where this route ends.

Route 9: Río Borosa

8 HOURS - FULL DAY
MODERATE

Deservedly Cazorla's most popular signposted hike.
Splendid river gorge and mountain landscape with a rare flora
and fauna.

Best season
April-July
Of interest
Year-round

Habitats river, riverine woodland, cliffs, forest glades, pinewood, oak wood
Selected species Spanish Ibex, Dipper, Spanish Algyroides, Eelgrass-leaved
Butterwort*, Dense-flowered Orchid, Spanish Midwife Toad, Yellow Clubtail,
Orange-spotted Emerald, Mercury Bluet, Chapman's Green Hairstreak, Two-
tailed Pasha

The Río Borosa is one of Cazorla's scenic mountain streams and is easily explored via a track (later a trail) that runs along its entire length to the source. The walk combines amazing views of narrow gorges, high mountains and, after rain, spectacular waterfalls, with good chances of encountering some of the region's rarest endemics. If you want to explore the Cazorla on foot, this is the walk that cannot fail to be part of your schedule.

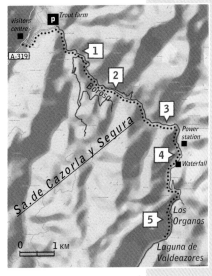

Starting point The Sierra de Cazorla visitors' centre along the A-319.
Across the street from the visitors' centre, a tarmac road (signposted *Sendero Río Borosa*) takes you to a trout farm. Just before, there is a large car park. Continue on foot from here. The route starts after a barrier just beyond the trout farm. Scan the verges of the road for Mercury Bluet on the way over.

1 The beautiful Río Borosa attracts some very typical species. Dipper and Grey Wagtail are common and Cetti's Warbler can often be heard. Otter also occurs here but seeing one remains a matter of great luck.

Along the first section of the trail there are many Strawberry Trees, which attract two interesting butterflies: Chapman's Green Hairstreak and the Two-tailed Pasha. Large Tortoiseshell is common and typical for this habitat as well. Rosemary Broomrape, Grass-leaved Buttercup and Narrow-leaved Helleborine are among the interesting wildflowers. Southern Midwife Toad inhabits the mountain streams in this sierra but is difficult to find.

Where the river cuts through a deep ravine, the trail continues on a rather spectacular boardwalk, suspended from the cliff face on the righthand side of the river.

2 The ravine is the place to see the rare and endemic Eelgrass-leaved Butterwort* (*Pinguicula vallisneriifolia*), a carnivorous plant that catches insects on its sticky leaves. It grows on the wet cliff in great numbers, together with Maidenhair Fern. In summer, thousands of Oak Yellow Underwing (a moth) rest in this gorge during daytime and fly up as you walk along – a spectacular sight. On the river, Common Goldenring and Beautiful Demoiselle are two frequent dragonflies.

The trail leads along an absolutely splendid wet cliff, carpeted with the endemic, insectivorous Eelgrass-leaved Butterwort* (*Pinguicula vallisneriifolia*).

3 In the next section, the river flows more gently and beautiful vistas open up of the surrounding mountains and (seasonal) waterfalls. Crag Martins are numerous. Look for Dense-flowered Orchid, which grows in the woodland on the right side of the trail. Common Grape Vine (*Vitis vinifera*), the wild ancestor of table and wine grapes, can be seen in the riparian vegetation. As a liana, it spirals up the trees to reach its place in the sun. This is also a good stretch to look for Spanish Algyroides, a rare lizard which is endemic to the Sierra de Cazorla and the adjoining mountain ranges. It inhabits rocky woodlands in the vicinity of fast-flowing mountain streams and is not uncommon here.

The official *Sendero de Río Borosa* ends at a small power plant. The seasoned hiker is recommended to continue up the trail that snakes up the cliff on the left.

4 Scan the slopes for Spanish Ibex. Alpine Swift and Crag Martin wheel by. The limestone cliffs host some interesting plants. On moist and shady spots, there are more specimens of Eelgrass-leaved Butterwort, while the rare and local *Sarcocapnos baetica* grows on dry cliffs. The trail takes you through tunnels which have been dug in the cliff to supply the power plant with water. This is an adventurous stretch – very dark, wet and narrow. Bring a flashlight!

From a distance, the Spanish Algyroides may not appear very spectacular. On closer inspection, its keeled scales give them a very different appearance from the widespread Iberian Wall Lizard. The Spanish Algyroides is endemic to the Sierra de Cazorla and nearby mountains.

5 After the last tunnel, the trail is level again, following a small channel to an upland reservoir. Cuatrecasas Narcissus* (*Narcissus cuatrecasasii*), endemic to Andalucía, grows along the channel. At the *Embalse de los Órganos*, the trail splits. The lefthand branch is a short stretch which takes you to the source of the *Aguas Negras*, an impressive sight in springtime when crystal clear water is ejected out of the mountain with force. The righthand branch continues to the *Laguna de Valdeazores*, an attractive stretch for wildflowers and birds.

Small waterfall from the limestone cliffs at the end of the Sendero de Río Borosa.

Route 10: The plateau of Campos de Hérnan Perea

5 HOURS
EASY

!
Little shade

Little visited, upland karst plateau with a rich flora and fauna.

The barrier is open
from 9.00 – 21.00

Best season
April-June

Habitats hedgehog scrub, stony grassland, open pinewood
Selected species Woolly Viper's-bugloss, Spanish Ibex, Lataste's Viper,
Lammergeier, Melodious Warbler, Orphean Warbler, Spectacled Warbler, Cirl
Bunting, Ortolan Bunting, Rock Bunting, Brown Bluebell, Mother-of-Pearl
Blue, Natterjack Toad

The Campos de Hernán Perea is one of the hidden gems of the Sierra de Cazorla. This highland plateau is situated at 2,000 metres above sea level and presents the visitor with some outlandish landscapes. It is also a silent witness to the waning agricultural practice of transhumance. Ecologically, the plain lies fair and square in the hedgehog broom zone, which, with its extreme annual and daily temperature fluctuations, gives rise to a unique flora and fauna.

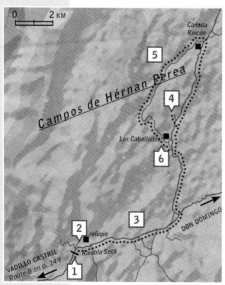

Starting point Control de Rambla Seca

Getting there From Arroyo Frío, head out on the A-319 towards Cazorla and take the road signposted *Nacimiento Río Guadalquivir*. Follow these signs until the bridge over the Guadalquivir at *Cerrada de Utrero*. At a fork in the road shortly after the bridge, turn left. Follow this road, later turning onto a dirt track, all the way to the Control de Rambla Seca. Park at the gate and proceed on foot.

1 The Control de Rambla Seca is a control station where cattle are counted. The Campos de Hernán Perea is a summer ground for grazing cattle. With plant growth peaking in spring and

The high altitude dry karst plateau of Hérnan Perea boasts a unique, harsh climate – cold in winter, hot in summer and dry and exposed to the elements all year round.

summer, it is a very suitable area to bring cattle when the winter grazing grounds at lower altitudes have been depleted. Cows, horses, sheep and goats roam freely across the plain. The sound of cow bells and singing birds on an early morning hike over this tranquil plateau makes for an enchanting experience.

After entering the gate, follow *Pontones / Don Domingo.*

Lataste's Viper is hard to find, but not uncommon on the Hérnan Perea plateau.

2 On the short stretch beyond the gate, the trees gradually give way to the open landscape of the plateau. This 'transition zone' is an excellent spot to look for Woodlark, Corn Bunting, Cirl Bunting, Iberian Grey Shrike and many Serins. The presence of Black-veined White, Adonis Blue, Large Tortoiseshell, Cardinal, Grayling and Marbled Skipper illustrates the diversity in butterflies here.

At the *Refugio Rambla Seca* mountain hut, start following *Campo del Espino.*

160

In summer, damp patches on the trail attract hundreds of 'mud-puddling' blues.

3 Here the plain truly opens up before you. Steppe grassland and juniper bush, boulders, solitary trees, herds of cattle and the gently undulating terrain define the landscape. The mountains surrounding the plateau on all sides form a constant reminder of the fact that you are not on a lowland steppe but still at 2,000 metres altitude. This habitat is favoured by the rare Lataste's Viper. The scrub supports a special birdlife with Woodchat Shrike, Spectacled, Subalpine, Orphean and Melodious Warblers. Northern Wheatear, Hoopoe, Thekla Lark and Short-toed Lark scurry about on the ground. Always keep an eye on the sky. Booted Eagle, Golden Eagle, Griffon Vulture or the rare Bonelli's Eagle may be seen on patrol. If you are lucky you may even spot one of the Lammergeiers that once again roam the skies of the Sierra de Cazorla (see page 86). The diminutive Brown Bluebell grows on the rocky soils. The more conspicuous Andalucian Stork's-bill* (*Erodium cheilanthifolium*) are also present. More locally, you can find Woolly Viper's-bugloss* (*Echium albicans*) and Silver-leaved Bindweed* (*Convolvulus boissieri*; p. 70), two specialists of the hedgehog zone.

Some 2,700 m beyond the *refugio*, follow the track to the left towards *Campo del Espino*. 2500 metres after this turn you will arrive at the *Refugio de los Caballistos* where the trail splits. Follow the right branch and some 500 metres beyond the mountain hut, a small dirt track to the left leads to a spring and several drinking troughs for cattle.

4 Limestone plateaux are notoriously dry. As rainwater seeps away in cracks almost immediately, permanent surface water is scarce. Hence this site is a true oasis, used by amphibians to lay their eggs in, and by large numbers of birds that come to drink. Rock Buntings, Linnets and many others can be seen flying to and fro for a refreshing sip of water. Rock Sparrow is present in large numbers as it nests in the stone walls of the trough. In summertime, permanent waters such as these are ideal spots for mud-puddling butterflies. The rare Mother-of-pearl Blue may be found between the scores of Southern Brown Argus, Silver-studded Blue and Escher's Blue.

Return and continue along the main track. After 2,500 metres you will find another mountain hut on the left: the *Refugio de Pastores Cañada del Rincón*. Leave the main track and turn left onto the small trail that leads past the mountain hut.

5 The terrain becomes a little more rugged, with rocky outcrops replacing the gentle hills. Pines also become more prominent. This is the place to look for plants like the saxifrage *Saxifraga trabutiana* and Olive-leaved Daphne* (*Daphne oleoides*). Black Redstart, Coal Tit, Rock Bunting and Red-billed Chough are some of the birds you may encounter here. Ocellated Lizard and Iberian Wall Lizard can be seen basking on the rocks.

At a fork, turn left to return to the *Refugio de los Caballistos*. From there, return via the same trail.

6 This mountain hut has a small reservoir of water which again attracts large numbers of thirsty birds. Pick a good spot to observe the reservoir, take your binoculars and sit still as scores of Serins, Linnets, Rock Bunting and other birds come and go. Dragonflies like Black-tailed Skimmer and Red-veined Darter also favour this small body of water to hunt and to lay eggs.

Rock Sparrows are just one of the attractive birds that are common on the plateau.

162

Route 11: Sierra Mágina

**6 HOURS, 34 KM
EASY**

Best season
April-July

A car route through the heart of the Sierra Mágina.
Wide variety of habitats from lowland dehesa to a limestone peak.

Habitats hedgehog scrubland, pine forest, dehesa, rivers
Selected species Spanish Ibex, Golden Eagle, Griffon Vulture, Blue Rock
Thrush, Alpine Swift, Hoopoe, Ring Ouzel, Southern Midwife Toad, Spanish
Chalk-hill Blue

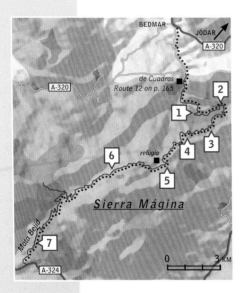

The Sierra Mágina is an isolated limestone mountain range. Spectacular vistas, jagged limestone cliffs and a splendid dehesa form the main scenic attractions. This car route crosses the length of the Sierra Mágina from Bedmar to Mata Bejid. It traverses all major habitats the Sierra has to offer, from green riverine valleys and shady pine forests to Mediterranean and hedgehog dwarf scrub, broom scrub, the high limestone peaks and the dehesa of Mata Bejid.
This is an adventurous route, following dirt tracks over its entire length. Some may be in bad state so always use common sense when contemplating whether or not to continue.

Starting point Bedmar
Arriving in Bedmar from Jódar, a road to the left is signposted *Cuadros*. The turn is very sharp and it is advisable to overshoot the turning, turn round and take this road from the opposite direction. After 3.5 km, turn left, signposted *Área Recreativa de Cuadros*. Several tracks depart at the car park. Follow (by car) the one signposted *Caño del Aguadero*, marked in yellow and white, up the mountain on the dirt track left of the car park.

1 The first stretch of the climb takes you through a pine forest. Scan the trees and listen for Crossbill, Crested Tit, Coal Tit and Firecrest. A viewpoint can be found at an information panel. Park the car here and enjoy the view. Scan the sky for Short-toed and Booted Eagles. Open patches in the forest are carpeted with wildflowers and scrub. These are good spots to look for butterflies like Southern Gatekeeper and Great Banded Grayling.

After approximately 5 km, a sharp left turn departs from the signposted track. Park here and explore the area.

2 This is a rich spot for butterflies. Spanish Chalk-hill Blue, Sage Skipper, Grayling and False Ilex Hairstreak are common.

Return to the car and continue along the signposted track.

3 On the right side, spectacular vistas open up to the north. You look out over Europe's largest wood of Turpentine Trees. As the name suggests, in historic times this tree was the source of turpentine. The bark of the trees was cut and the resin the wounded tree secreted was collected and distilled to produce the valuable fluid.

The high parts of the Sierra Mágina are clad in a superb hedgehog vegetation (top). Iberian Ibex are a common sight in these parts (bottom).

4 The landscape becomes more rugged. Keep an eye on the cliffs on the left for Red-billed Chough, Peregrine, Rock Bunting, Blue Rock Thrush and Alpine Swift. Ibex Ibex can be seen along the cliffs and the scree slopes. Large Phoenician Junipers dot the flanks of the mountain. Rock Grayling is a butterfly which feels at home in this habitat.

164

5 The signposted trail ends at *Caño del Aguadero*, an old farmhouse. A small spring keeps several water troughs filled, where Southern Midwife Toad lays its eggs. The mountain pastures around the farm are good spots to look for Ring Ouzel (winter / early spring) and butterflies.

Continue along the track.

6 Trees become less and less frequent and Spiny Alison* (*Hormatophylla spinosa*) and other shrubs of the high mountains become more prominent. On the left side, the limestone cliffs of the *Karst de Sierra Mágina* are visible. Spanish Ibex can be seen here and Rock Bunting and Blue Rock Thrush are again possible. Stonechats, Black Redstart and Subalpine Warbler perch on rocks and shrubs to sing. Red-legged Partridge also occur. Be sure to scan the skies for raptors. Golden Eagle is frequently seen here.

The dehesa in the Sierra Mágina (top). The open woodlands with rocks and scattered bushes form the ideal habitat for Rock Buntings, which should not be difficult to track down (bottom).

About 7.3 km after the *Caño del Aguadero* the dirt track ends at a T-junction, turn left here.

7 This is the *Dehesa de Mata Bejid* – a beautiful dehesa with some magnificent, ancient Holm Oak trees. Hoopoe is quite common here and the ruins of the *Castillo de Mata Bejid* make for an attractive landscape. The beautiful Spanish Saint Bernard's Lily is among the flowers you can find here.

The track ends at the A-324. Turn left to visit the visitors' centre and for the road back to Bedmar / Jódar.

Route 12: Las Viñas

> **3 HOURS, 10 KM**
> **MODERATE**
>
>
>
> A short introduction to the Sierra Mágina and its habitats.
>
> **Habitats** Mediterranean scrublands, pine forest, rivers
> **Selected species** Wild Oleander, Iberian Green Woodpecker, Cetti's Warbler,
> Black Wheatear, Common Crossbill, Cirl Bunting

Best season
April-June
Of interest
Year-round

This short hike makes for a scenic stroll through some of the habitats of the Sierra Mágina. It starts at the Río Bedmar, a lovely mountain stream with a beautiful and well-developed Oleander thicket, and takes you through the pine forests to the orchards and eventually to the *Torreón de Cuadros*, an ancient military outpost which once guarded the pass over the Sierra Mágina against Moorish incursions.

Starting point Área recreativa de Cuadros

See previous route for directions to this recreational area. Follow the footpath *sendero Las Viñas*.

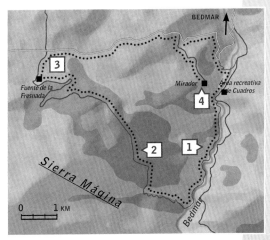

1 The first section of the route leads through the valley of the Río Bedmar with its magnificent Oleander thicket. Cetti's Warbler can be heard, Spotted Flycatcher occurs on passage and Golden Oriole sings from the trees in the valley.

After approximately 5 km, a sharp left turn departs from the signposted track. Park here and explore the area.

166

2 After the trail leaves the valley of the Río Bedmar, it starts climbing. This stretch takes you through a pine forest, where Long-tailed, Crested and Coal Tit, Crossbill, Bonelli's Warbler, Goldfinch, Firecrest, Sardinian Warbler and Turtle Dove are some of the birds you may encounter. Mastic Tree also grows here. This small tree is primarily known for its resin, the dried form of which is known as Mastic gum.

3 When the trail starts to descend, the tree cover becomes less dense until eventually the forest makes way for olive orchards interspersed with large patches of scrub. This is a good spot to look for Mediterranean songbirds like Sardinian, Dartford and Melodious Warblers. Iberian Green Woodpecker, Hoopoe, Cirl Bunting and Bee-eater may be found. At the *Fuente de la Fresneda*, a small spring, check the water basin for amphibians and butterflies.

Two widespread Andalucían birds you may encounter in Las Viñas: Hoopoe (top) and Long-tailed Tit (bottom), a distinctive race of which occurs on the Iberian Peninsula.

Shortly before you reach the Río Bedmar again, a short detour to the right takes you to the *Mirador Torreón de Cuadros*.

4 This tower was once part of a chain of fortifications which separated the Christian kingdoms in the north from the Moorish Caliphate in the south. This particular tower guarded the pass across the Sierra Mágina from Mata Bejid to Bedmar (see route 11). Rock Bunting can be seen here and with some luck, a Spanish Ibex may cross your path. You can also enjoy the view over the splendid Oleander vegetation and the lowlands to the north.

Return to the dirt track and turn right, shortly afterwards you meet the Río Bedmar again and the trail takes you back to the car park.

Additional sites in Cazorla

A – Mirador de Palomas

The A-319 main road from Cazorla snakes up from Burunchel to the Mirador and Puerto de Palomas. You can explore the area between the open area of the *mirador* and pass of *Puerto de Palomas*, which are approximately 700 metres apart.

Of interest
Year-round

The area offers scenic views over both the Guadalquivir valley and the olive groves around Cazorla. A short stroll brings you to a summit from where you have a splendid view and a good chance of seeing raptors. Bonelli's, Golden, Booted and sometimes Spanish Imperial Eagles can be seen from here. The surrounded pine forest is the domain of Citril Finch (a recent colonist), Firecrest and Crossbill, while Rock Bunting, Woodlark, Mistle Thrush and Rock Thrush inhabit the more open rocky areas. In winter, Alpine Accentor is seen here.

Among the interesting wildflowers, look for the Spanish Snapdragon* (*Antirrhinum hispanicum*), despite its name an endemic confined to Eastern Andalucía, and the iconic Cazorla Violet* (*Viola cazorlensis*). The latter grows in rock crevices in either side of the road. Sage Skipper, Tree Grayling and Cleopatra are among the butterflies.

The endemic Cazorla Violet (top) flowers on cliffs near the Mirador de las Palomas. From the mirador, you have splendid views into the central valley of the Sierra de Cazorla (bottom).

From the hide at *Puerto de Palomas* you have excellent views over the valley and may see raptors that soar along the ridge. If you want to explore the area more closely, you can hike from the small stream in the village of Arroyo Frío, crossing the Guadalquivir and zigzag up via scrubland to Puerto de Palomas. This route is 2.5 km long and takes about one hour.

The eastern Sierra Morena and Guadalquivir basin

The Sierra Morena is a huge range of low, rolling hills that forms the southern edge of the great Spanish *Mesetas*. The Sierra Morena stretches out all along the northern border of Andalucía from the Portuguese border to Cascada de la Cimbarra (route 14). The eastern and most rugged part lies in the area covered in this guidebook.

Much of the eastern end of the range falls within the Sierra de Andújar – the wildest, most remote and least inhabited part of this enormous range (route 13 and sites A and B on page 178). It was little visited by naturalists – most of whom went to Extremadura or the western, more accessible parts of the Sierra Morena, until it became known as *the* place in Spain to see the very rare and endangered Iberian Lynx. This is still the main reason to visit Andújar, although the Mediterranean woodland and vast stretches of dehesa are attractive for birdwatching too. As in most of these sierras, there are many raptors, which include good numbers of Spanish Imperial Eagle and Black Vulture, and many Azure-winged Magpies. The Sierra de Andújar is also one of the last areas where the Wolf, sadly now very rare here, is found in southern Spain.

East of the Sierra de Andújar, two smaller natural parks are worth visiting. The first is Parque Natural Despeñaperros (site C on page 179). It is a very scenic area and of great historic importance as the natural gateway between east Andalucía and central Spain), The second is Paraje Natural de la Cimbarra – famous for its beautiful waterfall and rich flora and fauna (route 14).

From Andújar, it is not far to Córdoba. This beautiful historic town has some great surprises for naturalists as well (site D on page 180).

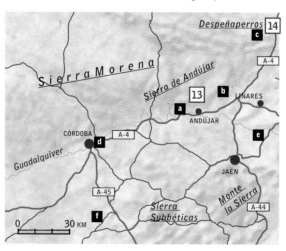

Overview of the Sierra Morena area. The letters refer to the sites described on page 178-182.

Route 13: Exploring the Sierra de Andújar

**FULL DAY OR MORE
EASY**

The single best route to see Iberian Lynx in the whole of Spain.
An excellent side show of mammals and birds, in an extraordinary, wild landscape.

Best season
March-May
Of interest
Year-round

Habitats dehesa, scrubland, river
Selected species Iberian Lynx, Mouflon, Red Deer, Otter, Egyptian Mongoose, Spanish Imperial Eagle, Black Vulture, Golden Eagle, Black Kite, Great Spotted Cuckoo, Azure-winged Magpie, Ortolan Bunting, Rock Bunting, Orphean Warbler

Anywhere else in Spain the presence of a good population of Spanish Imperial Eagles would be the star attraction, but the Parque Natural de Sierra de Andújar has something even more impressive: it is one of the last refuges of the Iberian Lynx plus a small population of Iberian Wolf. Whilst the latter are virtually impossible to find, seeing a lynx is, with perseverance, reasonable weather and a bit of luck, a distinct possibility. With this in mind, we dedicate this route to optimising your chances of seeing this endangered species, with other mammals and birds a pleasant sideshow. Because finding Lynx requires staying on a single place rather than walking around, we pay less attention to the flora and small fauna.

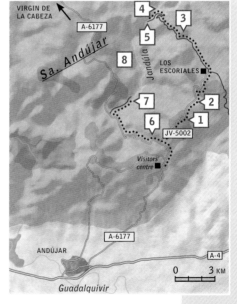

Seeing lynx is something of a lottery. Chance and weather play an important role, so set aside 3 or 4 days to explore this route several times if necessary.

Starting point Centro de Visitantes Viñas de Peñallano

The grand prize of a trip to the Sierra de Andújar – a glimpse of an Iberian Lynx.

Top tips for Lynx watchers

- Be prepared to wait! Most sightings are made from good vantage points across suitable habitat after a long vigil.
- Plan to stay for 3 to 4 days. You might get lucky on your first day, but it might easily take a bit longer.
- Bring a folding chair – it makes the wait more comfortable and thus helps concentration.
- Dress suitably – it can be cold in the mountains.
- Bring a telescope – animals can be distant.
- A visit in late winter/early spring (January – March) when Lynx tend to be more active optimizes your chances, but the animals may be seen throughout the year.
- Lynx tend to be most active during early mornings and dusk.
- Watch and listen to the birds (esp. magpies) which often spot – and noisily harangue – the lynx before you manage to see it!
- Communicate with other lynx watchers – they will have news of the latest sightings. (Swapping mobile numbers can be a useful strategy).

From the visitors' centre take the A-6177 towards *Santuario Virgen de la Cabeza* (a well signposted destination). Immediately after the *Complejo Turístico Los Pinos* (1.7 km) take the minor JV 5002/JH 5002 road on your right, signposted *Pantano del Jándula*.

1 This narrow tarmac road snakes its way up into the hills and provides your first chance of finding Lynx. It may be seen anywhere from (or even crossing) the road, but chances increase the further you drive along this route. Meanwhile, Azure-winged Magpies are abundant in the dehesa, while in the skies above Griffon and Black Vultures patrol, occasionally joined by a Golden or Spanish Imperial Eagle.

2 A particularly good vantage point to stake out Lynx is the long gentle hill through the scrubland just after the *Cerrajeros finca* (approximately 6 km from the A-6177). The views are good, but the downside is the lack of convenient places to park. If you do park, make sure you are off the tarmac – otherwise you risk a hefty fine (see also page 220). At Los Escoriales (about 3.5 km further along the road) the tarmac gives way to a gravel. Turn left at the remains of an electricity substation beyond Los Escoriales and head for the *Mirador del Embalse del Jándula*. The bumpy track continues through open dehesa inhabited by fierce 'torros bravas', but soon passes through denser woodland and more scrubby areas. Continue, watching all the while for both Lynx and raptors.

3 About 5 km from the junction, you reach a downward sloping section of the track, marked by large concrete blocks, some of which are painted white. This is one of the primary sites for seeing Lynx. Scanning the dehesa below you will likely see Red Deer, possibly Wild Boar or Mongoose, and certainly some rather nervous Rabbits. However be prepared to wait several hours for Lynx. Time to get those chairs out of the boot! Fortunately, there is plenty to entertain you here, from Rock and Ortolan Buntings and Sardinian Warblers in the scrub to Red-billed Chough and eagles in the skies above. Black Vulture is another diverting treasure to be seen here.

Continuing further along the track, you'll reach the *Mirador del Embalse del Jándula* (superb views of the embalse and the surrounding hills). The track then drops sharply down to the small settlement of La Lancha and the dam beyond.

The extensive and sparsely populated landscape of the Sierra de Andújar.

172

4 From the dam you have a chance of spotting Otter whilst Crag Martins and, in summer, Red-rumped Swallows enjoy swooping by at arm's length. The tunnel on the far side of the dam often has roosting bats.

5 To your left as you approach the dam you can opt for a pleasant short walk (about 600m) to the *Mirador del Rey*. Scan the rock faces here for Mouflon and Spanish Ibex, and Blue Rock Thrush and Black Wheatear. In winter Alpine Accentor regularly turn up and Wallcreeper is a rare visitor.

Return all along the track and road to the A-6177 and turn right towards the *Santuario Virgen de la Cabeza*. Road signs showing a lynx quickly remind that, even along this busier road, a sighting is possible and urges you to keep your speed down (*Recuerde el Lince* – mind the Lynx).

6 *El Peregrino Mirador* (well signposted on your right) offers a superb view over the Sierra de Andújar, and another opportunity to scan for raptors. In the summer check the swifts carefully for the scarce White-rumped.

The scenic Jádula river (top). Some rocks in the river, upon closer inspection, turn out to have eyes! They are Spanish Terrapins, of which there are many on the river (bottom).

After crossing the river Jándula, turn right along a track which follows the river. The recreation area gives some opportunities to explore the river itself.

7 The highest point of the track (about 1.5km), clearly marked by more white concrete blocks and some railings, is perhaps the best area to see Lynx. Red Deer, sometimes joined by Fallow Deer, can be seen as well, while Otter occurs in the river.

8 Those less anxious to 'stake out' Lynx, are advised to walk along the path besides the track for another 1.5 km to the dam. The river holds a good range of amphibians (e.g. Iberian and Stripeless Tree Frog, Iberian Midwife Toad), reptiles (e.g. Montpellier and Viperine Snake), dragonflies (e.g. Violet Dropwing and Orange Featherleg) and the usual range of butterflies like Spanish Festoon and Provence Orange-tip. Naturally, the eagles and vultures mentioned elsewhere may fly over, while smaller birds here may include Great Spotted Cuckoo, Wryneck, Iberian Green Woodpecker, Melodious Warbler and Rock Sparrow. Azure-winged Magpies are ubiquitous and often quite tame here. Once you reach the dam you have a splendid view over the river, where Spanish Terrapins are basking on the rocks. Note that this area can be popular with picnickers at weekends in the warmer months.

Black Kite with Azure-winged Magpies – the birdlife of the Sierra de Andújar is superb.

PRACTICAL PART

Route 14: Cascada de la Cimbarra

4 HOURS
EASY

Best season
February-June
Of interest
Year-round

A walk through a small but very scenic natural park.

Habitats cliffs, scrubland, dehesa, river and riverine forest
Selected species Viperine snake, Azure-winged Magpie, Kingfisher, Golden Oriole, Alpine Swift, White-rumped Swift, Morena Purple Foxglove*, Stripeless Tree Frog, Viperine Snake, Orange Featherleg, Epaulet Skimmer, Violet Dropwing, Orange-winged Dropwing, Marsh Fritillary, Nettle-tree Butterfly

The Cascada de la Cimbarra is a small *Paraje Natural* (protected landscape) just east of the Despeñaperros. It is named after a beautiful waterfall but the riverine habitats along the river are equally impressive with some paradisiacal stretches along the trail.

The area has a good selection of birds, but above all, it is the dragonfly fauna that stands out. A late spring or early summer visit is the most rewarding.

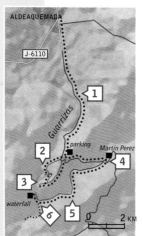

Starting point Aldeaquemada.
Follow the signs *Cimbarra* and *Paraje Natural*.

1 The stream is flanked by lush riparian growth. Look and listen for Golden Oriole. Hoopoe, Scops Owl and Iberian Green Woodpecker. Kingfishers hunt from the waterside perches as do many species of dragonfly. Blue Emperor, Western Clubtail and Epaulet Skimmer are among the residents of the Río Guarrizas, as is Stripeless Tree Frog.

Continue until you reach a small car park from which you continue on foot on the signposted trail to Cascada de la Cimbarra.

2 The short trail takes you to the waterfall. The first stretch overlooks the Río Guarrizas upstream from the waterfall. Golden Orioles are again seen and heard around the treetops and Rock Bunting and Blue Rock Thrush are present on the rocky slopes. A short side trail to the right takes you down to the base of the waterfall – a highly recommended detour! Beneath the waterfall, you'll find a small lake, several small pools and the ruins of an old watermill, together making for a fairy-tale-like scenery. Keep an eye out for Crag Martin, Grey Wagtail and Kingfisher. Dainty Bluet, Blue Emperor and Orange Featherleg are among the dragonflies present here. The margins of the pools are frequented by Nettle-tree Butterflies and Spanish Purple Hairstreak.

Return to the trail and continue to a magnificent viewpoint overlooking the waterfall.

View of the Cascada de Cimbarra in summer, when the river carries only little water.

3 This is a good spot to scan for raptors. Griffon Vulture, Bonelli's Eagle, Golden Eagle and Spanish Imperial Eagle (the latter rare) are among the possibilities. In wintertime, the area is also frequented by Black Vultures.
Striped Grayling, Dusky Heath and Spanish Gatekeeper are common butterflies.
Continue the trail that leads back to the car park and follow the signs to *Área Recreativa Arroyo de Martín Perez.*

4 This recreational area is a good place to spot Azurewinged Magpie. The Arroyo Martín Perez is a small stream to the left, where dragonflies

A lush 'gallery' forest of Narrow-leaved Ash trees lines the Guarrizas river (top). This is an excellent environment for two orange odonates: the Orange-winged Dropwing (centre), which has colonised Andalucía with spectacular rapidity. The Orange Featherleg (bottom) is a lot less conspicuous.

(e.g. Keeled Skimmer) hunt over the water. The stream houses a sizable population of Viperine Snakes.

Follow the trail *Arroyo de Martín Perez* that starts at the far end of the recreational area.

5 This trail runs along the Martín Perez brook to its confluence with the Río Guarrizas. The riverine forest is again good for Golden Oriole. When the trail crosses the arroyo, follow a sign that reads *Formación*

Geológica. This short detour takes you into a splendid little gorge. The rare Morena Purple Foxglove* (*Digitalis purpurea mariana*) grows on the rocks and many Trout can be seen swimming in the crystal-clear water. Also keep an eye out for Grey Wagtail and Ocellated Lizard.

The Morena Purple Foxglove (top) is an endemic of the Sierra Morena. It is closely related to the well-known Purple Fox-glove (which doesn't occur here) and sometimes regarded as a subspecies of the latter.

Once at the Río Guarrizas, you can follow its banks upstream in the direction of the waterfall for a while (signposted *El Negrio*).

6 You arrive at a beautiful lake with waterfall. Spanish Terrapin can be seen basking along its shores and Kingfisher hunt over the water. During late spring and summer, carefully scan the scores of swifts flying overhead as a few White-rumpeds may be among the far more numerous Alpine and Common Swifts. Several pairs breed in the area. The small lake is again a dragonfly hotspot with beauties like Purple and Orange-winged Dropwing, Small Pincertail and Copper Demoiselle all present.

The Río Guarrizas is also home to a population of Otter and even Iberian Lynx occurs in the general area.

The Dusky Heath is beautifully patterned, but well camouflaged. It flies in summer when it blends in perfectly in the dusty brown environment.

To get back to the car, return the way you came. If you fancy some further exploration, follow the Río Guarrizas downstream. Similar species can be found there.

Additional sites in the Sierra de Andújar

A – Along the Río Jándula - La Ropera

Best season
February-July

The confluence of Río Jándula and the Guadalquivir at the foot of the Sierra Morena is cloaked in Mediterranean scrub and woodland – a beautiful backdrop to a pleasant and easy circular walk of approximately 7.5 km – *the Sendero de la Ropera*. The walk crosses dense, riverside vegetation of Black Poplars, willows and tamarisks, where Grass Snake and Penduline Tit live alongside Olivaceous Warbler and introduced Waxbills. In stretches with open Mediterranean woodland, there are Azure-winged Magpies, Woodchat Shrike, Great Spotted Cuckoo and the usual raptors of the Sierra Morena.

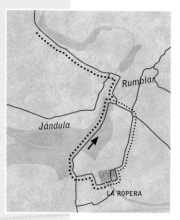

At places where you can approach the river, you might be lucky enough to see an Otter, or dragonflies like Orange Featherleg and Western Clubtail. Near the Rumblar Canal, make a detour over the wide track that branches off to the left. It leads to some farmland that is a favourite hunting place for Black-winged Kite.

Once back at the Rumblar Canal, either complete the circuit (through an area with young olive groves) or retrace your steps along the river.

To get there from the village of La Ropera (which is 5 km northwest of Andújar), simply follow the sign *Sendero La Ropera* to the starting point.

B – Baños de la Encina

Best season
March-June

Those who want to explore a bit more of the Sierra de Andújar on foot, should consider walking the GR-48 hiking trail from the recreational area of Pozo Nuevo. Pozo Nuevo lies along the JH-5042 just east of Baños de la Encina.

The path leads through olive groves, pinewoods, holm oak woods and pastureland and offers splendid views over the Embalse del Rumblar. Much of the area has maintained the untamed character of the Sierra Morena. On your walk in spring, you are accompanied by butterflies like Spanish Festoon and Provence Orange-tip, while the delicate Pallid Narcissus and Mirror Orchid are plentiful beneath the trees. The birdlife is great, with

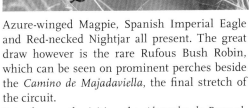

Azure-winged Magpie, Spanish Imperial Eagle and Red-necked Nightjar all present. The great draw however is the rare Rufous Bush Robin, which can be seen on prominent perches beside the *Camino de Majadaviella*, the final stretch of the circuit.

It is also worth visiting the *Alcazaba de Bury al-Hamman* (or Castillo de Burgalimar), an ideal viewpoint for raptors. The castle also has a Lesser Kestrel colony and is home to Iberian Wall Lizard, Mediterranean House and Moorish Geckos. Other species recorded here include Pallid and Alpine Swifts, Booted Eagle, Blue Rock Thrush, Egyptian Vulture, Golden Eagle and, occasionally, Spanish Imperial Eagle.

Hoopoes (left) and Azure-winged Magpies are among the more common and easily seen birds on the trail to Baños de la Encina.

C – Parque Natural Despeñaperros – the Barranco de Valdeazores trail

In the Despeñaperros Nature Park, a wonderful trail takes you along the *Barranco de Valdeazores* to a magnificent viewpoint overlooking the famous Despeñaperros pass, the dramatic gateway into Andalucía from the central *meseta* highlands. The area is known for its well preserved stands of original Mediterranean forest with Holm Oak, Cork Oak, Austrian Pine and Strawberry Tree, the latter of which attracts Two-tailed Pasha. Crossbill, Coal Tit, Crested Tit and Firecrest are frequent around the

Best season
March-June
Of interest
Year-round

180

The cliffs of Despeñaperros.

pines and Iberian Chiffchaff breeds in the area. Check the streams and temporary pools along the trail for Fire Salamanders and their larvae. The viewpoint at the end of the trail offers a splendid look over the pass. The pillars of quartzite that have been forced upward by tectonic pressure on the other side of the pass are aptly called *Los Órganos* – The Organs. The pass has always been of great strategic importance as the gateway to Andalucía. Signs of military presence date back to Roman antiquity and the pass was famously used during the Reconquista by King Alfonso VIII of Castile to mount a surprise attack on a Moorish army (see page 50).

The historic viewpoint is a good place to scan the sky for Golden Eagle, Spanish Imperial Eagle and Griffon Vulture. White-rumped Swift also occurs, but it is rare. Among the mammals, Red Deer and Spanish Ibex are common, the first in the forests, the latter on the cliffs. Iberian Lynx and Iberian Wolf occur in very small numbers and are seldom, if ever, seen.

To get to the start of the trail, take the A4 from Santa Elena in the direction of Madrid, take exit 244 (*Venta de Cardenos*). Turn left at the roundabout to the other side of the motorway. After 1 km, a dirt track on the right takes you to the start of the trail. To park, however, drive on for another 300 metres to find a large car park on the left.

D – Córdoba city – Sotos de Albolifia

Of interest
Year-round

Surprisingly, one of the few stretches of well-preserved riverine forest and river banks of the Guadalquivir lies right in the city centre of Córdoba. So if you come for a cultural visit to this historic place (which we highly recommend!) don't forget to go to the Roman Bridge that overlooks the *Sotos de Albolifia* to watch Night Herons, Little Bittern and Cattle Egret which roost here. Little Ringed Plover, Common Sandpiper, Serin, Bee-eater, Pallid Swift, Kingfisher, Melodious Warbler and Lesser Kestrel may also be around. The site is particularly great at sunset, when the Night Herons collectively fly out to forage.

This site offers dragonfly enthusiasts the most daunting experience possible: the rare Faded Pincertail *(Onychogomphus costae)* flies here at the hottest spot in Europe during the hottest time of the year, in a place with very little shade. To make things worse, this species is not easy to find among the mix of Orange and Violet Dropwings, Epaulet Skimmers, and White Featherlegs (but then again, these are attractive species too!).

E – Laguna Grande

The Laguna Grande, a *Paraje Natural*, is a small oasis in an otherwise uninterrupted landscape of dry olive groves. It is well signposted from the A-316 between Mancha Real and Baeza. Before reaching the site itself you will pass the Hacienda de Laguna Grande, which has a small information centre.

Of interest
Year-round

A circular track leads all the way around this small wetland. Several small artificial lakes are fringed by tamarisks, reedbeds and patches of riverine forest. It harbours a heron colony with Night, Squacco and Purple Herons, Little and Cattle Egrets. The marshland is home to Purple Gallinule, Little Grebe and other waterfowl. Both Penduline Tit and Marsh Harrier nest, while the woods are home to Golden Oriole, Nightingale, Iberian Green Woodpecker, Hoopoe, Azure-winged Magpie and Turtle Dove. Sand Martin and Bee-eater – both colonial birds that nest in sandy banks, frequently fly by.

Summer at Laguna Grande – the Banded Groundling, immediately recognisable by its black wing markings, flies low over the mudflats and trails.

Ocellated Lizard is common along the track while good numbers of Spanish Terrapins can be seen basking on tree trunks in the water. Amphibians to be found here (especially on wet days) include Sharp-ribbed Newt, Western Toad and both European and Stripeless Tree Frog. The reservoir is home to some sought-after, southern dragonflies like Epaulet and Long Skimmers, Violet Dropwing and hordes of damselflies like Iberian Bluetail, Small Red-eye, Small Spreadwing, and Dainty Bluet. In terms

of wildflowers, it is not all that great, but Stinking Iris (actually an attractive flower) may put a smile on the botanist's face.

F – Laguna de Zoñar and del Rincón

Of interest
Year-round

In the south of Córdoba Province, not far from the main road to Málaga, lie several endorheic lakes of great importance for waterfowl. The largest of them, Laguna de Zoñar, has played a crucial role in the conservation of the rare and endangered White-headed Duck. In the late 1970s, when the species was in the most perilous state, Zoñar was its last refuge in Spain. Since then, a protection and recovery programme has boosted its numbers.

Today the permanently wet Laguna de Zoñar and nearby Rincón lake, are an important hotspot for wildfowl, including White-headed Duck, Crested Coot (reintroduced in Laguna del Rincón), Pochard, Red-crested Pochard, Great Crested and Little Grebes and Purple Gallinule. Reed, Great Reed and Melodious Warbler occur in the reedy fringes while a few Rufous Bush Robins are known to breed in the surrounding olive groves.

Laguna de Zoñar is signposted from the big roundabout on the A 304 just south of Aquilar de la Frontera. There are signposted trails from the visitors' centre that lead to a hide and there is a track that bends around the lake on the east side and offers good views from the north, but then you have the disadvantage of looking into the sun.

The Crested Coot has been introduced in the Laguna del Rincón.

Getting to Laguna del Rincón is possible from the west and from the east. The walk from the western side is a little longer (1 km vs 700 metres), but parking is better. Coming on the A3132 from the north, park on the left side of the road just before the *Arroyo de la Limosna* and follow the track to the southeast (the one crossing the *arroyo*).

Alternatively, find the access track off the CP-101 signposted *Laguna del Rincón*.

The Sierra Nevada

The Sierra Nevada is without doubt a highlight of your visit to eastern Andalucía. This impressive mountain range, part of the larger Sierra Baetica (see page 12), dominates the landscape and climate of the entire region. Blocking the stream of moist Atlantic air from the west, the Nevada is responsible for the dry semi-desert climate of south-east Andalucía. The Sierra Nevada itself is, with a maximum altitude of 3,478 metres (the Mulhacén), high enough to form an Alpine enclave in the middle of the Mediterranean region. As a result, many species have evolved into unique forms – the Sierra Nevada endemics.

Travelling from the lower reaches of the mountain range to its peaks, the visitor is treated to a rapid succession of habitats. Lush river valleys (routes 16, 17, 18 and 19) are followed by holm oak woodlands (route 17), pine plantations (routes 17 and 19) and the hedgehog broom zone (routes 17 and 19). Moving even higher, you will eventually find barren rock, snow-capped peaks and *borreguiles* or mountain peatlands (routes 17 and 19).

Overview of the Sierra Nevada area. The letters refer to the sites described on page 204-207.

In contrast to most of the ranges of Andalucía, the Nevada is dominated by acidic schists, rather than limestone. There are limestone areas around the base of the massif though (most notably the Sierra de Huétor; route 15), which boast a very different flora than the rest of the Nevada.

Historically, the region is of tremendous significance. The Alpujarras, Nevada's southern extension, was the last stronghold of the Moors in Spain (see page 53). It is in places like Capileira and Trevélez that their cultural heritage is still very alive and visible. Centuries of Moorish architecture and agricultural practices have shaped the Alpujarras into the attractive region it is today (routes 18 and 19). It is a well-known destination for hiking.

The Sierra de Huétor, a separate mountain range to the north of the Sierra Nevada, also merits a visit. It is more rugged and has a rich flora (many orchids), superb butterfly spots and large numbers of Spanish Ibex (routes 15).

Route 15: Sierra de Huétor

Best season
March-July

FULL DAY, 7 KM
EASY

Day trip connecting several great sites of Sierra de Huétor.
One of the best butterfly and orchid routes in eastern Andalucía.

Habitats forest, grassland, scrubland, river, pinewood
Selected species Yellow Pheasant's-eye, Southern Early Purple Orchid*,
Spanish Omega Orchid*, Dull Bee Orchid, Mirror Orchid, Fan-lipped Orchid,
Giant Orchid, Violet Bird's-nest, Spanish Ibex, Azure-winged Magpie, Bonelli's
Eagle, Mother-of-Pearl Blue, Spanish Chalk-hill Blue, Dwarf Mantis

The limestone area of the Sierra de Huétor, just north of the Sierra
Nevada, is often ignored by visiting naturalists. This is a pity as it has an
amazing butterfly fauna and a rich flora, in particular orchids – and this
just a stone's-throw away from Granada and the Alhambra. In fact, the
latter is situated on one of the foothills of the Sierra de Huétor.
To appreciate the richness of the orchids, be here in April or early May.

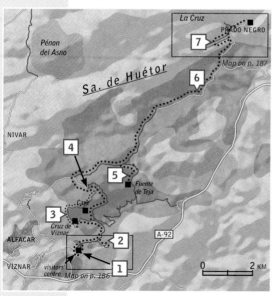

The butterflies peak, both in
quantity and diversity in early
summer. The area also prides
itself in having a large population of Spanish Ibex and is a
reliable area for seeing Azure-
winged Magpie. During the
Spanish Civil War, the Sierra
was of strategic importance.
Many remains of fortifications bear silent testimony to
this fact.
This is a short car route, connecting several easy rambles
on well-marked trails.

Starting point Visitors' centre *Puerto Lobo* at Km 8 on the
GR-3103 east of Víznar. Park
by the bend just before the

visitors' centre on the track to the *Área Recreativa La Alfaguara* and near a small electricity tower.

1 Follow the short 460m *Puerto Lobo* trail over a limestone hill with a sublime collection of orchids, both in number and diversity. Look for Mirror, Yellow Bee and Spanish Omega Orchids* (*Ophrys dyris*), which grow in profusion. Southern Early Purple Orchid* (*Orchis olbiensis*) is simply everywhere while Naked-man Orchid grows here and there in small clumps. The rare Fan-lipped Orchid, an early species that finishes flowering before the end of April, is more solitary. Search for it near the top of the hill. Azure-winged Magpies will be your noisy companions along the walk. Also keep an eye out for Ocellated Lizards.

From the electricity tower, follow the GR-3103 in the direction of the Alfaguara recreation area. Stop after approximately 750 m at the start of the *Sendero Trincheras del Cerro del Maulo*.

The Sierra de Huétor route is arguably the best one for finding orchids in eastern Andalucía. Near the visitors' centre in spring, you can find, amongst others, Spanish Omega Orchid* (Ophrys dyris; top and far left), Naked-man, Fan-lipped and (far right) Spanish Early-purple Orchids.

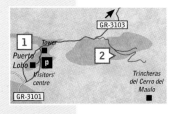

2 This 900m walk leads through pine forest and dry scrubland, where in spring the Morels and Pink Crown mushrooms are conspicuous. You'll find more Southern Early Purple Orchid* (*Orchis olbiensis*) and the pretty Rusty Toadflax* (*Linaria aeruginea*). Red Squirrel is common in these pinewoods and uprooted soil is a sure sign Wild Boar is present. Look for the foundations of trenches of a military stronghold during the Spanish Civil War (see page 55). From here, a stunning panorama appears of Granada and the summits of the Sierra Nevada. This is also a good spot for 'hill-topping' butterflies and a viewpoint for raptors.

Red Squirrels are remarkably rare in eastern Andalucía. The Sierra de Huétor is a welcome exception. Here this adorable animal is frequently encountered.

Return to your car and drive on for 1.2 km. Park in the hairpin bend at the lowest point of the wooded valley. The *Cruz de Víznar trail* starts here.

3 The trails leads up the hill and it won't take long before you will see some Spanish Fir (*Pinsapo*) trees. This tree is native only to the Serranía de Ronda in western Andalucía, but was planted here to minimise the chance of its extinction. Violet Bird's-nest Orchids, Wild Tulips and both Western Peony and *Paeonia coriacea* grow in the forest. An open area, *Collado de Víznar*, appears from where you can go left to the *Cruz de Víznar*, 300m ahead for another splendid view. Look here for butterflies which congregate at this hilltop, and for Wolf Spiders (tarantulas) which hide in holes in the ground. Retrace your steps to the car or, if you fancy a longer hike, you can continue to the *Cueva de Agua* and on to the GR-3103 road, where you turn right to return to the car (8 km in total).

Continue and after approximately 2.7 km you reach the recreational area *La Alfaguarra*. Park here for a visit to the Botanical Garden, which is actually an arboretum. Access is free.

4 Of the many different trees in the garden, the 30 m tall Cedars are the stars. The characteristic Strawberry Tree is the host plant for the Two-tailed Pasha, that glides along the

canopy in summer. The cone-shaped Spanish Firs grow both inside and outside the arboretum. The open areas are sublime spots to observe hundreds of butterflies in summer. Black Satyr, High Brown Fritillary and Amanda's Blue are possibilities, but Great Banded Grayling and Spanish Marbled White are most abundant. The typical birds of coniferous forests (Coal and Crested Tits, Short-toed Treecreeper and Crossbill) may appear here. In spite of this being a botanical garden, the wildflowers here were not planted and boast some eye-catching species like jonquils, peonies, Yellow Pheasant's-eye, Naked-man Orchid and Sunset Foxglove.

Continue to a T-junction where you turn right to Fuente la Teja at the junction. The tarmac soon gives way to gravel. Check the open areas for butterflies (e.g. Spanish Marbled White, Rock Grayling and Panoptes Blue). After 3 km park near the barrier and walk the *Sendero Fuente de Teja* (1.7 km one way).

5 All along the trail in spring, the forest floor is carpeted with jonquils. Scan the rocky slopes opposite for Spanish Ibex and open, grassy patches for butterflies, such as Provence Orange-tip, Blue-spot Hairstreak and Spanish Festoon in spring, and Striped Grayling, Dusky Heath and Dark Green Fritillary later in the season. Notice the Rosemary Broomrape that parasitises Rosemary in the scrubland. The tree-lined source offers a steady flow of water throughout the year. This site is home to dragonflies like Common Goldenring and Large Pincertail. You'll see them chasing along the stream in summer, joined by many Beautiful Demoiselles.

Continue further along the main gravel road and you will find tarmac again near the electricity wires. One km beyond these wires, the road snakes in an open patch along the stream.

6 The presence of Spanish Purple Hairstreak justifies a short stop in summer at the point where a stream and electricity wires cross the road. Dragonflies like Copper Demoiselle, Common Goldenring, Keeled and Southern Skimmer are present as well.

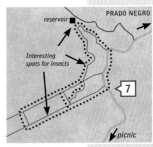

Drive further and turn left in the direction of Prado Negro at the recreational area. The large picnic site can be very busy in the weekend. After 1.5 km, you can park the car near a broad track on your left and walk the small loop indicated in the map.

7 In spring many birds of scrub and open woodland are present, including Subalpine and Bonelli's Warbler and the elusive European Nightjar. Under the Kermes Oak, Southern Early Purple Orchid* (*Orchis olbiensis*) and peonies flowers in spring. In summer, this spot is rewarding for its insects and you can spend hours here sorting out the different species of butterflies. They occur in large numbers and we've found over 60 species in a single day, including Mother-of-Pearl, Spanish Chalkhill and Spanish Zephyr Blues, Cinquefoil Skipper, Hermit and Cardinal. The European Dwarf Mantis* (*Ameles spallanzania*) and the conspicuous Thread-winged Lacewing, a relative of the ant-lions, are present here too.

Continue to the village of Prado Negro, where this route ends.

Additional remark From the village of Prado Negro it is possible to climb to the mountain top. On the slopes you may encounter Blue Rock Thrush, Rock Bunting and Subalpine Warbler. This is a good site for Griffon Vultures and Golden Eagles too. Giant Orchids are scattered in the scrubland, while the surroundings of the village form a hotspot for Golden Oriole, Cetti's Warbler and Nightingale.

The landscape near Prado Negro.

Route 16: Río Genil

5 HOURS
EASY

Best season
April-July

A scenic stroll through the canyon of the Río Genil.

Habitats oak woods, scrubland, cliffs, riverine forest
Selected species Sunset Foxglove, Robust Marsh Orchid, Green-flowered
Helleborine, Dipper, Marsh Fritillary, Spanish Purple Hairstreak

The Río Genil is the largest river to flow from the Sierra Nevada and the second largest of Andalucía (after the Guadalquivir). This route explores its upper reaches. The river, lined with shady riparian forest, has beautiful cascades and rapids whilst the slopes above are clothed in dry Mediterranean scrubland, evergreen oaks and broom scrub.

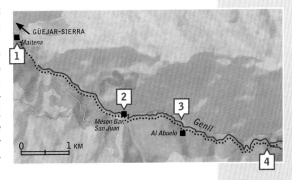

Starting point Restaurante Maitena

Getting there From the centre of Güejar Sierra, follow the signs *Río Genil / Río Maitena*. The restaurant is just beyond a hairpin bend on your right side.

1 Walk down the valley, where the Río Maitena meets the Río Genil. Birds of more temperate regions like Wren, Blackcap, Chaffinch and Spotted Flycatcher live in the lush riverine habitats. Turtle Dove, Golden Oriole and Bee-eaters are frequently seen. The tunnels along this section of the route were originally constructed for a tramway which took visitors from Granada into the Sierra Nevada until 1962. Scenically, it is an attractive spot.

Continue. The tarmac road ends at restaurant *Mesón Barranco San Juan*. Leave your vehicle in the car park and cross the little bridge on foot.

2 This footpath follows the river upstream. The valley of the Río Genil shows a typical cross-section of a Mediterranean river. The north facing slope (to the right as you look upstream) is covered with Holm Oak, the bottom of the valley supports a lush riverine forest with Pyrenean Oak, Chestnut and Elm, while the south facing, sun-exposed slope to the left is covered with Mediterranean scrub. Check the river for Dipper, Grey Wagtail and Kingfisher. Melodious Warbler can also be heard. The footpath crosses several gullies with seasonal streams and two streams with permanent water. Muddy spots along these streams attract numerous butterflies including Lesser Spotted Fritillary, Spanish Purple Hairstreak, Large Tortoiseshell and Marsh Fritillary. Shady and moist patches along the streams are also sites for Robust Marsh Orchid and Narrow-leaved Helleborine.

The fast-flowing Genil river (top). The riverside vegetation is a favourite haunt of Large Tortoiseshell.

3 After 1 km, the trail arrives at a magnificent ancient Chestnut, the *Abuelo Vereda de la Estrella*. Enthusiastic botanists should keep an eye out for both Purple and Sunset Foxglove, both of which are fairly common along the trail. The succulents *Pistorinia hispanica* and *Mucizonia hispida* can be found on rocky substrates. In summer, the pretty Thread-winged Lacewing flutters about in more exposed, scrubby terrain.

4 The route ends at the confluence of the Río Genil and the Río Vadillo. A trail to the left descends to a bridge across the Río Genil, another good spot to look for Dippers and Grey Wagtails and enjoy a picnic.

Return via the same way.

Route 17: The Pico Véleta

**6 HOURS - FULL DAY
21 KM**

Cross-section of the Sierra Nevada's habitats.
from its base to its highest peaks.

Best season
Late May-August

Habitats scrublands, evergreen oak forest, pine forest, hedgehog scrub, borreguiles, rivers
Selected species Nevada Butterwort*, Spanish Fritillary, Sierra Nevada Violet, Snowy Plantain*, Golden Eagle, Alpine Accentor, Spanish Ibex, Apollo, Nevada Blue, Nevada Grayling, Spanish Brassy Ringlet, Zullich's Blue

This is the perfect route to gain a first impression of the Sierra Nevada as it takes you from hot, Mediterranean lowlands all the way up to one of its highest peaks. Along the way, you pass through evergreen oakwoods, pine forests, the hedgehog broom zone, the rocky Alpine slopes and the famous *borreguiles* (mountain peatlands) with its endemic flora. The entire route is splendid for wildflowers.

Getting there Güejar Sierra

In Güejar Sierra, follow the main road to *Río Genil / Río Maitena*. At a fork with many wooden signposts on the edge of the village, turn right (signposted *Restaurante La Fabriquilla*). This road takes you to a bridge over the Río Genil.

1 This is the point where the Río Genil flows into the Embalse de Canales. Swifts and Red-rumped Swallows hunt over the water while a glance at the sky may reveal a Booted Eagle or other raptors. A metal flight of stairs takes you down to the river bank.

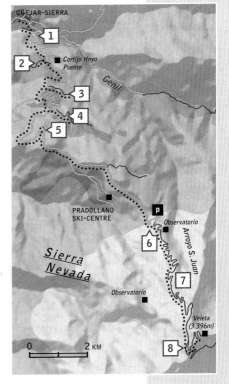

Sunset Foxglove flowers in late spring. It is an indicator of acidic soils.

This is a good spot to scan the river for Dipper, Grey Wagtail and Kingfisher. Beyond the bridge, a dirt track skirts the edge of the reservoir. The sparsely vegetated shore here is good for Violet Dropwing while Viperine Snakes may be seen hunting in the water.

Return to the car and continue across the bridge. The road starts snaking up the mountain. After 3.4 km from the bridge you will find a large sign on the left that reads *Cortijo Hoyo Puente*. Park and explore the track into the oak woods opposite this sign.

2 This is a good spot to get a taste of the evergreen oak zone, the lowest of the vegetation zones of the Sierra Nevada. Holm Oak is the dominant species here. In spring and summer, the bright yellow flowers of broom colour the landscape, especially in more open patches. Keep an eye out for Sardinian and Dartford Warblers. Some interesting wildflowers like Western Peony, Sunset Foxglove and Common Gladiole grow along this track. In summer, there are some attractive butterflies, like Marsh Fritillary, False Ilex Hairstreak and Spanish Marbled White.

Return to the car and continue up the mountain. After 1.6 km you arrive at a T-junction. Turn right here. The road leads through some narrow gorges, so be wary of oncoming traffic. After exiting the last of these narrow gorges, take a dirt track to the left, signposted *Apartamentos Rurales Altos de las Catifas*. Find a suitable place to park.

3 Here the deciduous trees have made way for pine trees. On the left side of the track you can enjoy some splendid views over the valley of the Río Genil. The dirt track ends at the apartment complex but several side trails enable you to explore the pine forest and scrub more thoroughly. Spanish Marbled White and Mother-of-Pearl and Argus Blues are some of the butterflies to be seen here, especially around patches of Spanish Lemon Thyme* (*Thymus baeticus*). With some luck you may already have seen an Apollo here, although they are more frequent at higher altitudes. Common Crossbill and Coal Tit are about and sometimes Booted Eagle shows itself.

Return to the road and continue. After 600 m, at a T-Junction just before the El Dornajo visitors' centre, take a sharp left. Continue for 2.4 km after this crossing to a dirt track on the left, which leads into an open area. Park the car here and continue along this track on foot.

4 The track explores the hedgehog broom zone. Holly Flax – (*Santolina rosmarinifolia*), Evergreen Milkvetch* (*Astragalus giennensis*) and Nevada Toadflax* (*Chaenorhinum glareosum*) are common shrubs, between which flowers like Boissier's Milkwort (*Polygala boissieri*) and Woolly Thrift (*Armeria villosa*) grow abundantly. Chimney Sweeper, a conspicuous black diurnal moth, flutters about. Stonechat, Rock Bunting, Sardinian and Subalpine Warbler are all present. After 450 m the track crosses the *Barranco Seco* and further ahead the *Barranco de los Tejos*. The vegetation in the gullies of these seasonal mountain streams is denser and lusher than the vegetation on the dry slopes. Look here for Robust Marsh Orchid.

In summertime these are excellent spots for butterflies, such as Silver-studded, Amanda's and Mother-of-Pearl Blues, Black-veined White and Marbled Skipper.

Return to the car and continue along the road. After 3.4 km take the dirt track on the left to a viewpoint (accessed via a gap in the guardrail). Park the car here and continue to the viewpoint on foot.

Some of the larger butterflies engage in 'hill-topping' to mate. Both males and females fly up-slope and meet each other around hill-tops, which thus can become crowded with butterflies. On this route, we found both Swallowtail (top) and Spanish Scarce Swallowtail (bottom) common around hillocks in summer.

5 You are now well above the tree line and right in the middle of the Hedgehog Broom zone. This is one of the few areas in the Sierra Nevada with limestone soils, hence the vegetation shows more similarities with that of the the limestone sierras than with that of the rest of the Sierra Nevada. The beautiful blue-flowered Hedgehog Broom occurs alongside Spiny Vella* (*Vella spinosa*) and Evergreen milkvetch. Walk back along the road to find calcareous wildflowers like Andalucian Stork's-bill* (*Erodium cheilanthifolium*) and Silver-leaved Bindweed* (*Convolvulus boissieri*). Stonechat, Subalpine Warbler, Linnet, Black

Redstart, Tawny Pipit and Northern Wheatear are birds of this area. The butterflies are represented by both Swallowtail and Scarce Swallowtail.

Return to the car and continue along the main road. After another 1.4 km, turn left, to Veleta and again after 3 km, once more signposted Veleta. The road ends at a car park near a military station. This is where the trail to the summit starts.

6 This last stretch is the most spectacular section of the route. The cold fierce winds have sculpted the vegetation into low dwarf forms. Most of the surface is barren rock with a few patches of Common Juniper (the ground hugging variety *depressa*) but amongst the rocks some very special wildflowers may be found like Glacier Buttercup, Spanish Fritillary, Glacial Eryngo* (*Eryngium glaciale*), Nevada Violet* (*Viola crassiuscula*), and Nevada Saxifrage* (*Saxifraga nevadensis*). As their names suggest the latter two are Sierra Nevada endemics. In this zone, another Sierra Nevada endemic can be found: the flightless grasshopper *Eumigus rubioi* (p. 202). Butterflies of high altitude are found in sheltered places. The endemic Nevada Blue occurs in great numbers and Apollo is frequent. Spanish Argus, Spanish Brassy Ringlet and Nevada Grayling are other specialities of this area.

Alpine river just beneath the Pico Véleta. The grassy banks hold many interesting wildflowers.

Left of the track you see an abandoned observatory. Climb up there to get a good view of the valley to the east.

7 This is the valley of the *Arroyo de San Juan*, one of Pico Véleta's many meltwater streams. Along this stream several deep green patches can be seen. These are some of the famous *borreguiles* of the Sierra Nevada. If you carefully descend into the valley you can take a closer look. This is

especially rewarding if you are interested in the rare, endemic flora of the
Sierra Nevada, as some of the region's
most sought-after plants grow exclusively in this habitat type. The carnivorous Nevada Butterwort* (*Pinguicula
nevadensis*), and Sierra Gentian*
(*Gentiana sierrae*) are among the
most striking examples. The Snowy
Plantain* (*Plantago nivalis*), readily
distinguishable by the silvery hairs on
the leaves, grows near the edges of the
borreguiles.

8 The experienced hiker may
want to continue all the way up to the summit
of Pico Véleta, but bear in mind that the weather
can be treacherous here. The surroundings will get
more barren as you proceed. With some luck, butterfly enthusiasts may be able to add Zullich's Blue
to their tally here. This is another Sierra Nevada endemic, which depends on the presence of Vitaliana
(*Androsace vitaliana*), its host plant, and
only occurs above 2,700 m altitude.
Close to the summit, look around for
Alpine Accentor. In spring and summertime the highest summits of the Sierra
Nevada are the only places in Andalucía
where you can reliably find this species.

Return via the way you came.

The high slopes of
the Pico Véleta are
a treasure trove of
endemic, cold-
adapted butterflies
and wildflowers,
including from top
to bottom, Zullich's
Blue, Snowy Plan-
tain*, the ragwort
Senecio Boissieri, and
Nevada Toadflax*
(*Chaenorhinum
glareosum*).

196

Route 18: The Poqueira valley

HALF A DAY, 7 KM
MODERATE

Best season
April-July

A scenic circuit through one of Alpujarras highest and most impressive valleys.

Habitats river and riverine forest, scrubland, grassy slopes
Selected species Dipper, Common Rock Thrush, Blue Rock Thrush, Black
Wheatear, Apollo, Marsh Fritillary, Purple-shot Copper

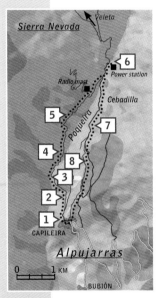

The steep Poqueira valley is one of the highlights of the Alpujarras as well as a gateway to the higher Sierra Nevada. A gentle circular trail leads into a steep gorge, cut out by the Poqueira river. This wonderful walk offers amazing views over narrow gorges, scrub and broad-leaved forest. The flora and fauna is rich in general, but in particular the birds and butterflies are attractive. This route is a must for any visitor to the Alpujarras.

Getting there Village of Capileira
When entering Capileira from the south, take a sharp left to the main car park. On foot, keep right at the water tap (*fuente del cubo*) and turn right, leaving the village.

1 You soon arrive at a platform (*Eras de Aldeire*) formerly used for drying hay. It offers a good overview of your walk. From here you can see the Alpine Swifts dashing through the valley, while Booted and Golden Eagle may fly over to inspect the area from above.

Continue the track down on the *Camino Abuchite*.

2 You pass the last fields of Capileira and will soon find some springs on your right, where in late spring the pink spikes of the Robust Marsh Orchids are conspicuous. The small streams next to the trail form the perfect habitat for the Common Goldenring. The surroundings are good for

The springs near the last fields of Poqueira village (top). Robust Marsh Orchid is common in wet spots in this area (bottom).

songbirds too. Golden Oriole and Nightingale sing from deep within the vegetation, while Sardinian Warbler frequents the shrubs and Bonelli's Warbler inhabits the pines. In the evening, the Scops Owl may start calling.

The path drops steeply down into the valley where you head on to the *Puente Abuchite*. This brings you into the scenic Poqueira valley with a small bridge that crosses the fast-flowing river.

3 Large Tortoiseshell and Spanish Festoon are frequently seen near the bridge. Songbirds struggle to make themselves heard against the background noise of the rapids. Look for Dipper on the river. Butterflies such as Marsh Fritillary and the endemic subspecies of the Heath Fritillary visit the brambles for nectar, often accompanied by Purple-shot Copper, Escher's Blue, Provence Orange-tip, Cleopatra and Cardinal.

4 Further along the track note the Large Psammodromuses, which are plentiful here. Some remarkable, tall Pyrenean Oaks along the path play host to Mistle Thrush and Serin.

PRACTICAL PART

198

5 Further on you enter a stunning, damp broad-leaved forest. Bonelli's Warbler, Hawfinch and Iberian Green Woodpecker are frequent here. Beyond the forest, you enter a dry scrubland. This is again a great stretch for butterflies. In season Apollo is on the wing together with more inconspicuous species like Marbled Skipper, Spanish Fritillary, Blue Spotted Hairstreak, Southern Brown Argus and Southern Gatekeeper.

The patch of damp, broad-leaved forest near point 5 is an enchanting place (top). Near the river, keep an eye out for Dipper (bottom).

The trail drops down again and you then pass a house. At the radio mast, walk down the valley towards the hydro-electric power station. You can already see the abandoned village of Cebadilla.

6 The hydro-electric power station is built at a section of the river that runs through a narrow canyon. Crag Martin, Black Redstart, Rock Dove, Peregrine Falcon and Rock Sparrow are residents, while Rock

Thrush is a summer visitor. If you haven't seen Dipper or Grey Wagtail yet, here you have another chance.

From Cebadilla power station you can continue along the trail towards the refugio to explore that section of the Sierra Nevada, which is more rugged, with rocky and bushy grasslands. The fit hiker may climb all the way up to the peak of the Véleta.

To continue our route, retrace your steps to the power station. Cross the river and follow the road. Beyond Cebadilla the route diverges from the road and comfortably leads you back to Capileira. On this side of the river, the landscape is more rocky and less green.

Marsh Fritillaries are rather common along the trail in summer.

7 The scrub provides shelter for Cirl Bunting, Sardinian and Subalpine Warblers. The rocky slopes on this section are excellent for Black Wheatear, Rock Bunting and Blue Rock Thrush, perching on rocky outcrops.

Keeping right at the junction in the pine forest, you arrive at a white house where Capileira is indicated to the right.

8 The scrub slowly gives way to arable land as you draw close to Capileira. An ingenious and remarkable irrigation system carries the water to Capileira and its arable land. Look around the small channels for Southern Skimmer. White Banded Grayling, Knapweed Fritillary and Long-tailed Blue are at home in this agricultural land and become more abundant as you proceed.

From the trail you have a splendid view over the valley and extensive arable lands of Capileira. Red-rumped Swallows welcome you back in the village, where you keep right for the car park and celebrate the end of a beautiful route in one of the most famous white villages of Andalucía.

Route 19: From Trevélez to the Mulhacén

FULL DAY STRENUOUS

A spectacular climb to the barren summit of Mulhacen. Superb flora and fauna with many Sierra Nevada endemics. Only recommended to the trained walker.

!
High mountain route: dangerous in bad weather!

Strenuous walk only suited for experienced hikers

Habitats high mountain slopes, riverine forests, scrublands, borreguiles
Selected species Nevada Columbine*, Nevada Butterwort*, Sierra Gentian*, Spanish Ibex, Dipper, Rock Thrush, Northern Wheatear, Apollo, Zullich's Blue, Nevada Blue, Nevada Brassy Ringlet

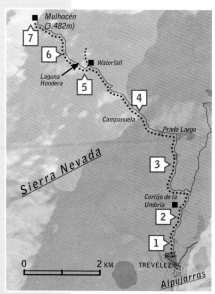

The ascent to the summit of Mulhacén, the highest mountain of mainland Spain, ought to be on the list of anyone visiting the Sierra Nevada. The route takes you through all the habitats the Sierra has to offer. Unlike the Sierra's second peak, the Pico Véleta, the landscape around the Mulhacén is relatively unspoilt. Many of the special Sierra Nevada endemics can be found along the route. As you gain altitude, you'll witness the neat succession of habitats from lush river valleys, scrub, low pine forest, hedgehog broom zone, *borreguiles* and finally barren rock and snow of Mulhacén's peak.

The Mulhacén is not an easy summit to conquer, though. This walk, splendid as it may be, is very long and demanding. Between the starting point and the peak, you'll have to climb over 1,900 metres, which makes this more than a day's walk for unfit or inexperienced ramblers. Consider booking a night in the hut near the Mulhacén and making it a 2-day trip. Alternatively, you can make it a shorter but still highly attractive walk making *La Campinuela* (point 4) or *Laguna Hondera* (point 5) your destination rather than the peak.

Best season
June-July
Of interest
May-September

Starting point Trevélez

From the village, follow the signs *Mulhacén / Siete Lagunas*. These take you to the beginning of a trail, the PRA-27, signposted with wooden poles with white and yellow markings.

1 The first part of this trail leads you through the green valley above Trevélez. Rock Sparrows frequent the sheepfolds along the trail. You cross brooks, lined with patches of riverine forest, where Golden Oriole, Wren and Blackcap thrive and Robust Marsh Orchid and Purple Foxglove grow in abundance. Early Marsh Orchid also occurs, but is much rarer. The lush character of these valleys is not entirely natural. It is the product of a Medieval irrigation system which can be traced back to the Moors. This age old system of weirs and channels (*acequias*) still supports agriculture in these valleys. On this route you can admire a well-preserved example of such an irrigation system.

2 As you climb higher, the vegetation, and with it the wildlife, changes. The landscape has a decidedly more Mediterranean character. Scrub with broom dominate in this section and birds like Subalpine Warbler, Woodchat Shrike, Stonechat, Black-eared Wheatear, Rock and Cirl Buntings can all be seen. Ocellated Lizard may be basking along the trail too. The flashy, purple flowers of Nevada Columbine* (*Aquilegia nevadensis*) can also be found.

Cascade of meltwater near the top of the mighty Mulhacén.

3 The next section of the trail takes you through two patches of low pine forest interspersed with broom scrub. Woodlark is common here.

4 When you leave the last patch of pine trees at La Campinuela, you enter the hedgehog broom zone. Here you are really getting the feel of the Sierra's highest peak.

The vegetation becomes much thinner. The beautiful, large Sierra Nevada subspecies of the Apollo butterfly is common. Among the birds, Black Redstart and Northern Wheatear are frequent on the slopes, while Grey Wagtail can be seen flying to and fro along the streams. The endemic grasshopper *Eumigus rubioi* can be found here along with *Baetica ustulata*, an endemic cricket. At *La Campinuela* you can also see the first of the *borreguiles*, the Sierra Nevada's typical mountain peatlands. With a very high level of endemism, these deep green patches of moist grassland are a botanist's dream.

The strange grasshopper *Eumigus rubioi* owes its somewhat maggot-like appearance to its lack of wings. Its immobility, together with its adaptation to the cold, contributes to its confinement to the high parts of the Sierra Nevada.

Near the cascade, the trail crosses a stream. Find a suitable place to jump across and continue on the trail towards the waterfall.

5 After climbing the trail to the right of the waterfall you are treated to a spectacular sight: *Laguna Hondera*, a beautiful meltwater lake with its extensive *borreguiles* and the summit of the mighty Mulhacén. These *borreguiles* are well worth exploring as they are accessible and sport a very rich flora. All the endemics associated with this habitat type can be found here: Nevada Butterwort* (*Pinguicula nevadensis*), Sierra Gentian* (*Gentiana sierrae*), Snowy Plantain* (*Plantago nivalis*) and the bird's-foot trefoil *Lotus glareosus* are some striking examples. Herds of Spanish Ibex usually linger in the vicinity of the lake. This is an excellent spot to take a lunch break and soak up the atmosphere.

The *Siete lagunas* (seven lakes) trail continues to the right. If you don't want to climb the summit and if snow conditions allow it, you can follow this trail to several other lagunas. Our route continues on the other side of the Laguna Hondera, across the ridge and to the summit. This trail is no longer officially signposted but hikers have taken it upon themselves to mark the path with piles of rocks.

6 The climb to the summit is strenuous but it is well worth the effort. The rocky substrate supports more local endemic wildflowers like Nevada Saxifrage* (*Saxifraga nevadensis*), Nevada Violet* (*Viola crassiuscula*), Cold Fleabane* (*Erigeron frigidus*), Nevada Toadflax* (*Chaenorhinum glareosum*) and the rare and endangered Granada Wormwood* (*Artemisia granatensis*). On good days in springtime, thousands of Small Tortoiseshells dance around the summit. Look here too for the local endemic butterflies, like Spanish Brassy Ringlet and Golgus and Zullich's Blues. Alpine Accentor is fairly frequent.

The Nevada Violet is an endemic flower of the highest parts of the Sierra Nevada (top). This is also the area to look for the Alpine Accentor (bottom).

7 The summit is the final destination of this route. The exhilarating feeling of having conquered the Iberian Peninsula's highest mountain alone makes it worth the effort, but for the naturalist, this peak has more in store. A small shrine and the ruins of an old mountain hut form the background while the peak is marked with a short stone pillar. Here you have a magnificent view over the Sierra Nevada's north side, which is much more rugged than the southern slope you have just ascended. This dramatic view over the steep cliffs, the sharp peaks and the Pico Véleta are an awe-inspiring sight. On clear days, the Mediterranean Sea is visible to the south while the Sierra de Huétor stands out in the north with the Granadan plain rolling away to the west. A close encounter with one or more Spanish Ibex is again very possible. Also spectacular are the scores of Common, Pallid and Alpine Swifts that loudly swoosh by at close range hunting for insects.

Return by the way you came.

204

Additional sites in the Nevada

A – Puerto de la Ragua

Best season
May-July

The A-377 is the only national road that cuts through the Nevada massive to connect its northern and southern flanks. The section between La Calahorra in the north and Laroles in the south makes for a scenic drive which gives a truly Alpine feel. The pass *Puerto de la Ragua* is known for its skiing facilities, but also well known by naturalists. Starting at 2,000 metres, *Puerto de la Ragua* offers an easy access to high mountain habitat.

At the car park, look for the small flocks of the Citril Finch, belonging to the most southernmost population of this European endemic bird. This species seems to be a recent colonist, first being proved to breed here as recently as 2004. Iberian Wall Lizards take shelter in the foundations of the terrace and are rather tame.

The *Barranco Maja Caco* is a small stream which cuts through a peaty grassland scattered with spiny bushes and small trees. On hot days, many butterflies can be found here around the mud, including Heath and Meadow Fritillaries and Panoptes, Silver-studded and Idas Blues, the latter belonging to the endemic subspecies of the Nevada. Reptiles are, as usual, not easy to find, but the general area around the pass is home to Lataste's Viper, Smooth Snake and Large Psammodromus. The plants chip in as well, with local endemics like Nevada Broom* (*Cytisus galianoi*), Spiny Globula* (*Globularia spinosa*) the bellflower *Campanula herminii* and the Nevada Mullein* (*Verbascum nevadense*).

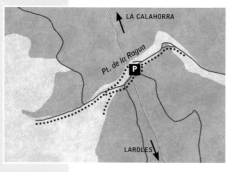

Puerto de la Ragua is a superb site to observe migratory butterflies. In some years you can count thousands of Clouded Yellows or Painted Ladies on their northward migration in spring. The pass is good for migratory birds too. From *Puerto de la Ragua*, various walking trails lead higher up into the mountains, where more butterflies can be found. Violet Copper, Spanish Brassy Ringlet, Panoptes Blue, Mountain Argus and Apollo are quite easy to find, but you need to allow some time to find the cryptic Nevada Hermit, resting in the shade of rocks. Attractive plants include Marsh

Gentian, Nevada Wallflower* (*Erysimum nevadense*), Pyrenean Eryngo* (*Eryngium bourgatii*), Iberian Pink* (*Dianthus pungens*) and the endemic subspecies of Purple Foxglove. Birdlife can be surprisingly rich in this area, with a mixture of temperate species like Raven, Coal Tit, Sparrowhawk, Buzzard, Grey Wagtail, Crested Tit, Firecrest, and Short-toed Treecreeper, mixed with southern species like Iberian Grey Shrike, Rock Bunting, Subalpine and Bonelli's Warblers.

B – Charca de Suárez

  Close to the beaches and hotels of Motril lies the Charca de Suárez reserve – the most important protected marshland of Granada. Many volunteers are involved in the conservation of this area and maintain the network of trails and hides. The 'core' opening times are 9.00 – 13.00 year round and variable in the afternoon – check on site for the most recent opening times or contact the reserve at **info@motril-turismo.com**.

The hides offer good views of waterfowl, which include attractions like Purple Gallinule, White-headed Duck, Ferruginous Duck and many waders in spring. The Crested Coot has been introduced here as part of the Spanish breeding program. Water Rail, Cetti's Warbler, Night Heron, Little Bittern and Squacco Heron are regularly seen, and there is a colony of Red Avadavats. This is the only breeding site in Málaga Province for Savi's Warbler whilst in winter Moustached Warblers may turn up.

The area is superb for insects, especially for rare dragonflies with an essentially African distribution, like Long Skimmer, Black Pennant, Black Percher, Orange-winged Dropwing and Banded Groundling. Monarchs are sometimes present and other coastal butterflies like the African Grass Blue and Mediterranean Skipper are

Of interest
Year-round

The Violet Dropwing, another colonist from Africa, is just one of the spectacular dragonflies of the Charco de Suárez.

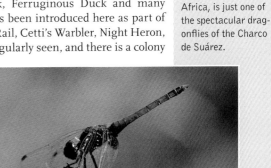

frequently seen above the sparse vegetation. The Stripeless Tree Frog and the elusive Common Chameleon (a recent colonist) are some of the herpetological delights, among the more widespread species like Horseshoe, Montpellier, Viperine and Grass Snake and Spanish Terrapin.

Apart from the trail around the reserve, you can scan the area from the eastern boulevard of the adjacent Playa Granada. Park in the north at the end of *Calle Rector Frederic Mayor Zaragoza*. Scanning the sea may reveal some seabirds as well.

C – Laguna de Padul

Of interest
Year-round

The Laguna de Padul is a nature reserve in the foothills of the Sierra Nevada. It harbours extensive reedbeds, interspersed with rough grassland and arable fields that, combined, support a rich birdlife. You can walk a circuit through the reserve and observe wildlife from platforms and hides.

The area is magnificent for raptors. Golden, Short-toed and Booted Eagles and Griffon Vultures are regular and even Bonelli's Eagle sometimes comes down from the mountains. The freshwater marshes attract Kingfisher, Marsh Harrier and Great Reed Warbler, in winter joined by Bluethroat, Reed Bunting, Water Pipit and Water Rail. Among the reptiles, Spanish Terrapin, Viperine Snake and Ocellated Lizard are listed

There is nothing better for banishing the winter blues than watching Bluethroats on a warm, sunny February day as they explore the undergrowth at Laguna de Padul. For refugees from the chill north it is one of the joys of Andalucía in winter.

for the reserve. Just like the Charca de Suárez, Padul has a rich insect life, featuring many African species. Violet Dropwing, Banded Groundling, Long Skimmer and Mediterranean Bluet are frequent dragonflies, while African Grass Blue and Monarchs are noteworthy butterflies.

It is best to start at the Visitors' Centre, where you can pick up detailed information and backgrounds about the reserve and its wildlife.

To get to the Visitors' Centre, take the main road N-323 from Padul to Motril. About 700m beyond the village of Padul turn right at the first junction. Here you find the small *Aula de la naturaleza*, from where the walk starts.

The nearby plains west of Padul along the A4050 may still support a small and declining population of the very rare Dupont's Lark.

D – The Alhambra

Without doubt the Alhambra in Granada can be regarded as the cultural highlight of Andalucía. For those who want to visit this UNESCO World Heritage, reservation for the palace is highly recommended since the number of visitors per day is limited. Reservations can be made online.

Of interest
Year-round

The museum and the gardens are both worth visiting and offer some wildlife too. Monarch, Common Goldenring, Crag Martin, Lesser Kestrel and Iberian Water Frog are residents of the Alhambra.

More information about tickets, schedules, recommended routes, events and the most interesting places of the monumental complex can be found on the official website: **www.alhambra-patronato.es**

View of the Alhambra UNESCO world heritage site.

Almijara and Tejeda region

The provincial boundary between Málaga and Granada neatly bisects the huge Parque Natural Sierra de Almijara Tejeda y Alhama into an equal north and south part. The region is known for the white villages such as Frigiliana and Compéta, where the Moorish influences are still present in the architecture and some cultural habits. It is surprising to reflect that this range was once so remote that it was the last refuge of anti-Franco guerillas who persisted here into the late 1940s and early 1950s.

The landscape is rugged and mountainous and supports the typical range of Mediterranean birds of mountains, like Alpine Swifts, Blue Rock Thrush, Rock Bunting and Golden and Bonelli's Eagles. There are scores of orchids and other attractive wildflowers, but what truly sets this region aside from the other areas described in this book, is the presence of several very rare and localised butterflies and dragonflies, which is why we have selected a route especially devoted to finding these specialities.

Apart from the route described in this bok, there are many more hiking trails in the Parque Natural (site A on page 212), which are easily accessible from Nerja and Frigiliana in the south.

The nearby Costa del Sol is rather touristy and spoilt in places, except for the Acantilados de Maro-Cerro. This rough and rocky coastline marks the terrestrial border of the Sierra Tejeda, but the range continues below sea level, where the diving or snorkelling naturalist will find a world to explore extending into the Mediterranean (site B on page 212). The caves and rocks under water are worth exploring and form a unique and little known habitat.

The northern section of the Parque Natural is laced by a network of small rivers, gorges and Mediterranean scrubland, but there are also marshes with an interesting birdlife (the Alhama de Granada; site C on page 213). This is another site where Crested Coot is introduced It is also an excellent spot for dragonflies.

Overview of the Sierra de Almijara area. The letters refer to the sites described on page 212-213.

Route 20: The Río Chíllar

**FULL DAY
MODERATE**

Splendid river valley with rich dragonfly and butterfly fauna.

Best season
April-July
Of interest
Year-round

Habitats river, pinewood, scrubland
Selected species Pink Butterfly Orchid, Mirror Orchid, Dipper, Black Wheatear, Blue Rock Thrush, Bonelli's Eagle, Orange-winged Dropwing, Epaulet Skimmer, Ringed Cascader, Two-tailed Pasha

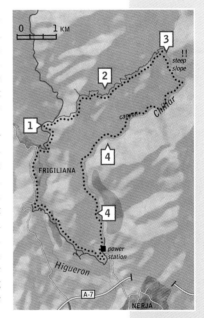

This route explores the southern flank of the Sierra Almijara along the rivers Higueron and Chíllar. The contrast between the dry slopes with Mediterranean scrub and the lush valleys and mountain streams form a striking feature of the landscape of this route. The true highlight however, is the occurrence of several dragonflies and butterflies of African origin.

This route may be covered as two separate linear routes along the river valleys, or as a long circular route. Note that taking the circular version (as described below) can become quite strenuous, particularly in the summer heat. Furthermore, note that considerable stretches run straight through the river beds of both rivers, so you won't keep your feet dry! In times of heavy rains, it is not possible to return through the riverbed. In summer, though (when the dragonflies are active) the trip through the river is a blessing rather than a curse. Hence the walk through the Chíllar riverbed is a popular summer outing.

Starting point Frigiliana
Park at the car park next to the small roundabout in the centre of Frigiliana. On foot, go right at the roundabout into the centre and take the narrow alley right of the *Unicaja Bank* down into the canyon of the Río Higueron. Follow its valley upstream.

Upstream, the river passes through a spectacular gorge.

1 The Río Higueron is fringed by Oleander. A couple of other interesting plants occur in the valley, although most of them are quite rare and are not necessarily found on this short stretch. Among them are the conspicuous Ladder Brake Fern and the orchid Two-leaved Gennaria (flowering at the end of winter). Sardinian Warblers and Blackcaps are common in the scrub, Crag Martin flies overhead and Blue Rock Thrush can be seen on the cliffs. The first dragonflies can already be noted here. Copper Demoiselle frequents the stream, while a number of other, generally fairly common species, occur in the small reservoir on the left side of the valley. Keep an eye out too for basking snakes and search the sky for Bonelli's Eagle.

Just beyond the reservoir the trail (marked white and red) leaves the valley and starts ascending the slope on the right. Follow it if you're planning to do the circular route. Alternatively, return to Frigiliana after point 1 and take the car down to Nerja (see map below). Turn left at the N-340 into Nerja and turn left again on the third roundabout to *Cahorros del Rio Chíllar* (*Calle Julio Romero*). After some 150m turn right, signposted *Mercadillo* on the *Av. de la Constitution*. After 800 m you turn left on the *Calle de Mirto* at the end of the village, easy to find by the electric wire and arable field. Turn right and follow the track under the viaduct and park after 500 m near the former power station. Please note the parking instructions.

Follow the Chíllar river upstream, passing first point 4 and then point 3 of the above description.

2 The landscape soon becomes drier as you leave the valley. In spring, this area sports a rich flora. Mirror and Pink Butterfly Orchid accompany you along the trail together with the small and pretty Blue Bindweed* (*Convolvulus siculus*), Woolly Viper's-bugloss* (*Echium albicans*) and White Rock-rose. Spiny-footed Lizard and Large Psammodrumus can

Over most of its length, there is no trail along the Río Chíllar – the riverbed is the trail (top). The river is one of the few sites for the spectacular Ringed Cascader, a specialist of fast-flowing rivers (bottom).

be seen basking on sunny patches. Towards the summer two curious insects, the Thread-winged Lacewing and Hooded Praying Mantis* (*Empusa pennata*), occur in this habitat, together with the butterflies Dusky Heath and Striped Grayling. To the right some splendid vistas to the Mediterranean Sea and the city of Nerja open up.

After 4 km, the trail arrives at the Río Chíllar.

3 The Río Chíllar is a fast-flowing mountain stream. Its valley is lush and green and brims with life. Dippers and Grey Wagtails may be spotted as they fly up and down the river, but it is the dragonflies that are of most interest. Depending on the time of year, you may encounter Copper Demoiselle, Common Goldenring, Large Pincertail, Western Spectre and Ringed Cascader hovering over the water. African species like Epaulet Skimmer and Orange-winged Dropwing overlook their territories from perches.

Cleopatra, Provence Orange-tip and Spanish Festoon search for nectar flowers on the steep slopes and even the beautiful Two-tailed Pasha may be seen here.

!

This section involves wading through the river.

4 Downstream, the river takes you through more splendid riverine habitat. You will be able to find more of the dragonflies described at point 3 here, with the addition of Keeled Skimmer. The birdlife includes Crag Martin, Blue Rock Thrush and Black Wheatear, Kestrel and Peregrine.

PRACTICAL PART

212

Additional sites in the Almijara region

Best season
March-May

Of interest
October-June

A – Walking in the Parque Natural de Sierras de Tejeda, Almijara y Alhama

The Sierras de Tejeda rise up like a steep wall from the Mediterranean behind the town of Nerja. This is a classical southern sierra · rocky, with large areas of Mediterranean scrub and pinewoods, intersected by deep limestone gorges. There are plenty of birds and other wildlife, plus a fine range of orchids. In a way, this Sierra reminds one of the Sierra de Grazalema and Sierra de las Nieves in western Andalucía, although the Tejeda is not nearly as well-known. The birdlife is similar, with Bonelli's, Golden, Booted and Short-toed Eagles, Griffon Vulture, Eagle Owl, Blue Rock Thrush, plus Black Wheatear and Alpine Swifts in the gorges, and a large variety of warblers in the scrub.

The beautiful Two-tailed Pasha is a common butterfly the Sierras de Tejeda and Almijara.

The gorges offer some fine walking, even in hot summers as they are shady. Some of them are quite popular for canyoning.
Many fine walking trails depart from the beautiful A-4050 that intersects the Sierra from the south (Otívar) and Fornes and Játar in the north.

B – Acantilados de Maro-Cerro

Of interest
Year-round

On the very edges of the Sierra Almijara dramatic steep limestone cliffs (*acantilados*) plunge down into the sea. This near-virgin coastline with offshore stacks, arches and undersea caves stretches out for 12 km east of Nerja and crosses the border of the provinces of Málaga and Granada. It forms a unique ecosystem that is home to a great variety of flora and fauna, including fields of the submarine 'meadows' of the endangered Neptune Grass. The great views over sea might yield sea birds like Audouin's Gull, shearwaters and terns. The Shag, a scarce bird in the Mediterranean, is occasionally seen here.
Inland, rocky outcrops are suitable habitat for Rock Bunting, Blue Rock Thrush, Black Wheatear and Alpine Swift.

C – Alhama de Granada and surroundings

The village of Alhama de Granada is a good starting point to explore the local wetlands, such as the Pantaneta de Alhama pool along the Río Alhama. Cetti's and Reed Warblers occur here and in 2008 Crested Coot has been introduced. To the south, the Alhama gorge leads to the dam of the Río Alhama reservoir.

Best season
March-June

Numerous footpaths through the eroded limestone offer chances to see Blue Rock Thrush, Golden Oriole, Sardinian Warbler and Dipper. Among the butterflies are African Grass Blue and Cleopatra. Dragonflies feature Copper Demoiselle and Epaulet Skimmer. The surrounding scrub is dominated by Kermes Oak and Mediterranean Buckthorn, interspersed with some Gibraltar Hare's-ear that indicates basic soils. The area hosts Azure-winged Magpie, Iberian Grey Shrike and Bonelli's Eagle and wildflowers like Wide-leaved Iris* (*Iris planifolia*) and various bee orchid species (*Ophrys*).

A second site nearby, the gorge and the Embalse del Río Cacín, can be reached by the A-402 and A-338 from Alhama to Pantano de Bermejales. Crested Coot, Night Heron and Bonelli's Eagle are resident around the embalse, while Great Spotted Cuckoo is a migrant albeit one that may arrive as early as December! Shoveler, Pochard, Tufted Duck and occasionally Ferruginous Duck spend the winter here. Old buildings in this hamlet host bats like the Greater Horseshoe.

Natterjack Toads can look a little grumpy. They are common in most of the region, including at Alhama de Granada.

PRACTICAL PART

TOURIST INFORMATION & OBSERVATION TIPS

Travel

Travelling to eastern Andalucía
Eastern Andalucía is easy to reach by car, train or plane. Most visitors to the region will come by plane. Sevilla, Málaga or Almería all enjoy regular services and many charter flights. Some airlines also offer flights to Granada-Jaén, usually with a transfer in Madrid. From Granada there is one train connection to Almería via Guadix.

Travelling in eastern Andalucía
The car is by far the easiest means of transport for this region. There are many car rental companies in all the airports and major cities. Economy class cars are not expensive, but carefully check rental details as some companies have restrictions and consider buying your insurance in advance as it is often cheaper.
Public transport connecting the smaller villages is, just like in many other places in Spain, close to non-existent. The few buses that connect the communities leave only once a day or once a week, so it is hard to organise a trip based on them. However, most villages have a taxi service, which can transport you to and from the start and finish of the walking routes. Travelling by public transport is inexpensive, great fun, adventurous, but also time consuming. Speaking at least rudimentary Spanish is a great help if you wish to tackle the region by public transport.

Planning your trip

When to go
Eastern Andalucía is of interest throughout the year. Spring, when flowers and insects emerge and birds are singing and nesting, is the most rewarding period. The onset of spring is delayed at higher altitudes, so this favourable period extends from February around Cabo de Gata to well into July on the heights of the Sierra Nevada. In January and February, when the winter sports season in the snow-capped Sierra Nevada is in full swing, the first bulbs are blooming on the coast and birds start to display. The semi-desert and coastal area is most rewarding in February to April.
From late March to early June the lower mountain ranges offer a feast of wildflowers. Late March and April is also the prime time for witnessing the spring bird migration so that by early May, most breeding species should be present in good

numbers. Thus mid to late April offers often the perfect compromise with a bit of everything. In late May and June the temperatures rise, which is perfect for finding insects and reptiles and yet still good for spotting some late breeding birds like the White-rumped Swift and the Rufous Bush Robin. By the start of July temperatures in the lowlands easily reach over 35°C on midday and long hikes are out of the question. Most plants have flowered and birds are quiet. In the high mountains of Sierra the Nevada and Sierra Cazorla though, the Alpine flora peaks together with the butterflies and other insects. Deciduous forests and secluded rivers with permanent water and shade are refreshing and offer large numbers of dragonflies and butterflies (e.g. route 8 and 9) and we recommend the Río Chillar (route 20) where you even can wade through the river during hot days. From late August to late September, the autumn migration, whilst not nearly as pronounced as at Tarifa, makes for a wonderful spectacle, with autumn flowers appearing between October and November. At this time of year, the coastal marshes and badlands of Almería are wonderful again.

Accommodation

Eastern Andalucía is far too large to cover from a single base. We suggest travelling through the area and staying a few days in each zone. Which zones to visit and which to skip depends of course on your interests, the season and the length of your total stay. Here are some helpful suggestions:

Cabo the Gata and the Desierto de Tabernas are of interest for birdwatchers, naturalists and nature and landscape photographers. The best season is autumn to spring (October – May). Accommodation is plentiful on the coast, in places such as Níjar, Almería, Roquetas and San José with a few hostels further inland, in Tabernas and Sorbas for example. There is a camp site in San José and one in Cabo de Gata.

The Cazorla area is of interest for birdwatchers, botanists and naturalists alike, and most attractive from April to October. The town of Cazorla and the village close to it, La Iruela, are good bases. The small village of Arroyo Frío inside the park has plenty of accommodation and is even closer to the best sites, but rather busy in the high season. There are at least four camp sites in the same area.

Sierra Nevada and Alpujarras are most attractive in summer (May – September) and form a great destination for ramblers and hikers, butterfly and wildflower lovers. There are two main access points.

From the north, the area of Granada and Güejar Sierra is the logical access point. It offers the highest diversity within short distance. You have good access to the high Nevada at La Pileta and the Genil river, but also to the Sierra de Huétor and even the Hoya de Guadix is just an hour's drive. Towards the southwest, the Mediterranean

Eastern Andalucía through the year

January	Wintering birds at the coast, flocks of steppe birds, winter flowers at Cabo de Gata.
February	More early spring flowers (daffodils, toadflaxes), first migrant birds (swallows, Great Spotted Cuckoo). Reptiles emerge on warm days.
March	Early spring wildflowers peak and orchids appear in the lowlands. Towards the end of the month, the big wave of migrant birds emerge. Reptiles and spring butterflies emerge.
April	Peak of wildflowers in lowlands, early flowers (bulbs, orchids) are starting to bloom in the mountains. Birds take in their territories as most migrants arrive in this period. Reptiles and spring butterflies are plentiful.
May	Tail end of wildflower season in the lowlands, the mountain flora (up to 2,000 m) peaks. Dragonflies emerge. Early half of May, the breeding season for birds is in full swing – late arriving birds take in their territories.
June	Spring flora in mountains disappears, replaced by summer species. High mountain flora emerges. Butterfly season peaks, lots of dragonflies emerge. Birds become silent except in the mountains.
July	In Early July, the summer butterflies peak, as do dragonflies. Wildflowers are at their best in the high mountains. In the lowlands, adult praying mantises and grasshoppers become frequent and some summer flowers emerge. Tourism season is getting in full swing.
August	Tail end of butterfly season, first migrant birds arrive from the north. Tourism season peaks.
September	Bird migration at the coast peaks 2nd half of the month. At that time, the tourists have largely disappeared and the weather invites for walks. Autumn butterflies (e.g. Monarch) peaks.
October	Autumn flowers (bulbs) are at their best, while bird migration is coming to an end. A few late butterflies and dragonflies linger.
Nov – Dec	Winter birds and a few winter flowers. Usually mild weather, inviting for walks.

and the edges of the Sierra de Almijara are roughly an hour by car. Obviously, there is plenty of accommodation in Granada and surrounding villages.

From the south, you can access the high Nevada from villages like Capileira and Treveléz. These are the bases to choose if you prefer the long hikes. In the middle of the Alpujarras, the surroundings are lovely and hiking options are endless. This area is less suitable if you plan to do excursions further afield as travelling out of the Alpujarras over all those winding roads is time consuming.

There is plenty of accommodation in villages like Zanfarón, Capileira, Treveléz and all others on road A-4130 that runs along the southern edge of The Sierra Nevada National Park.

The Hoya de Guadix and Baza are of interest to birdwatchers, nature and landscape photographers and anyone who craves the romance of deserted landscapes. The high plateaux are bitterly cold in winter and boiling hot in summer, leaving spring and autumn as the best seasons. As the area is not very easily accessed, your options for exploration are somewhat limited (unless you have a 4x4). You could choose to stay in Guadix town (plenty of accommodation) or in one of the few smaller guesthouses in the villages (e.g. Gorafe has a fine guest house), or decide to cover the Hoya Guadix from Granada and combine a visit to Hoya de Baza with a trip to Sierra María-los Vélez (with accommodation both in Baza and María).

Andújar area, Despeñaperros, Córdoba and the Guadalquivir basin This large area can be covered conveniently from the town of Andújar, but it may be more attractive to choose several accommodations or skip part of this huge area. If you are trying your luck with the Iberian Lynx, you'll wish to stay in the heart of Parque Natural de Sierra de Andújar. Many naturalists stay at the *Complejo Turístico Los Pinos* or *Villa Matilde*, where often a lively exchange of information takes place among Lynx watchers. Accommodation can also be found along the A-6177, particularly near the visitors' centre in Viñas or in Baños de la Encina. From there, it is about a 1.5 hours drive to Cascada de la Cimbarra or Córdoba.

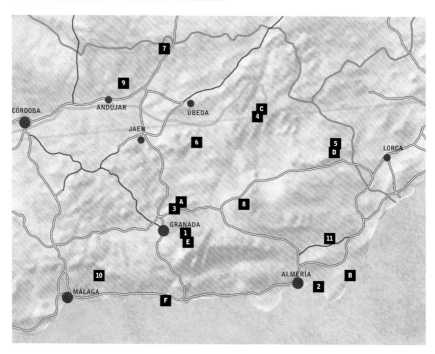

Visitors centres (numbers) and botanical gardens (lettres) in eastern Andalucía.

The best accommodation is of course in places where the owners are dedicated to low or zero environmental impact, often suplementing their enterprise with organic farming. You can find such eco-friendly accomodation at **www.ecotur.es**. Other rural tourism sites (not necessarily eco-friendly) are **www.toprural.com** and **www.andalucia-turismorural.com**.

For camp sites, check out **en.camping.info/spain/andalusia/campsites**.

Visitors' Centres

Most National and Natural Parks have a visitors' centre (*centro de visitantes*). They are good sources for guidebooks, leaflets on walks, postcards, etc. All have toilets and frequently also displays about the area (usually only in Spanish but a few have an explanatory English language booklet, often downloadable as a pdf; see below). Staff generally only speak Spanish. Details of all of Andalucia's visitors' centres can be found at **www.reservatuvisita.es** or via an interactive map at **www.juntadeandalucia.es** and search *visitguide*. Opening times vary from centre to centre, but as a general rule, most are closed on Monday and opening times are usually from around 09:00 until 14:00.

1 **Sierra Nevada** El Dornajo, on the A-395 near km. 23, Güéjar Sierra
2 **Cabo de Gata-Nijar** Las Almoladeros, on the AL-3115 near km. 7, Almería
3 **Sierra de Huétor** Puerto Lobo, on the Víznar-Puerto Lobo road, Km. 43, Víznar
4 **Sierras de Cazorla, Segura y Las Villas** Torre del vinagre, on the A-319, km 48,5, Santiago-pontones
5 **Sierra de María-Los Vélez** Almacén del Trigo, Avda. Marqués de los Vélez, Vélez Blanco
6 **Sierra Mágina** Castillo de Jódar, on the Ubeda-Iznalloz Jódar road, km. 24, Jódar
7 **Despeñaperros** Llano de las Américas, on the A4 motorway exit on km 257, Santa Elena
8 **Sierra de Baza** Narváez, on the A-92 motorway, exit km. 28
9 **Sierra de Andújar** Viñas de Peñallana, on the Andújar-Santuario, Virgen de la Cabeza road, km 13, Andújar
10 **Sierras de Alhama** Tejeda y Almijara Sedella, calle Villa del Castillo 11, Sedella
11 **Karst y Yesos de Sorba** Los Yesares, calle Terraplén, Sorbas

Botanical Gardens

The Andalucían Network of Botanical Gardens operates from 2001 and hold magnificent collections of native flora. All gardens are situated in the natural environment itself. In this way, plants grow in natural conditions with minimal human intervention. To become familiar with the local flora and see what is flowering in what time of the year, we recommend to visit the local botanical gardens.

A **La Alfaguara (arboretum)** Sierra de Huétor, Alfacar, on the GR 3103 east of Nívar
B **El Albardinal** Cabo de Gata-Níjar, near the church of Rodalquilar
C **Torro del Vinagre** Sierra de Cazorla, on the A-319, km 48,5
D **Umbria de la Virgen** Sierra María-Los Vélez, on the A-317 from María to Orce, near the chapel of Virgen de la Cabeza
E **Hoya de Pedraza** Sierra Nevada, Sierra Nevada road, Km. 27, Monachil
F **El Majuelo** Avda. Europa, Almuñecar

Convenient Travel and Safety Issues

Annoyances and hazards

There are a couple of things you need to be aware of when travelling in Andalucía:
Law and regulation Most of the legal do's and don'ts in Andalucía are straightforward. However, keep in mind that in Spain it is illegal to park in the roadside outside of towns and villages. The only legal way to park is with all four wheels off the tarmac. The Guardia Civil are very keen on fining any vehicle that pulls over at the side of the road to look for birds. You won't be the first naturalist whose holiday suddenly became a lot more expensive on that lovely minor road where hardly a car passes except for the Guardia Civil.

Furthermore, note that much of the land in Andalucía is private. Entering fenced off land is not appreciated and doing so, apart from arguments or worse, gives nature conservation (which you are representing once you have your bins on your neck) a bad reputation.

Theft In much of eastern Andalucía theft and muggings are exceptionally rare. However, since the economic crisis, you need to take the risk serious, especially in touristy places on the coast. Theft from rental cars is the biggest risk. Leave nothing of value in your car when you are out walking, not even pocket change. Don't cover anything up with jackets either. Simply show potential thieves there is nothing to gain from braking into your car. In touristy places, consider parking in public places such as residential areas rather than in the car parks designed for tourists.

Risks for hikers – terrain and climate The extremes of the eastern Andalucían climate call for special preparations for hikers, which we've outlined on page 222.

Dangerous animals There is one poisonous snake and a few other animals which theoretically could injure you, but that risk is close to zero. However, once you start turning stones to actively look for them, you should be careful with scorpions, Megarian Banded Centipedes and snakes.

Permits and restrictions

No permits (or entrance fees) are required for the routes described in this book. Note that in all nature parks there are specific rules you'll have to abide by (e.g. on picking flowers, bringing nets or traps, etc.). They are listed on the access roads of the parks.

Responsible Tourism

There is no such thing as an environmentally friendly trip to Andalucía since you are relying on car or plane. But there are ways to minimise your impact on the environment. Ecotourism is often promoted as a sustainable form of local development, which can coexist and even support nature conservation. The positive impacts of your visit are most when you consume local foods and products in small establishments. In Spain, these products are often labelled *denominación de origin*, declaration of origin. Buying wine with cork as a stopper (instead of plastic) supports the maintenance of the valuable cork oak dehesas.

Water consumption is another issue. Over the last decades massive reservoirs have been created to meet the sharply increasing demand for freshwater. Help to control the water demand and do not use more than is strictly necessary. One example which is easy to carry out is requesting your hotel to change the towels and sheets only once a week.

Obviously it is important to keep a low profile on your trip, not only to prevent disturbing wildlife, but also to increase your chances of observing it. Coastal lagoons and freshwater ponds are important resting spots for migratory birds. When you go out birding, keep in mind that these sites are small and birds are easily disturbed. Especially at the coast, with busy tourism anyway, disturbance is a problem. So keep your distance.

Traffic takes a big toll on wildlife each year. Casualties vary from lizards, toads and newts to Iberian Lynxes. Keep this in mind and don't drive too fast in Nature Parks and forested areas. In some places, like in Sierra de Andújar, special signs are placed to warn against speeding.

The greatest and most devastating threat to Mediterranean nature is the risk of forest fires. Be extremely cautious with fire and never throw away cigarette butts or glass in the field.

You can contribute to nature conservation by sharing your wildlife records. Many internet portals offer facilities for uploading your records (e.g. **www.observado.org**). These datasets are frequently used by NGOs for conservation matters and distribution maps.

Hiking in East Andalucía

The mountains of eastern Andalucía have an elaborate network of walking routes. Most of them are well signposted, but be careful not to rely on signposting too much

– some markings are hidden, overgrown or have miraculously disappeared. Local routes range from just a few hundred metres to 15 km or more and are usually signposted with a PR-A code. The Alpujarras, Sierra Nevada, Sierra de Huétor, Sierra Mágina, Sierra Cazorla y Segura and Cabo de Gata offer the best hiking options. You can find routes as a printed leaflet at the local visitor centre or download them from special trekking websites.

Within the framework of European long distance trails, the famous red-white marked distance *Senderos de Gran Recorrido* (GR), the GR7 trail runs through most areas described in this guidebook. From this southern branch it winds further via the Alps up to Greece.

Take into account that many trails are linear routes, often from one village to another. For naturalists in search of flora, fauna, or geological or ecological phenomena, this isn't a big problem: walking a shorter stretch and returning via the same route is just as productive and interesting as doing a proper loop. Hikers for whom this is not a satisfactory option, are advised to find a taxi service to return you to your point of departure. Mind you, by 'taxi service', we don't mean a 'taxi company'; the driver is usually either the owner of the local bar, his brother or his brother-in-law. In any case, your best chance is to ask for a ride in the local bar. If you don't speak enough Spanish to feel safe about organising a ride back yourself, have the hotel, campsite or B&B where you're staying make arrangements in advance. To avoid any risk of getting stranded, consider parking at your proposed destination and organise a taxi to your starting point.

If you want to truly get in touch with nature, consider a multiple day trek through the mountains. Usually this kind of hiking should be arranged in advance, especially when you want to spend the night in a refuge. Some travel agencies can organise your overnight stays and baggage transport, allowing you to hike, free as a bird, from one place to another. You can either bring your own backpack and explore e.g. the summits of the Sierra Nevada which can be ascended in one or two days.

Preparations for walking

The sunny, warm and stable weather is one of the great perks of Andalucía. Nevertheless the land is known for its extremes. There are very open, arid and hot areas in the lowlands of Almería, but also extremely exposed areas high up in the mountains, where the UV-radiation is even higher, while temperatures are much lower.

For hikers this entails risks. Sun stroke, sunburn, overheating and dehydration are serious dangers, but so is hypothermia in the mountains. Much of the terrain in eastern Andalucía has few trees, so shade is sparse. A combination of sun and wind causes sunburn within minutes and dehydration only lagging behind a little. This happens much faster than your body is able to warn you. Add to this the bright light reflected from rocks or snow patches that is a constant strain on the eyes, which can cause dizziness and, in severe cases and in combination with dehydration, disorientation. The weather in the higher sierras is changeable in every season except summer. Fog, rain, sleet and snow are not uncommon between autumn and spring. Combine this with trails that often have inadequate marking and mountainous, sometimes chaotic terrain and the danger of getting lost should be clear. Sadly, each year people get seriously lost, in a few cases resulting in injury and even death.

We don't mention this to put you off, but to encourage careful preparation. That preparation is twofold.

On the one hand, bring the right gear: use sunblock and wear a hat and sunglasses. Wear layered clothing, not only against the cold, wind or rain, but also against the sun. There are now shirts available with densely woven cloth impregnated with a UV-blocking substance. Also bring good footwear and consider using a trekking pole for balance. Drink plenty of water and bring salty food to eat on hot days. Don't rely on water sources in the field, although water from underground sources (*fuentes*) is usually drinkable (never drink from surface water like streams or ponds!).

On the other hand, stock up on information. Check the weather forecast in advance (the free app *eltiempo* is excellent!). Make sure you don't go out with at least a good hiking map, but better still is a good gps device, fully charged and with your starting point marked. Bring your mobile phone too, but be aware that not every area has reception. When going out on more adventurous routes, make sure you tell someone about your itinerary and planned return.

Additional information

Recommended reading

Apart from the usual field guides, the following books and websites are recommended.

Guidebooks on individual nature parks There are two nature guide series to the *parques naturales* of Andalucía: the *Guía del Parque* and the *Guía Oficial del Parque Natural*. Both are good, but tend to focus rather strongly on history, traditions, culture and gastronomy, rather than natural history. The 'official' is more informative and has more information on natural history. Neither of them is very practical and both series are only available in Spanish. They are quite expensive, but you can download them for free as pdf (in parts) from **www.juntadeandalucia.es/medioambiente** and subsequently following *ventana de visitantes de espacios naturales* and subsequently *publicaciones*.

A positive exception is the *Visitor's Guide to the Sierra Nevada* of the *Parques Nacionales* (ISBN 84-8014-620-6), which is in English and has lots of information on the flora and fauna.

Wildflowers The two books to buy are *Wild Flowers of Eastern Andalucía* by Sarah Ball (2014; ISBN 978-0956396112) and the *Field Guide to the wild flowers of the western Mediterranean* by Chris Thorogood (2016; ISBN 9781842466162). Both books are published by Kew Gardens. For German readers, *Die Neue Kosmos Mittelmeerflora* by Ingrid Schönfelder (ISBN 9783440107423) is the book to use. If you read some Spanish, you could combine the above with the generous number of local flower books on the local nature reserves. They are for sale in visitors centres but also in many cafes in the area. They deal only with a limited number of species – those that have a special conservation interest. The most comprehensive flower "guide" is the *Flora Iberica*, which' 21 volumes together are a hugely extensive (and expensive!) key to the entire flora of Spain (except the Canaries). It is a work that demands respect, but completely impractical in the field. For reference, parts of it can be downloaded as pdf at **www.floraiberica.es**.

Butterflies European butterfly field guides offer general information, so some local work is recommended. *Las mariposas diurnas de Sierra Nevada* (2011), *Butterflies of the Sierra Nevada and Alpujarras* by F. Javier Olivares et al. (ISBN 978-84-92807-72-7) are both in Spanish.

Birdwatching guides There are many books, leaflets and brochures about birding in Andalucía. Additional websites, trip reports, forums and blogs might help you to find your bird of interest. We recommend *Where to watch birds in Southern and Western Spain* by Ernest Garcia and Andrew Paterson (ISBN: 978-0713683158), *Birdwatching on Spain's Southern Coast* by John Butler (ISBN-13: 978-8489954380) and *Finding Birds in Andalucía* by Dave Gosney (ISBN: 9781907316005).

Walking and naturalist guides Various walking guides are written about Andalucía. We selected a few. *Walking the GR7 in Andalucía* by Kirsti Shirra and Michelle Lowe describes the GR7 throughout Andalucía (ISBN 978-18-52846-93-0). *Walking in the Sierra Nevada – Walks and multi-day treks* by Andy Walmsley (ISBN 978-18-52844-35-6). Circular routes of half to a full day are given in: *Walking in Andalucía* by Guy Hunter Watts (ISBN 978-84-89954-92-2). An overview of walking routes is provided by **www.fedamon.com/senderos/prs/prs.htm**.

Don't forget to check the following websites in preparation for your trip: **www.treksierranevada.com** or **www.topwalks.net/es/andalucia.htm**, where you find additional walking routes and backgrounds. For more information about trekking and climbing in the Sierra Nevada, check **www.spanishhighs.co.uk/walking-sierra-nevada-high-peaks.html**.

Maps

The Michelin and the Freytag & Berndt map of southern Spain provide a good overview of the entire area and are adequate when combined with the maps in this book. For more thorough explorations, use the good quality and detailed maps of the

individual nature parks, which are for sale in the local visitors' centres. Local brochures and walking guides have small maps of good quality that are indispensable
if you wish to walk routes other than the ones described in this book. Again, most of
these local maps can be found in visitor centres or in tourist shops.

Nearby destinations worth visiting

If you want to venture beyond the borders of this guide then, if you are heading
west, we recommend the sister volume of this guide on Western Andalucía which
describes this diverse area in detail. The closest site is Laguna Fuente de Piedra,
one of Europe's main breeding sites for Flamingo and home to many other birds.
Further west, the calcareous Sierra de Grazalema is of great botanical interest, especially for orchids and as the home of the unique Pinsapar fir forest. It is also rich in
raptors. To the south-west are the lower sandstone mountains of the Alcornocales,
named after the Cork Oaks that cloak its flanks. On its southern rim lies Gibraltar
and Tarifa which offer spectacular numbers of migrating raptors and storks in
spring and autumn. Flowing south from Sevilla to disgorge into the Atlantic, the
Guadalquivir is flanked by marshes, salinas, dunes and umbrella pine forests. Here
the famous Coto Doñana is home to the Iberian Lynx and Spanish Imperial Eagle
plus a huge number of other birds, insects and reptiles. Along the province's northern border the Sierra Morena has many sites with a unique flora and fauna.
If you are heading north instead, the Tablas de Daimiel and Cabañeros National
Parks are worth visiting. To the north-east are the lowlands of Murcia and Albacete.
The world is yours as these areas are famous for their fantastic birdlife and traditional landscapes of dehesas and steppes which turn into a colourful carpet of
wildflowers in spring.

Food and drinks

The Andalucían way of life was and is recently recognised by UNESCO as world
cultural heritage. The Spanish love to dine out. Hence reasonably priced restaurants
(*ventas*) are almost everywhere. From the early morning to lunchtime, various bars
serve the classic Andalucían breakfast, which is *tostada* (toast) with *mermelada* or
Jamón Serrano or cheese with olive oil and crushed tomato, finished with a coffee. In
the afternoon (12:00-16:00) bars serve a three course meal of the day, the *menú del
día*. This is a quick inexpensive meal for a fixed, low price (around € 8,00- € 12.00).
If you are near the coast, head to the nearest *chiringuito* – a small beach-side restaurant where they serve paella or freshly caught fish. A great way to spend an evening
is going out for tapas. There is even a verb for this – *tapear*. In many bars you get a
free tapa with each drink. In many places you can have a complete meal of tapas by
ordering larger portions, called *raciones.*

Vegetarians have a hard time when dining out, except in the larger towns, where the tendency to cut down the meat consumption – either for health or moral reasons – is most evident. In village bars and restaurants, pork, beef, lamb and mutton feature prominently on the menu. Minced meatballs (in an almond sauce) and stuffed peppers; the loin marinated and roasted; the fillet braised in orange-Sherry sauce and off course the famous *Jamón Ibérico* from the Ibérico Pig and chorizo are well known pork dishes. Typical lamb dishes are slow-cooked shepherds' stews (*caldereta de cordero*). Sheep's and goat's cheeses are also worth seeking out.

Some people struggle to get used to the late dinner times in Spain. The kitchen is usually closed before 21:00, although in many touristy places it is possible to have dinner earlier. Keep in mind that vegetables are not usually part of the main course so have to be ordered separately. After dinner, don't be surprised when your glasses are filled again or an aperitif appears. This often happens when you have spent time and money in a bar or restaurant.

Dishes to try

If you visit Andalucía, you'll find some delicious epicurean traditions, which have been passed down from mothers to daughters. Try some of these:

Arroz marinero *caldoso* (soupy) rice with seafood that may have *almejas* (clams), *mejillones* (mussels) or *gambas* (prawns).

Cabrito en ajo caballón A strong tasting goat stew. Great in winter.

Espetos - sardines or freshly-caught sea fish covered in coarse sea salt, speared and cooked over an olive-wood fire until golden, tender and tasty, with that unmistakable smoky barbeque flavour. A popular traditional Spanish dish in beach restaurants.

Gazpacho a chilled tomato soup, served with diced vegetables. Very nice on a hot day!

Huevos a la flamenco eggs fried with ham, chorizo and vegetables. A colourful speciality.

Paella the famous rice dish from a two-handled frying pan. Added to the rice were once other ingredients, but seafood or chicken are most famous nowadays.

Rabo de toro bull's tail *estofado* (stew).

Salmorejo a thicker version of Gazpacho, served with chopped boiled egg and ham.

Solomillo al whisky pork fillet cooked in brandy.

Shops – opening hours

The traditional 'Siesta' is a result of the hot climate. This means that shops are usually open at 8:00 or 9:00 close at 13:00. They open again in the afternoon from 17:00 to 21:00 or 22:00. Large supermarkets don´t close in the afternoon. Banks and Post-offices open only in the morning, mostly from 9:00 to 14:00. Many bars open early for breakfast and are often already busy at 7:00. Remember too that religious feast days and local holidays are widely observed.

Observation tips

Finding orchids

The first thing you ought to know when you go out looking for orchids in eastern Andalucía is that they are very local. Vast areas in the arid south-east, the *hoyas* and the Guadalquivir basin lack orchids entirely, while acidic mountains like the Sierra Nevada, las Apjarras and the Sierra Morena have but a few species.

The predisposition towards limestone areas – for orchid lovers a familiar trait of these wonderful flowers – is quite extreme in eastern Andalucía. As always, though, there are exceptions.

So pick your destinations carefully: Sierra de Almijara, Sierra de Huétor, Sierra Mágina and Sierra de Cazorla (all limestone mountains) are the places to head for, plus Yesos de Sorbas (page 132) where ultra-basic soils also suit the particular requirements of orchids. In these places, Narrow-leaved Helleborine, Mirror, Dull Bee, Yellow Bee, Sawfly and Spanish Early-purple Orchid* (*Orchis olbiensis*) are the more frequently encountered species.

If you're not familiar with the noble pastime of orchid hunting, you need to be aware that European representatives of the wonderful group of flowers are rather small. The full frame pictures in books (including this one), in combination with images of the potted orchids in grandma's window, distort expectations and send off many nouveau naturalists searching for flowers far bigger than they are in reality. Granted, the spikes of Naked-man and Southern Early Purple Orchids* (*Orchis olbiensis*) with their congregation of flowers, are conspicuous, but you need to develop an eye for the small flowers of the bee orchid genus (*Ophrys*). Out in the field, the pale, rather thick stems usually capture your attention first.

Most orchids grow in places which are regularly grazed or mown, albeit not too often. In heavily grazed areas, they 'hide' underneath prickly bushes or near fences. The ideal orchid habitats are grassy roadsides, edges of picnic spots and other ungrazed but regularly mown sites.

The best period for flowering orchids is from March to May, but altitude matters greatly in determining when the flowers come into bloom. A Mirror Orchid in Yesos de Sorbas can have finished by the end of March, but may yet have to open its first flower in the Sierra de Baza. Rich orchid haunts in eastern Andalucía are:

Sierra de Cazorla y Segura (route 8, 9) About 55 species: including Algerian Butterfly Orchid* (*Platanthera algeriensis*), Cazorla Orchid* (*Orchis cazorlensis*), Dense-flowered Orchid, Bird's Nest Orchid, Robust Marsh Orchid, Narrow-leaved and Red Helleborines and many *Ophrys* species.

Sierra Mágina (route 11) About 20 species: Bee Orchid, Early Spider Orchid, Spanish Omega Orchid* (*Ophrys dyris*), Sawfly Orchid, Mirror Orchid, Southern Early Purple Orchid, Pyramidal Orchid, Lady Orchid and Narrow-leaved Helleborine.

Sierra de Huétor (route 15) several bee orchid species including Spanish Omega Orchid* (*Ophrys dyris*), Dull Bee Orchid, Woodcock Orchid and Mirror Orchid plus Naked-man Orchid, Giant Orchid, Fan-lipped Orchid, Southern Early Purple Orchid* (*Orchis olbiensis*) and Violet Bird's-nest.

Sierra de Almijara (page 212) Over 45 species: Pink Butterfly Orchid, Dull Bee Orchid, Spanish Omega Orchid* (*Ophrys dyris*), Mirror Orchid, Sawfly Orchid, Bug Orchid, Dense-flowered Orchid and Man Orchid.

Yesos de Sorbas (page 132) Giant Orchid, Fan-lipped Orchid, Sawfly Orchid, Mirror Orchid.

Finding snakes, spiders, scorpions and the like

A good thing about snakes, spiders and scorpions is that if you do not want to see them, they remain hidden, but if you do, there are ways to find them. The best way to go about it is to head for a scree field or stony karst landscape and start turning over stones (always remembering to put them back in place). Beneath them you find a wonderful hidden life of creatures that appear on too many menus to afford the luxury of a 'place in the sun'. They come out at night to hunt and avoid being hunted by crawling under a rock.

Mostly you will find ants and their nests, but every now and then you will stumble upon a scorpion, wolf spider (related to the tarantulas), snake, Megarian Banded Centipede or one of the more drought-resistant amphibians. If you are lucky you might even find a Worm Lizard.

Flat stones or old pieces of plastic yield most success. Lift them up on one side, turn them over and step back. Be aware that some animals can cause painful stings or bites. Keep in mind that turning over stones is very invasive for the animals that are hiding beneath them. Many of them have worked hard to create a nest in their shelter. Therefore, make sure that you do not disturb the subterranean life too long and place the stone back in exactly the same position as you found it.

Some snakes are particularly active at night. They often warm themselves on the surface of small country roads. A drive or walk at dusk can reveal Ladder, False Smooth and Southern Smooth Snakes. In spring and summer other snakes and lizards use these places to warm up for the day. Grass and Viperine Snakes are, with some luck, more easy to spot at the edges or in shallows of small streams.

Snorkelling

Cabo de Gata-Níjar Nature Reserve is a popular destination for snorkellers and scuba divers because the water is crystal clear and there is a variety of marine life. There are lots of fish including larger species absent from most parts of the overfished Mediterranean. Diving clubs offer guided scuba diving tours to iconic sites in the area such as the shipwreck of *El Arna* and *the Cueva del Francés*.

It is also possible to enjoy the sea life and the beautiful underwater landscapes without a permit or scuba equipment. If you bring a mask, a snorkel and fins, snorkelling is possible anywhere. The best sites are the small beaches of Acantilados de Maro-Cerro (page 212), Cala de las Hermánicas near San José (Cabo de Gata) and the southern end of Playa de los Muertos (a bit further northeast, near Mesa Roldán). For a quick snorkel any beach with rock formations in the water is worth a try (e.g. Playa de Mónsul; route 2).

Typically, you can find large amounts of polyps, sea squirts, sponges and sea urchins on or near the rocky substrates. Among the large number of fish species you can find are the Ornate Wrasse (*Thalassoma pavo*), Painted Comber (*Serranus scriba*) and Mediterranean Moray (*Muraena helena*) as well as many Damselfish (*Chromis chromis*) and several species of blennies (*Blennidae*). Octopus (*Octopus vulgaris*) is a master in camouflage but if you see a cavity in the rocks with parts of shells and crabs in front of it, it is worthwhile to take a closer look. In sandy parts the endangered Neptune Grass can form underwater meadows. Here you can find the Noble Pen Shell (*Pinna nobilis*), a large 'mussel' that stands vertical on the sea floor. The Red Mullet (*Mulus surmuletus*) can be seen using their barbells to find invertebrates in the sand, they are often accompanied by Sea Bream (*Sparidae*) or Rainbow Wrasse (*Coris julis*) that take advantage of any food stirred up by the goatfish.

Birdwatching list

The following bird list includes all breeding and wintering birds and regular passage migrants (note that spring starts in February/March for many species). Numbers between the brackets (...) refer to the routes from page 114 onwards.

Shearwaters, storm-petrels, gannets, auks and cormorants From headlands along the Mediterranean coast (1, 2, site B on page 131) you have a chance of seeing Cory's (both forms) and Balearic Shearwaters, particularly during passage. Reports of Yelkouan Shearwater have declined markedly since the 1970s. Shag breeds, but numbers are low. In winter (and on passage), Gannet, skuas, Cormorants and Razorbill can be seen. European Storm-petrel has a single population on Isla de Terreros but is very rarely seen from coastal vantage points.

Herons, egrets, Glossy Ibis and Greater Flamingo Little Egret is the most numerous of the herons and egrets and is found on most wetlands. Little Bittern breeds in areas with reedbeds (4, site A on page 178, site D on page 133 and site B on page 205). Grey Heron, Cattle Egret and Squacco Heron are rather uncommon (best are site D and E on page 133-34 and site B on page 205). Night Heron breeds in Córdoba (site D on page 180) and Punta Entinas-Sabinar (4). Glossy Ibis is rather scarce (site D and E on page 133-34) The estuaries of Cabo de Gata (1) and Punta Entinas

Sabinar (4) are good for Greater Flamingo. Purple Heron and Spoonbill are irregular visitors during migration. Spoonbill also winters (1, 4).

Storks Both Black and White Storks are occasionally seen during migration. White Stork is a rare breeding bird in the Guadalquivir basin.

Ducks, grebes and other waterfowl Cañada de las Norias (site E on page 134), Rambla de Morales (1), the estuaries of Punta Entinas Sabinar (4), Cabo de Gata (1) and the marshes of Charca de Suárez (site B on page 205), Laguna Grande and Zoñar (site E and F on page 181-82) and Laguna de Padul (site C on page 206) all hold many species of waterfowl, especially during migration. Among them are some sought-after species, such as the Marbled Duck (1, 4), White-headed Duck (most of the above sites, but especially 1, 4 and site B on page 205, D on page 133, and F on page 182) and Crested Coot (4, site B on page 205 and F on page 182). Purple Gallinule is found on 4, site B on page 205, site E on page 181, site D on page 133 and site F on page 182). Little Grebe is common in most reservoirs (1, 4, 17 and most of the mentioned sites). Red-crested Pochard is often seen on 1, 4, site F on page 182, Pochard is seen on 1, 4, site E on page 181 and Shelduck on 1, 4. During winter you might encounter Teal, Pintail, Gadwall, Mallard and Shoveler at these sites too. Water Rail is found on most marshes, especially in winter.

Vultures Egyptian Vultures can be seen, generally in low numbers, on routes 8, 13, and site B on page 178. Griffon Vultures are present on cliffs in various mountain ranges (large numbers on routes 5, 7, 8, 10, 11, 13 and 14 and site A on page 167). Lammergeier has been introduced into Sierra de Cazorla (8, 10) but have wandered as far as the Sierra Nevada. Sierra de Andújar (13) is home to Black Vultures (very unusual elsewhere in the area covered in this guide).

Eagles and other raptors Most raptors are absent from or much less frequent in the arid south-east. Sierra de Cazorla (8, 9, 10) hosts the greatest density of Golden Eagles in Europe, but this impressive bird can be seen in most mountain ranges of Eastern Andalucía (e.g. 7, 12, 13, 15, 17, 18). Spanish Imperial Eagle can best be observed in Sierra de Andújar (13) and occasionally in Sierra de Cazorla (Site A page 167). Short-toed and Booted Eagles occur throughout, except in the arid zone of Almería. Bonelli's Eagle is uncommon but widespread in the mountainous parts of the area. Within the range of this book, it is best found in the Almería province, Huétor and Alpujarras (1-3, 5, 15 and site A on page 212). Goshawk and Sparrowhawk are present in forested regions (e.g. 8, 12, 13, 14, 15, 16). Black-winged Kite prefers open areas and is mostly seen in the Guadalquivir basin (site A and, less often, E and F on page 178-82 and site C on page 206). The Black Kite breeds in the Guadalquivir basin and Sierra Morena (13, 14 and sites A-F on pages 178-82). Red Kite is now a very scarce breeding bird although numbers increase in winter. Osprey is present during migration, mostly seen along the Guadalquivir and on the coast (1 and 4). Honey Buzzard is rare during migration, mostly in the western part. Buzzard is uncommon but widespread. Marsh Harrier nests in Laguna Grande (site E on page 181) and irregularly winters in Cabo de Gata (1) and Entinas de Sabinar (4). Montagu's Harrier prefers agricultural lands and steppe (5, 6, 14).

Falcons and Kestrels Peregrine Falcon is an uncommon breeding bird of mountains and coastal cliffs (1, 2, 4, 7, 8, 10, 12, 14, 18, 20). Lesser Kestrel is quite scarce but breeds colonially in ruins, ancient urban areas and steppe areas (5, 6 and la Alhambra). Common Kestrel is frequent throughout the area.

Partridges Red-legged partridge is common in scrublands and agricultural land. It is often secretive, but as it is bred and released as game bird, you may sometimes come across very tame birds. Common Quail is an elusive bird of grasslands and agricultural land (5, 6).

Waders, Stone Curlew and Collared Pratincole Due the paucity of wetlands, waders concentrate in areas that are of particular interest to birders. Route 1, 4 Laguna Grande (E on page 181), Laguna Padul (C on page 206), Charca de Suárez (B on page 205) and Playa the Vera (D on page 133) are most rewarding for waders.
In coastal saline wetlands (1, 4) Avocet, Black-tailed Godwit, Common Redshank, Curlew Sandpiper, Dunlin, Kentish Plover and Black-winged Stilt are most frequent. The latter two are breeding, whilst the rest is seen during migration and in winter. Less common in the same sites are Spotted Redshank, Grey Plover, Golden Plover and Lapwing. The latter two are often seen on the Cabo de Gata beach, together with Sanderling and Ringed Plover. Inland, waders are usually found near reservoirs and rivers. Here you may expect Little Ringed Plover, Common and Green Sandpiper and sometimes Greenshank. Stone Curlew prefers stony and open grasslands (E.g. Hoya de Baza; page 147, and routes 1, 2, 4, 5, 6). Collared Pratincole is found at Entinas-Sabinar (4) and is frequenty observed in the saline marshes of Cabo de Gato (1).

Gulls and terns Audouin's, Mediterranean and Slender-billed Gulls are often present on beaches (1, 2, 4 and site D on page 133). Little Gull occur on passage. Gull-billed Tern, Sandwich and Little Terns are usually also present at the same sites. Whiskered and Black Tern are frequently seen on passage. Again, routes 1, 2, 4 and site D on page 133 offer the best chances. Yellow-legged Gulls are found at the same sites but are much more widespread. Lesser Black-backed Gull winters in wetlands in the Guadalquivir basin and at the coast.

Sandgrouse and Bustards Black-bellied is the most common of the sandgrouse, preferring fallow and recently ploughed fields (1, 3, 5, 6, Hoya de Baza, page 147). Pin-tailed Sandgrouse is rare and prefers stony and short-grass steppes (5, 6). Little Bustard is very rare and hard to find on steppe areas (5, 6). Great Bustard occurs in the Guadalquivir basin, but is also very hard to find.

Owls Eagle Owl is an uncommon breeding bird of cliffs. Scops Owls occur in summer in open forests and trees near villages (listen for typical, soft *pjuup*-call).

Barn, Tawny and especially Little Owls are present in good numbers throughout the region. The latter is frequently seen on 5 and 6.

Cuckoos Common Cuckoo is indeed common throughout and best seen in spring. Great Spotted Cuckoo is local but quite common in areas of bushy steppes (5 and Hoya de Baza).

Pigeons and Doves Wood Pigeon is a common and Stock Dove a rare breeding bird of the countryside. Both are more numerous in winter. Collared Dove is a common resident of towns and villages. Turtle Dove is a fairly common breeding bird of lightly wooded agricultural land and riversides. Rock Dove is quite common in mountains and ramblas throughout the area.

Nightjars Red-necked Nightjars are common in the lowlands and often sit on roads at dusk after warm days. Listen for their typical *ka-Tok, ka-Tok* call, resembling the sound of an approaching train (e.g. 7, 13). Common Nightjar is scarce and breeds in the mountains of Nevada, Huétor and Alpujarras (e.g. 15, 18).

Swifts Both Common and Pallid Swifts can be found in villages and towns, with Pallid dominating the coastal areas and Common the mountains and inlands areas. Alpine Swift occurs throughout the mountains (3, 8, 9, 10, 11, 12, 17, 18, 19). White-rumped Swift is rather rare and breeds under bridges and protruding rocks in old nests of Red-rumped Swallow (13, 14 and site C on page 179).

Bee-eater, Roller, Hoopoe and Kingfisher Bee-eater is a widespread species. There is a large colony at site E on page 181. The elusive Roller has its stronghold in steppe areas, where it prefers sitting on wires and poles (5, Hoya de Baza on page 147). Hoopoe is frequent, mostly in agrarian lowlands. Kingfisher is a fairly common resident on all major water courses and lakes in the region (e.g. 8, 9, 11, 14, 16).

Woodpeckers Great Spotted and Iberian Green Woodpeckers occur in any wooded area – the latter most common along rivers. A small population of Lesser Spotted Woodpecker is found in the Sierra Morena in Jaen province. Wryneck is a rare breeding, wintering and migrating bird of open woodland.

Larks, pipits and wagtails Short-toed Lark is fairly widespread, especially in the Guadalquivir valley. Lesser Short-toed Larks occur in low numbers near the salt marshes of Cabo de Gata and Sabinar (1, 4) and in the Hoyas (5 and page 147). Woodlarks are frequent in dehesas and open forests (7, 8, 10, 12, 13, 17, 18, 19). Crested Larks are most common in the agrarian lowlands whereas Thekla Larks are common and prefer mountains and bushy terrain. In winter, Skylarks frequent the open coastal areas (1, 2, 4), while a few also breed on the highest tops of the mountains (10, 19). The elusive and very rare Dupont's Lark is known from Las Almoladeras (1), Desiertos de Tabernas (3) and near Padul.

Tawny Pipits can be found in any open dry area, from coast to mountains (1, 4, 5, 6, 10, 17, and 19). A few Water Pipits winter at 1 and 4 but they breed numerously in the Sierra Nevada (17, 19). Meadow Pipits winter in the coastal plains.

White and Grey Wagtails occur along rivers. The Spanish race of Yellow Wagtail breeds locally in low marshland (1, 4 site B on page 205) but other races pass through on passage.

Swallows and Martins Red-rumped Swallow is common in rocky areas near water. Swallow and House Martin are common throughout. Crag Martin is present in any rocky terrain. Sand Martin is a highly localised colonial breeder (1, site E on page 181).

Dipper, Wren and accentors Dipper inhabits larger mountain streams (8, 9, 16, 18). Wren is a common species in its preferred habitat of dense low undergrowth. Alpine Accentor breeds high up in the Sierra Nevada (17, 19) and is a winter visitor in Cazorla (10). Dunnock is local but more widespread.

Thrushes and allies The Blue Rock Thrush is common in rocky habitats up to roughly 2,000 metres. 'Common' Rock Thrushes are mostly found in high mountains (17, 18, 19). Mistle Thrush is fairly common in open forest. Bluethroat is quite a rare winter visitor (4, site B and C on page 204-5). Nightingale is numerous in thick vegetation along rivers. Blackbirds are widespread but the best chances for Ring Ouzel are from autumn to early spring and usually at high altitudes (11, 17, 19). Fieldfare and Redwing winter in small numbers on high ground too. Rufous Bush Robin is fairly widespread (but scarce and declining) in scrubland in the northern parts of Cabo de Gata-Nijar (1) and Sierra Morena (Site B on page 178) and in the olive groves in the Guadalquivir lowlands (e.g. F on page 182). It is one of the latest birds to arrive, being present from late May to August.

Wheatears, chats, redstarts The Black-eared Wheatear is a common bird of rocky scrublands. East Andalucía is the best region for Black Wheatear in Spain. Search for it on dry cliffs (1, 2, 3, 5, 6, 7, 13, 14, 18, 20). The Northern Wheatear takes the place of Black-eared Wheatear on the highest slopes (10, 17, 19) but is common elsewhere on passage. Stonechat is common in bushy scrub and grassland. Black Redstart is common in urban areas and rocky terrain. Common Redstart is a scarce breeding bird of Cazorla.

'Sylvia' warblers Subalpine and Dartford Warblers occur in low dense tangles in the uplands (4, 5, 6, 10, 11, 12). Sardinian warblers are common in any scrubland. Spectacled Warbler is rarer and prefers arid areas, mostly on the lowlands but also in steppe-like uplands (1, 2, 5, 13, 17). Whitethroat is scarce, preferring to breed on north-facing slopes. Blackcaps occur in moist, dense forests. The Western Orphean Warbler is a rather uncommon bird of open forests and olive groves in the lower mountains (2, 8, 13, 14 and site E on page 181).

'Brown' warblers Zitting Cisticola is most frequent along the coast in damp meadows and marshes (1, 2, 4 and site B on page 205). The Common Chiffchaff is a common wintering species, being present between September and March. It also breeds in the Sierra Nevada. The breeding range of Iberian Chiffchaff is imperfectly known but it is a very local breeding bird of the Sierra Morena and possibly elsewhere. Bonelli's Warbler is fairly common in pinewoods (6, 7, 8, 11, 15, 17). Cetti's Warbler is numerous in thick vegetation along rivers. The Melodious Warbler is numerous throughout (e.g. 8, 9). Olivaceous Warbler arrives late in May and June. It occurs in the ramblas (1, 2, 3, 5) and Guadalquivir basin (sites D, E and F on page 180-82). Common and Great Reed Warblers breed in freshwater coastal marshes (1, 4, site D and E on page 133-34). Savi's Warbler only breeds at Padul (site C on page 206).

Tits, Firecrest and Flycatchers Crested and Coal Tit and Firecrest are associated with pine forest (6, 7, 8, 11, 15, 16, 17). Widespread are Great, Blue and Long-tailed Tit. Penduline Tit breeds in trees along freshwater marshes (4, site D on page 180, sites B and C on page 205-6) and winters on the Almería coast. Spotted Flycatcher is a common breeding bird of open woodland. Pied Flycatcher is an uncommon migrant and very rare breeding bird of Sierra Morena.

Nuthatch, Treecreeper and Wallcreeper Nuthatch is common in older woodlands. Short-toed Treecreeper is fairly common throughout. Wallcreeper is a very rare winter visitor. (8, 17, 19).

Shrikes Woodchat shrike is fairly numerous in scrublands and open forests in summer. Iberian Grey Shrike is fairly common in karst landscape and steppe areas (1, 3, 5, 6, Hoya de Baza; page 147) and more widespread in winter.

Crows and allies The most conspicuous species of this group, the Azure-winged Magpie, has its stronghold in the Sierra Morena and locally elsewhere (13, 14, 15 and site A, B, C on page 178-79). Red-billed Choughs are numerous in all rocky regions and steppes (5, 6, 8, 11, 13). Raven is uncommon but present throughout the mountains. Jackdaw is fairly numerous and Carrion Crow surprisingly rare.

Starlings and Oriole Spotless Starling is common in and around urban areas. In winter it is joined by Common Starling. Golden Oriole is fairly common along tree-lined streams and stands of Poplar (e.g. 8, 11, 16 and 18).

Sparrows Rock Sparrow occurs in any rocky terrain or steppe (e.g. 2,3, 5, 6, 10, 13, 18, 19, site A on page 130). Carefully check flocks of House Sparrows as Spanish Sparrow is sometimes found amongst them (e.g. 13). Tree Sparrow is thinly spread and occurs in villages or agricultural lands.

Finches and allies Hawfinch, Chaffinch, Greenfinch, Goldfinch, Serin and Linnet are all common or fairly common in their preferred habitat. Bulfinch has a single isolated population at the Jandula River (13). Citril Finch reaches its southern limit in the Sierra Nevada (Puerto de la Ragua; site A on page 204) and Sierra Cazorla (Puerto Palomas; site A on page 167). Both Siskin and Brambling are scarce winter visitors in variable numbers. Trumpeter Finch is fairly common but hard to spot in the Gabo de Gata and Desiertos area, where it dwells in dry ramblas (1, 2, 3). Common Crossbill is indeed common in pinewoods (6, 7, 8, 11, 15, 16, 17).

Buntings Rock Bunting is common in any rocky areas in the Nevada and limestone mountains. The Cirl Bunting frequents agricultural land with tall trees and is most common in the Alpujarras (e.g. 18). Corn Buntings are very common in agricultural areas. Reed Bunting is a scarce winter bird in freshwater marshes in the region (e.g. site C on page 206). Ortolan Bunting has an isolated population in the Sierra Nevada (17).

Introduced species The most prominent alien species are parakeets. Both Ring-necked and, more commonly, Monk Parakeet occur particularly in cities on the coast (e.g. Motril). Of smaller species, the Red Avadavat and Common Waxbill have established localised colonies. Note that at Charca de Suárez (site B on page 205) Common Waxbill has been joined by Black-rumped Waxbill.

ACKNOWLEDGEMENTS

As with all Crossbill Guides, this book has only been made possible thanks to the help of many contributors. First of all, a huge thanks to Antoon De Rycke. We greatly appreciate his valuable input on the local flora and for all the enriching comments he made on our draft texts regarding the semi-deserts. The geology section could never have the clarity it has now, if Gino Smeulders hadn't shared his geological knowledge with us. Regarding the herpetofauna, we had great help from Wouter de Vries, both for the general background regarding which species were present and for his handy tips on locating those species we were most keen to find.

Stef Strik, we owe you a hot cocoa after wading through the Frigiliana river in mid-winter. Apart from filling in gaps on this route for us, you also made it clear we have to emphasise that this part of the route is really best covered in summer! Renske Wijtsma explored the Sierra María route in advance and literally did some of the legwork for us. More warm thanks go to Renate Kemner, who tested some of our routes, provided us (and you, dear reader) with some of the more jaw-dropping photographs in this book. In the process, she managed to discover some additional species of flora and fauna that now enrich those routes in the south-eastern part of the region. Next in line is Gertie Vliegenthart, to whom we are indebted for her comprehensive input during the research in Spain. She put the routes to the test and (to her surprise, but not to ours of course) she found the species exactly there where we mention them in the description of the routes.

Last but certainly not least, we are grateful for the local help we had from people in the visitors' centres, for illuminating chats with the parks' biologists, the people on the street and where we stayed. Nothing beats getting that completely unexpected insight from a casual chat with a biologist or birder over an evening beer, or that colourful story of a herdsman who fortuitously crossed your path whilst out exploring.

Still, if it wasn't for the rest of the Crossbill Guides team, this book wouldn't have materialised. A big thanks to Oscar Lourens, Horst Wolter and Alex Tabak for their excellent design, illustrations and maps that grace this book. We thank John Cantelo, Brian Clews, Kees and Riet Hilbers for their robust, if sometimes sobering, 'savaging' (John's words) of the manuscript. Kim Lotterman, of course, scrutinised all the species names in the book. This guidebook would not be complete without the images that grace its pages and we warmly thank all photographers for their contribution. We acknowledge them on the following page. In particular, of course, we thank Jan van der Straaten of our partner organisation Saxifraga Foundation. We'd rather not count the number of times we came back to Jan, asking for 'yet another image' to complete this guide. In addition to his skills as a photographer, we discovered that patience is another of his great virtues!

Albert Vliegenthart, Bouke ten Cate, Dirk Hilbers, Kees Woutersen
December 2016

PICTURE CREDITS

In the references that follow, the numbers refer to the pages and the letters to the position on the page (t=top, c=centre, b=bottom, with l and r indicating left and right).

Crossbill Guides / ten Cate, Bouke: 4 (2nd from top), 16, 28, 31 (t, c, b), 36, 38, 51, 69 (2nd from top), (73 (t, c, b), 82 (b), 84 (l), 88 (t), 102 (b), 106 (t), 108 (t), 118, 122 (b), 126, 133, 142 (b), 145 (t), 159 (t), 163 (t, b), 164 (t, b), 172 (b), 175, 176 (t), 177 (t), 179 (l), 180, 185 (1st, 2nd, 3rd, 4th on bottom), 190 (b), 194, 195 (2nd from top), 201, 202, 203 (t, b)

Crossbill Guides / Hilbers, Dirk: 39 (t), 42, 52 (l), 67 (t, b), 69 (1st and 3rd from top), 74, 75, 76 (t), 111(l), 115, 122 (t), 124 (t), 131 (bl, br), 132 (t), 138 (t), 151 (t+b), 154, 166 (b), 167 (t, b), 206

Crossbill Guides / Vliegenthart, Albert: 4 (3rd and 4th from top), 5 (t), 17, 33 (t, b), 39 (b), 44 (t), 58, 61, 68 (3rd from top), 71 (t, b), 76 (b), 100, 106 (b), 108 (b), 109, 111 (r), 112, 117 (t, b), 119, 121 (t, b), 124 (b), 128 (l, r), 130, 138 (b), 140, 142 (t), 144 (t), 146 (b), 152 (t, b), 153, 156, 157 (t, b), 160, 172 (t), 176 (c, b), 177 (b), 181, 185 (t), 188, 190 (t), 192, 193 (t, b), 195 (1st, 3rd, 4th from top), 197 (t, b), 198 (t), 199, 205, 210, 211 (t, b)

De Rycke, Antoon: 68 (1st, 2nd and 4th from top), 69 (b), 70 (t, b)

Fikkert, Cor: 80, 141 (t), 161, 173, 179 (r)

Franklin, Francis C. / Wikimedia Commons.org: 129

Fransen, Bernard: 104 (r)

Gaianauta / Wikimedia Commons.org: 132 (b)

Greef, Jan van der: 5 (3rd from top), 47, 170, 171

Hills, Lawrie: 102 (t), 144 (b)

Hoogenstein, Luc: 82 (t)

Jordan, Frank: 4 (t), 5 (2nd from top), 18, 35, 137 (t), 214

Kemner, Renate: Cover, 5 (b), 10, 13, 22, 30, 56, 78, 88 (b), 99 (t), 125, 207

Locati, Fabio Allesandro / Wikimedia Commons.org: 24

Mager, Jörg: 40, 86, 95, 145 (b)

Nijssen, Marijn: 131 (t)

Saxifraga / Hoogenstein, Luc: 141 (b)

Saxifraga / Munsterman, Piet: 94 (l, r), 198 (b)

Saxifraga / Remmerzwaal, Wim: 84 (r)

Saxifraga / Straaten, Jan van der: 52 (r)

Saxifraga / Uchelen, Edo van: 159 (b)

Saxifraga / Vastenhouw, Bart: 134

Saxifraga / Zekhuis, Mark: 62, 93, 182, 186

Smits, Stijn: 26 (b), 44 (b), 85, 91, 97 (t), 137 (b), 166 (t)

Sohler, Jan: 90, 97 (b), 146

Swaay, Chris van: 135, 212

Thompson, Martyn (Cabo de Gata photography) / Wikimedia Commons.org: 26 (t)

Veling, Kars: 104 (l)

Wild, Angela de: 99 (b), 213

GLOSSARY

Borreguiles Peat bogs in the Sierra Nevada.

Crevices Cracks or small fracture in a rock formation.

Dehesa Habitat typical of southwestern Spain. It looks most like open African savannah with pasture and scrubland underneath. Some dehesas are dense enough to resemble an extensive grove of oaks or even the Mediterranean evergreen forest. Dehesas form a beautiful and very valuable landscape that is virtually restricted to western Andalucía, Extremadura and adjacent Portugal and are fairly rare in eastern Andalucía.

Endemic / Endemism Species that occurs nowhere else in the world but in one small area. For example, Sierra Nevada Sandwort* (*Arenaria nevadensis*) is endemic to the Sierra de Nevada; it grows only there.

Endorheic lake Shallow lake in a closed basin. Small, often temporary streams flow down to the floor of the basin but the high evaporation prevents the basin from spilling over and the water flowing out into nearby river systems. Many endorheic lakes dry up every summer. Endorheic lakes have a very special ecology.

Hybridize To produce offspring from two different species. Orchids are known to create many hybrids between two species.

Hedgehog zone The southern Spanish version of subalpine vegetation. Instead of boreal-like coniferous forests, which dominate the subalpine zone in central-European mountains, the hedgehog zone is dominated by very sturdy, usually spiky tussock-forming plants, many of which are endemic to southern Spain. The most emblematic plant of the hedgehog zone is the blue-flowering hedgehog broom (p. 69).

Karst Typical landscape that is formed when limestone is exposed to high precipitation. Limestone easily dissolves in water, which causes gullies, cracks, caves, dolines and a series of other typical karst features.

Rambla Seasonal river, usually dry in summer.

Scree field Field covered with stones and boulders.

Ungulate Hoofed animal such as Red Deer, Fallow Deer etc.

SPECIES LIST & TRANSLATION

The following list comprises all species mentioned in this guidebook and gives their scientific, German and Dutch names. It is not a complete checklist of the species of Eastern Andalucía. Some names have an asterisk (*) behind them, indicating an unofficial name. See page 7 for more details.

Plants

English	Scientific	German	Dutch
Aizoon	*Aizoon hispanicum*	Spanisches Eiskraut	Spaans ijskruid
Alison, Andalusian*	*Hormathophylla baetica*	Andalusisches Steinkraut*	Andalusisch schildzaad*
Alison, Purple	*Hormathophylla purpurea*	Purper-Steinkraut*	Purperschildzaad*
Alison, Spiny	*Hormathophylla spinosa*	Dorn-Steinkraut	Stekelschildzaad*
Aphyllanthes, Blue	*Aphyllanthes monspeliensis*	Blaue Binsenlilie	Blauwe bieslelie
Ash, Narrow leaved	*Fraxinus angustifolia*	Schmalblättrige Esche	Smalbladige es
Asphodel, White	*Asphodelus albus*	Weisser Affodill	Witte affodil
Barberry, Spanish	*Berberis hispanica*	Spanische Berberitze	Spaanse zuurbes*
Bean-caper, Syrian	*Zygophyllum fabago*	Bohnenähnliches Jochblatt	Syrische kapperstruik
Bearberry	*Arctostaphylos uva-ursi*	Echte Bärentraube	Berendruif
Bindweed, Blue*	*Convolvulus siculus*	Sizilianische Winde	Siziliaanse winde*
Bindweed, Silver-leaved	*Convolvulus boissieri*	Boissier-Winde	Bossiers winde*
Bird's-nest, Violet	*Limodorum abortivum*	Violetter Dingel	Paarse aspergeorchis
Birthwort, Andalucian*	*Aristolochia baetica*	Baetische Pfeifenwinde*	Baetische pijpbloem*
Bluebell, Brown	*Dipcadi serotinum*	Schweifblatt	Bruine hyacint*
Box	*Buxus sempervirens*	Buchsbaum	Buxus
Boxthorn, Canary	*Lycium intricatum*	Sparriger Bocksdorn	Mediterrane boksdoorn
Broom, Hedgehog	*Erinacea anthyllis*	Igelpolster	Blauwe egelbrem*
Broom, Nevada*	*Cytisus galianoi*	Nevada Geissklee*	Nevadabrem*
Broomrape, Rosemary	*Orobanche latisquama*	Breitschuppige Sommerwurz	Rozemarijn-bremraap*
Buckthorn, Mediterranean	*Rhamnus alaternus*	Immergrüner Kreuzdorn	Altijdgroene wegedoorn*
Bulrush	*Typha sp.*	Rohrkolben	Lisdodde
Buttercup, Glacier	*Ranunculus glacialis*	Gletscher-Hahnenfuss	Gletsjerranonkel
Buttercup, Grass-leaved	*Ranunculus gramineus*	Grasblättriger Hahnenfuss	Grasbladige boterbloem*
Buttercup, Narrow-leaved*	*Ranunculus angustifolius*	Schmallblättriger Pyrenäen-Hahnenfuss*	Smalbladige pyreneeenranonkel*
Buttercup, Sorrel-leaved	*Ranunculus acetosellifolius*	Sauerkleeblättriger Hahnenfuss*	Klaverzuringboterbloem*
Butterwort, Eelgrass-leaved*	*Pinguicula vallisneriifolia*	Sierra-Fettkraut*	Sierravetblad*
Butterwort, Nevada	*Pinguicula nevadensis*	Nevada-Fettkraut*	Nevadavetblad*
Cabbage, Pink	*Moricandia moricandioides*	Grosse Moricandie*	Grote moricandia*
Caper, Wild	*Capparis spinosa*	Echter Kapernstrauch	Kappertjes

Caralluma	*Caralluma europaea*	Europaeisches Fliegenblume*	Schijncactus*
Catchfly, Pink	*Silene colorata*	Farbes Leimkraut	Kleurige silene*
Chestnut	*Castanea sativa*	Edelkastanie	Tamme kastanje
Cinquefoil, Nevada*	*Potentilla nevadensis*	Nevada-Fingerkraut*	Nevadaganzerik*
Cistanche, (Yellow)	*Cistanche phelypaea*	Gelbe Cistanche	Cistanche
Cistus, Grey-leaved	*Cistus albidus*	Weissliche Zistrose	Viltige cistusroos*
Cistus, Gum	*Cistus ladanifer*	Lackzistrose	Kleverige cistusroos*
Cistus, Laurel-leaved	*Cistus laurifolius*	Lorbeerblättrige Zistrose	Laurierbladige cistusroos*
Cistus, Narrow-leaved	*Cistus monspelliensis*	Montpellier-Zistrose	Montpellier cistusroos*
Cistus, Sage-leaved	*Cistus salvifolius*	Salbeiblättrige Zistrose	Saliebladige cistusroos*
Columbine, Nevada*	*Aquilegia nevadensis*	Sierra Nevada-Akelei	Nevada-akelei*
Columbine, Pyrenean	*Aquilegia pyrenaica*	Pyrenäen-Akelei	Pyreneese akelei
Coris	*Coris monspeliensis*	Stachelträubchen	Blauwe coris*
Coris, Spanish	*Coris hispanica*	Spanischer Stachelträubchen*	Spaanse coris*
Cotoneaster, Granada	*Cotoneaster granatensis*	Granada-Zwergmispel*	Granadadwergmispel*
Cottonweed	*Otanthus maritimus*	Strand-Filzblume	Katoenkruid*
Crocus, Saffron	*Crocus sativus*	Echter Safran	Saffraan
Daffodil, Nevada	*Narcissus nevadensis*	Sierra Nevada- Narzisse	Sierra Nevadanarcis
Daffodil, Sea	*Pancratium maritimum*	Strandlilie	Zeenarcis
Daffodil, White Hoop-petticoat	*Narcissus cantabricus*	Kantabrische Reifrock-Narzisse	Witte hoepelroknarcis*
Daphne, Olive-leaved	*Daphne oleoides*	Ölbaumähnliche Seidelbast	Olijfpeperboompje*
Elm	*Ulmus sp.*	Ulme	Iep
Eryngo, Glacial*	*Eryngium glaciale*	Eis- Mannstreu	IJskruisdistel
Eryngo, Pyrenean	*Eryngium bourgatii*	Spanischer-Mannstreu	Pyreneese kruisdistel
Fern, Ladder Brake	*Pteris vittata*	Gebänderter Saumfarn	Laddervaren*
Fern, Maidenhair	*Adiantum capillus-veneris*	Venushaarfarn	Venushaar
Fern, Rustyback	*Asplenium ceterach*	Milzfarn	Schubvaren
Flax, Beautiful	*Linum narbonense*	Französischer Lein	Frans vlas
Flax, Holy	*Santolina rosmarinifolia*	Rosmarinblättriges Heiligenkraut	Rozemarijnheiligenbloem*
Fleabane, Cold	*Erigeron frigidus*	Nevada-Berufkraut*	Nevadafijnstraal*
Foxglove, Fairy	*Erinus alpinus*	Alpenbalsam	Alpenbalsem
Foxglove, Morena Purple*	*Digitalis maríana*	Morena-Fingerhut*	Morenavingerhoedskruid*
Foxglove, Purple	*Digitalis purpurea*	Roter Fingerhut	Gewoon vingerhoedskruid
Foxglove, Sunset	*Digitalis obscura*	Dunkler Fingerhut	Spaans vingerhoedskruid
Fritillary, Spanish	*Fritillaria lusitanica*	Portugiesische Schachblume	Iberische kievitsbloem
Fungus, Maltese	*Cynomorium coccineum*	Malteserschwamm	Maltezer paddenstoel
Galingale, Dune	*Cyperus capitatus*	Dünen-Zypergras	Duincypergras*
Gennaria, Two-leaved	*Gennaria diphylla*	Zweiblättriger Grünstendel	Tweehartenorchis
Gentian, Marsh	*Gentiana pneumonanthe*	Lungen-Enzian	Klokjesgentiaan
Gentian, Sierra*	*Gentiana sierrae*	Sierra-Enzian*	Sierragentiaan*
Gentian, Spanish*	*Gentiana boryi*	Bory- Enzian	Spaanse gentiaan*

Germander, Cabo de Gata	*Teucrium charidemi*	Cabo de Gata-Germander	Cabo de Gata gamander*
Gladiole, Common	*Gladiolus communis*	Gewöhnliche Gladiole	Wilde gladiool
Globularia, Spiny*	*Globularia spinosa*	Dornige Kugelblume	Stekende kogelbloem*
Gold-coin	*Pallenis maritima*	Ausdauernder Strandstern	Dukaatbloem
Grape-Vine, Common	*Vitis vinifera*	Wilde Weinrebe	Wilde wijnstok
Grass, Esparto	*Stipa tenacissima*	Halfagras	Espartogras
Grass, False Esparto	*Lygeum spartum*	Espartogras	Vals espartogras*
Grass, Neptune	*Posidonia oceanica*	Neptungras	Neptunusgras
Greenweed, Bolina*	*Genista spartioides*	Binsenblättriger Ginster	Bezemstruikbrem*
Hare's-ear, Gibraltar	*Bupleurum gibraltaricum*	Gibraltar-Hasenohr	Gibraltarstruikgoudscherm*
Hellebore, Stinking	*Helleborus foetidus*	Stinkende Nieswurz	Stinkend nieskruid
Helleborine, Green-flowered	*Epipactis phyllanthes*	Grünblütige Stendelwurz	Groene wespenorchis
Helleborine, Narrow-leaved	*Cephalanthera longifolia*	Schwertblättriges Waldvögelein	Wit bosvogeltje
Helleborine, Red	*Cephalanthera rubra*	Rotes Waldvögelein	Rood bosvogeltje
Helleborine, Small-leaved	*Epipactis microphylla*	Kleinblättrige Stendelwurz	Kleinbladige wespenorchis
Horehound, Felty*	*Marrubium alysson*	Rotblütige Andorn	Rode malrove*
Horehound, Hairy	*Ballota hirsuta*	Behaarte Schwarznessel	Harige ballote*
Horned-poppy, Red	*Glaucium corniculatum*	Roter Hornmohn	Rode hoornpapaver
Horned-poppy, Yellow	*Glaucium flavum*	Gelber Hornmohn	Gele hoornpapaver
Houseleek, Nevada	*Sempervivum minutum*	Nevada-Hauswurz*	Nevadahuislook*
Hypecoum	*Hypecoum spec.*	Hypecoum*	Hypecoum*
Hypocist, Yellow	*Cytinus hypocistis*	Zistrosenwürger	Gele hypocist
Iceplant	*Mesembryanthemum crystallinum*	Kristall-Mittagsblume	IJsplantje
Iceplant, Small-leaved*	*Mesembryanthemum nodiflorum*	Knotenblütige Mittagsblume	Smalbladig ijsplantje*
Iris, Stinking	*Iris foetidissima*	Stinkende Schwertlilie	Stinkende lis
Iris, Wide-leaved	*Iris planifolia*	Flachblättrige Schwertlilie	Winterlis*
Ironwort, Hairy	*Sideritis hirsuta*	Behaartes Gliedkraut	Behaard ijzerkruid*
Jerusalem-sage, Iberian	*Phlomis lychnitis*	Filziges Brandkraut	Viltbrandkruid*
Jerusalem-sage, Purple	*Phlomis purpurea*	Purpur-Brandkraut	Paars brandkruid*
Jonquil, Rush-leaved	*Narcissus assoanus*	Binsenblättrige Narzisse	Rusbladige narcis*
Jujube Bush	*Ziziphus lotus*	Zickzackdorn	Zigzagdoorn*
Juniper, Common	*Juniperus communis*	Gewöhnlicher Wacholder	Jeneverbes
Juniper, Phoenician	*Juniperus phoenicea*	Phönizischer Wacholder	Phoenicische jeneverbes
Juniper, Savin's	*Juniperus sabina*	Sadebaum	Sevenboom
Kidney-vetch, Broom-like*	*Anthyllis cytisoides*	Ruten-Wundklee	Bremwondklaver*
Larkspur, Rocket	*Consolida ajacis*	Garten-Feldrittersporn	Valse ridderspoor
Lavender, Cut-leaved	*Lavandula multifida*	Farnblättriger Lavendel	Varenlavendel*
Lavender, French	*Lavandula stoechas*	Schopflavendel	Kuiflavendel
Lily, Spanish St Bernard's	*Anthericum baeticum*	Spanische Graslilie*	Spaanse graslelie*
Liverleaf	*Hepatica nobilis*	Leberblümchen	Leverbloempje
Mallow, Sea	*Lavatera maritima*	Meer-Strauchpappel	Zee-struikmalva*
Mantle, Virgin's	*Fagonia cretica*	Kretische Fagonie	Fagonia
Medick, Sea	*Medicago marina*	Strand-Schneckenklee	Zeerupsklaver
Milkvetch, Clusius'	*Astragalus clusii*	Clusius-Tragant*	Clusiustragant*

Milkvetch, Evergreen	Astragalus (sempervirens) giennensis	Ausdauernder Tragant	Overblijvende tragant*
Milkwort, Boissier's	Polygala boissieri	Boissiers Kreuzblümchen	Boissiers vleugeltjesbloem*
Mullein, Nevada*	Verbascum nevadense	Nevada-Königskerze*	Nevadakoningskaars*
Mushroom, Morel	Morchella sp.	Morchel	Morielje
Mushroom, Pink Crown	Sarcosphaera coronaria	Kronenbecherling	Kroonbekerzwam
Narcissus, Cuatrecasas*	Narcissus cuatrecasasii	Cuatrecasas- Narzisse	Cuatrecasasnarcis*
Narcissus, Pallid	Narcissus pallidulus	Blass-Narzisse*	Bleke narcis*
Narcissus, Whorl-leaved	Narcissus tortifolius	Andalusische Narzisse*	Andalusische narcis*
Oak, Cork	Quercus suber	Korkeiche	Kurkeik
Oak, Holm	Quercus ilcx	Stein-Eiche	Steeneik
Oak, Kermes	Quercus coccifera	Kermes-Eiche	Hulsteik
Oak, Portuguese	Quercus faginea	Portugiesische Eiche	Portugese eik
Oak, Pyrenean	Quercus pyrenaica	Pyrenäeneiche	Pyreneese eik
Oleander, Wild	Nerium oleander	Oleander	Oleander
Orchid, Algerian Butterfly	Platanthera algeriensis	Algerische Waldhyazinthe	Algerijnse nachtorchis*
Orchid, Bird's-nest	Neottia nidus-avis	Nestwurz	Vogelnestje
Orchid, Cazorla	Orchis cazorlensis	Cazorla-Knabenkraut	Cazorla orchis*
Orchid, Dense-flowered	Neotinea maculata	Gefleckte Keuschorchis	Nonnetjesorchis
Orchid, Dull Bee	Ophrys fusca	Braune Ragwurz	Bruine orchis
Orchid, Spanish Omega	Ophrys dyris	Marokkanische Ragwurz	Dyris orchis*
Orchid, Fan-lipped	Anacamptis collina	Hügel-Knabenkraut	Heuvelorchis
Orchid, Fragrant	Gymnadenia conopsea	Mücken-Händelwurz	Grote muggenorchis
Orchid, Giant	Himantoglossum robertianum	Roberts Mastorchis	Hyacinthorchis
Orchid, Man	Orchis anthropophora	Ohnsporn	Poppenorchis
Orchid, Mirror	Ophrys speculum	Spiegel-Ragwurz	Spiegelorchis
Orchid, Naked-man	Orchis italica	Italienisches Knabenkraut	Italiaanse orchis
Orchid, Pink Butterfly	Anacamptis papilionacea	Schmetterlings-Knabenkraut	Vlinderorchis
Orchid, Robust Marsh	Dactylorhiza elata	Hohes Knabenkraut	Grote rietorchis
Orchid, Sawfly	Ophrys tenthredinifera	Wespen-Ragwurz	Wolzweverorchis
Orchid, Southern Early Purple	Orchis olbiensis	Hyères-Knabenkraut	Kleine mannetjesorchis
Orchid, Spitzel's	Orchis spitzelii	Spitzels Knabenkraut	Spitzels orchis
Orchid, Yellow Bee	Ophrys lutea	Gelbe Ragwurz	Gele orchis
Palm, Dwarf Fan	Chamaerops humilis	Zwergpalme	Dwergpalm
Parsnip, Water	Berula erecta	Schmalblättriger Merk	Kleine watereppe
Pear, Prickly	Opuntia ficus-indica	Echter Feigenkaktus	Vijgcactus
Peony, Western	Paeonia broteroi	Westlicher Pfingstrose*	Westelijke pioenroos*
Pheasant's-eye, Yellow	Adonis vernalis	Frühlings-Adonisröschen	Voorjaarsadonis
Pine, Austrian	Pinus nigra	Schwarzkiefer	Zwarte den
Pine, Scots	Pinus sylvestris	Waldkiefer	Grove den
Pink, Charidem's	Dianthus charidemi	Charidem's Nelke*	Charidem's anjer*
Pink, Iberian*	Dianthus pungens	Iberische Nelke*	Iberische anjer*
Plant, Curry	Helichrysum stoechas	Mittelmeer-Strohblume	Mediterrane strobloem
Plantain, Snowy*	Plantago nivalis	Schnee-Wegerich	Sneeuwweegbree*
Polypody, Southern	Polypodium cambricum	Südlicher Tüpfelfarn	Zuidelijke eikvaren

Poppy, Purple	*Roemeria hybrida*	Basterd-Roemerie	Paarse klaproos*
Poppy, Pyrenean	*Papaver lapeyrousianum*	Pyrenäen-Mohn*	Pyreneese papaver*
Reed, Giant	*Arundo donax*	Pfahlrohr	Spaans riet
Reichardia, Coastal*	*Reichardia gaditana*	Gaditana- Reichhardie	Schijnmelkdistel*
Restharrow, Aragon	*Ononis aragonensis*	Aragon-Hauhechel*	Aragonstalkruid*
Restharrow, Branched*	*Ononis ramosissima*	Ästige-Hauhechel*	Vertakt stalkruid*
Rock-jasmine, Vandelli's	*Androsace vandellii*	Vandellis Mannsschild	Vandellis mansschild*
Rockrose, Almería	*Helianthemum almeriense*	Almeria-Sonnenröschen*	Almeriazonneroosje*
Rockrose, Thyme-leaved	*Fumana thymifolia*	Thymianblättriges Nadelröschen	Tijmbladig zonneroosje*
Rockrose, White	*Helianthemum apenninum*	Weisses Sonnenröschen	Wit zonneroosje
Rosemary, Wild	*Rosmarinus officinalis*	Rosmarin	Rozemarijn
Sage, Lavender-leaved	*Salvia lavandulifolia*	Lavendelblättriger Salbei	Spaanse salie
Saltwort, Andalucian*	*Salsola papillosa*	Andalusisch-Salzkraut*	Andalusisch loogkruid*
Saltwort, Opposite-leaved	*Salsola oppositifolia*	Gegenblättriges Salzkraut*	Paarbladig loogkruid*
Sand-crocus, Almería	*Androcymbium europaeum*	Europäisches Androcymbium	Spaanse zandcrocus*
Sandwort, Sierra Nevada*	*Arenaria nevadensis*	Sierra-Nevada-Sandkraut	Nevadazandmuur*
Saxifrage, Nevada	*Saxifraga nevadensis*	Nevada-Steinbrech	Nevadasteenbreek*
Saxifrage, Starry	*Saxifraga stellaris*	Stern-Steinbrech	Stersteenbreek
Sea-heath	*Frankenia corymbosa*	Andalusische Frankenie*	Andalusische zeehei*
Sea-lavender, Almeria*	*Limonium insigne*	Almeria-Strandflieder*	Almeria-lamsoor*
Sea-lavender, Large	*Limonium majus*	Grosse Strandflieder*	Groot lamsoor*
Sea-lavender, Lobe-leaved*	*Limonium lobatum*	Gelappte Strandflieder	Gelobd lamsoor*
Sea-lavender, Tabernas	*Limonium tabernense*	Tabernas-Strandflieder*	Tabernaslamsoor*
Sea-lavender, Winged	*Limonium sinuatum*	Geflügelter Strandflieder	Bochtig lamsoor
Sea-spurrey, Boccone's*	*Spergularia bocconei*	Boccone's Schuppenmiere*	Boccone's schijnspurrie*
Sedge, Pendulous	*Carex pendula*	Hänge-Segge	Hangende zegge
Silk-vine, Spanish	*Periploca angustifolia*	Schmallblättrige Baumschlinge	Smalbladige melkwingerd
Sisal	*Agave sisalana*	Sisal	Sisal
Snapdragon, Cabo de Gata	*Antirrhinum charidemi*	Cabo de Gata Löwenmaul*	Cabo de Gata leeuwenbek*
Snapdragon, Spanish	*Antirrhinum hispanicum*	Spanisches Löwenmaul	Spaanse leeuwenbek*
Speedwell, Nevada	*Veronica turbicola*	Nevada-Ehrenpreis*	Vevada-erenprijs*
Spurge-laurel	*Daphne laureola*	Lorbeer-Seidelbast	Zwart peperboompje
Stock, Sad	*Matthiola fruticulosa*	Kleine Levkoje	Struikviolier
Stork's-bill, Andalucian*	*Erodium cheilanthifolium*	Farnblättriger Reiherschnabel	Andalusische reigersbek*
Stork's-bill, Cazorla	*Erodium cazorlanum*	Cazorla-Reiherschnabel	Cazorlareigersbek*
Tamarisk	*Tamarix sp.*	Tamarisk	Tamarisk
Thrift, Nevada	*Armeria splendens*	Nevada-Grasnelke*	Pracht Engels gras*
Thrift, Woolly	*Armeria villosa*	Zottige Grasnelke	Behaard Engels gras*
Thymelea	*Thymelaea hirsuta*	Behaarte Spatzenzunge	Behaard vogelkopje*
Thyme, Nevada	*Thymus serpylloides*	Nevada-Thymian*	Nevadatijm*
Thyme, Spanish Lemon*	*Thymus baeticus*	Spanischer Zitronenthymian	Spaanse citroentijm*
Toadflax, Almería	*Linaria nigricans*	Almeria-Leinkraut*	Almerialeeuwenbek*

English	Scientific	German	Dutch
Toadflax, Antequera*	Linaria anticaria	Torcal-Leinkraut*	Torcalleeuwenbek*
Toadflax, Cartagena*	Chaenorhinum grandiflorum	Cartagena-Zwerglöwenmaul*	Cartagenaleeuwenbek
Toadflax, Glacial	Linaria glacialis	Gletscher-Leinkraut	Gletsjerleeuwenbek*
Toadflax, Nevada	Chaenorhinum glareosum	Nevada-Zwerglöwenmaul	Nevadaleeuwenbek
Toadflax, Pedunculate*	Linaria pedunculata	Gestieltes Leinkraut	Gesteelde leeuwenbek*
Toadflax, Rusty*	Linaria aeruginea	Kupfer-Leinkraut	Koperen leeuwenbek*
Tree, Carob	Ceratonia siliqua	Johannisbrotbaum	Johannesbroodboom
Tree, Olive	Olea europea	Ölbaum	Wilde olijfboom
Tree, Strawberry	Arbutus unedo	Erdbeerbaum	Aardbeiboom
Tree, Turpentine	Pistacia terebinthus	Terpentin-Pistazie	Terpentijnboom
Tulip, Wild	Tulipa australis	Südliche Tulpe	Zuidelijke tulp
Vella, Spiny	Vella spinosa	Dornige Vella*	Stekende vella*
Violet, Cazorla	Viola cazorlensis	Cazorla-Veilchen*	Cazorlaviooltje*
Violet, Nevada	Viola crassiuscula	Nevada-Stiefmütterchen*	Nevadaviooltje*
Viper's-bugloss, Woolly	Echium albicans	Weißlicher Natternkopf	Wollig slangenkruid*
Vitaliana	Androsace vitaliana	Goldprimel	Goudmansschild*
Wallflower, Nevada*	Erysimum nevadense	Nevada-Schöterich*	Nevadamuurbloem*
Wormwood, Granada*	Artemisia granatensis	Granada-Beifuss*	Granadabijvoet*

Mammals

English	Scientific	German	Dutch
Badger	Meles meles	Dachs	Das
Bat, Greater Horse-shoe	Rhinolophus ferrumequinum	Grosse Hufeisennase	Grote hoefijzerneus
Bat, Grey Long-eared	Plecotus austriacus	Graues Langohr	Grijze grootoorvleermuis
Bat, Lesser Horseshoe	Rhinolophus hipposideros	Kleine Hufeisennase	Kleine hoefijzerneus
Bat, Lesser Mouse-eared	Myotis blythii	Kleines Mausohr	Kleine vale vleermuis
Bat, Schreiber´s	Miniopteris schreibersii	Langflügelfledermaus	Schreibers' vleermuis
Boar, Wild	Sus scrofa	Wildschwein	Wild zwijn
Cat, Wild	Felis silvestris	Wildkatze	Wilde kat
Deer, Fallow	Damus damus	Dammhirsch	Damhert
Deer, Red	Cervus elaphus	Rothirsch	Edelhert
Deer, Roe	Capreolus capreolus	Reh	Ree
Dormouse, Garden	Eliomys quercinus	Gartenschläfer	Eikelmuis
Fox, Red	Vulpes vulpes	Rotfuchs	Vos
Genet	Genetta genetta	Ginsterkatze	Genetkat
Hare, Iberian	Lepus granatensis	Iberische Hase	Iberische haas
Hedgehog, Algerian	Erinaceus algirus	Wanderigel	Trekegel
Hedgehog, Common	Erinaceus europeus	Braubbustigel	Egel
Ibex, Spanish	Capra pyrenaica	Iberische Steinbock	Iberische steenbok
Lynx, European	Lynx lynx	Luchs	Lynx
Lynx, Iberian	Lynx pardinus	Pardelluchs	Pardellynx, Iberische lynx
Marten, Beech	Martes foina	Steinmarder	Steenmarter
Mongoose, Egyptian	Herpestes ichneumon	Ichneumon	Mangoest
Mouflon	Ovis (ammon) musimon	Mufflon	Moeflon
Otter	Lutra lutra	Fischotter	Otter
Pipistrelle, Common	Pipistrellus pipistrellus	Zwergfledermaus	Gewone dwergvleermuis

English	Scientific	German	Dutch
Pipistrelle, Soprano	*Pipistrellus pygmaeus*	Mückenfledermaus	Kleine dwergvleermuis
Polecat	*Mustela putorius*	Waldiltis	Bunzing
Rabbit	*Oryctolagus cuniculus*	Wildkaninchen	Konijn
Shrew, Mediterranean Water	*Neomys anomalus*	Sumpfspitzmaus	Millers waterspitsmuis
Squirrel, Red	*Sciurus vulgaris*	Eichhörnchen	Gewone eekhoorn
Vole, Snow	*Chionomys nivalis*	Schneemaus	sneeuwmuis
Vole, Southern Water	*Arvicola sapidus*	Westschermaus	West-Europese woelrat
Weasel	*Mustela nivalis*	Mauswiesel	Wezel
Wolf, (Iberian)	*Canis lupus*	Wolf	Wolf

Birds

English	Scientific	German	Dutch
Accentor, Alpine	*Prunella collaris*	Alpenbraunelle	Alpenheggemus
Avadavat, Red	*Amandava amandava*	Tigerfink	Tijgervink
Avocet	*Recurvirostra avosetta*	Säbelschnäbler	Kluut
Bee-eater	*Merops apiaster*	Bienenfresser	Bijeneter
Bittern, Little	*Ixobrychus minutus*	Zwergdommel	Woudaapje
Blackbird	*Turdus merula*	Amsel	Merel
Blackcap	*Sylvia atricapilla*	Mönchsgrasmücke	Zwartkop
Bluethroat	*Luscinia svecica*	Blaukehlchen	Blauwborst
Brambling	*Fringilla montifringilla*	Bergfink	Keep
Bulbul, Common	*Pycnonotus barbatus*	Graubülbül	Grauwe buulbuul
Bullfinch	*Pyrrhula pyrrhula*	Gimpel	Goudvink
Bunting, Cirl	*Emberiza cirlus*	Zaunammer	Cirlgors
Bunting, Corn	*Miliaria calandra*	Grauammer	Grauwe gors
Bunting, Ortolan	*Emberiza hortulana*	Ortolan	Ortolaan
Bunting, Reed	*Emberiza schoeniclus*	Rohrammer	Rietgors
Bunting, Rock	*Emberiza cia*	Zippammer	Grijze gors
Bustard, Great	*Otis tarda*	Grosstrappe	Grote trap
Bustard, Little	*Tetrax tetrax*	Zwergtrappe	Kleine trap
Buzzard, Common	*Buteo buteo*	Mäusebussard	Buizerd
Buzzard, Honey	*Pernis apivorus*	Wespenbussard	Wespendief
Chaffinch	*Fringilla coelebs*	Buchfink	Vink
Chiffchaff	*Phylloscopus collybita*	Zilpzalp	Tjiftjaf
Chiffchaff, Iberian	*Phylloscopus ibericus*	Iberischer Zilpzalp	Iberische tjiftjaf
Chough, Red-billed	*Pyrrhocorax pyrrhocorax*	Alpenkrähe	Alpenkraai
Cisticola, Zitting	*Cisticola juncidis*	Cistensänger	Graszanger
Coot, Common	*Fulica atra*	Blässhuhn	Meerkoet
Coot, Crested	*Fulica cristata*	Kammblässhuhn	Knobbelmeerkoet
Cormorant, Great	*Phalacrocorax carbo*	Kormoran	Aalscholver
Crossbill, Common	*Loxia curvirostra*	Fichtenkreuzschnabel	Kruisbek
Crow, Carrion	*Corvus corone*	Aaskrähe	Zwarte kraai
Cuckoo, Common	*Cuculus canorus*	Kuckuck	Koekoek
Cuckoo, Great Spotted	*Clamator glandarius*	Häherkuckuck	Kuifkoekoek
Curlew, Stone	*Burhinus oedicnemus*	Triel	Griel
Dipper	*Cinclus cinclus*	Wasseramsel	Waterspreeuw
Dove, Collared	*Streptopelia decaocto*	Türkentaube	Turkse tortel
Dove, Rock	*Columba livia*	Felsentaube	Rotsduif

Dove, Stock	*Columba oenas*	Hohltaube	Holenduif
Dove, Turtle	*Streptopelia turtur*	Turteltaube	Tortelduif
Duck, Ferruginous	*Aythya nyroca*	Moorente	Witoogeend
Duck, Marbled	*Marmaronetta angustirostris*	Marmelente	Marmereend
Duck, Tufted	*Aythya fuligula*	Reiherente	Kuifeend
Duck, White-headed	*Oxyura leucocephala*	Weisskopfruderente	Witkopeend
Dunlin	*Calidris alpina*	Alpenstrandläufer	Bonte strandloper
Dunnock	*Prunella modularis*	Heckenbraunelle	Heggenmus
Eagle, Bonelli's	*Hieraaetus fasciatus*	Habichtsadler	Havikarend
Eagle, Booted	*Hieraaetus pennatus*	Zwergadler	Dwergarend
Eagle, Golden	*Aquila chrysaetos*	Steinadler	Steenarend
Eagle, Short-toed	*Circaetus gallicus*	Schlangenadler	Slangenarend
Eagle, Spanish Imperial	*Aquila adalberti*	Spanischer Kaiseradler	Spaanse keizerarend
Egret, Cattle	*Bubulcus ibis*	Kuhreiher	Koereiger
Egret, Little	*Egretta garzetta*	Seidenreiher	Kleine zilverreiger
Falcon, Peregrine	*Falco peregrinus*	Wanderfalke	Slechtvalk
Fieldfare	*Turdus pilaris*	Wacholderdrossel	Kramsvogel
Finch, Citril	*Serinus citrinella*	Zitronengirlitz	Citroenkanarie
Finch, Trumpeter	*Bucanetes githagineus*	Wüstengimpel	Woestijnvink
Firecrest	*Regulus ignicapillus*	Sommergoldhähnchen	Vuurgoudhaantje
Flamingo	*Phoenicopterus roseus*	Flamingo	Europese flamingo
Flycatcher, Pied	*Ficedula hypoleuca*	Trauerschnäpper	Bonte vliegenvanger
Flycatcher, Spotted	*Muscicapa striata*	Grauschnäpper	Grauwe vliegenvanger
Gadwall	*Anas strepera*	Schnatterente	Krakeend
Gallinule, Purple	*Porphyrio porphyrio*	Purpurhuhn	Purperkoet
Gannet	*Morus bassanus*	Basstölpel	Jan-van-gent
Godwit, Black-tailed	*Limosa limosa*	Uferschnepfe	Grutto
Goldfinch	*Carduelis carduelis*	Distelfink	Putter
Goshawk	*Accipiter gentilis*	Habicht	Havik
Grebe, Great Crested	*Podiceps cristatus*	Haubentaucher	Fuut
Grebe, Little	*Tachybaptus ruficollis*	Zwergtaucher	Dodaars
Greenfinch	*Carduelis chloris*	Grünling	Groenling
Greenshank	*Tringa nebularia*	Grünschenkel	Groenpootruiter
Gull, Audouin's	*Ichthyaetus audouinii*	Korallenmöwe	Adouins meeuw
Gull, Lesser Black-backed	*Larus graellsii*	Heringsmöwe	Kleine mantelmeeuw
Gull, Little	*Hydrocoloeus minutus*	Zwergmöwe	Dwergmeeuw
Gull, Mediterranean	*Ichthyaetus melanocephalus*	Schwarzkopfmöwe	Zwartkopmeeuw
Gull, Slender-billed	*Chroicocephalus genei*	Dünnschnabelmöwe	Dunbekmeeuw
Gull, Yellow-legged	*Larus michahellis*	Weisskopfmöve	Geelpootmeeuw
Harrier, Marsh	*Circus aeruginosus*	Rohrweihe	Bruine kiekendief
Harrier, Montagu's	*Circus pygargus*	Wiesenweihe	Grauwe kiekendief
Hawfinch	*Coccothraustes coccothraustes*	Kernbeisser	Appelvink
Hemipode, Andalusian	*Turnix sylvatica*	Laufhühnchen	Gestreepte vechtkwartel
Heron, Grey	*Ardea cinerea*	Graureiher	Blauwe reiger
Heron, Night	*Nycticorax nycticorax*	Nachtreiher	Kwak
Heron, Purple	*Ardea purpurea*	Purpurreiher	Purperreiger
Heron, Squacco	*Ardeola ralloides*	Rallenreiher	Ralreiger
Hoopoe	*Upupa epops*	Wiedehopf	Hop

Ibis, Glossy	*Plegadis falcinellus*	Braunsichler	Zwarte ibis
Jackdaw	*Corvus monedula*	Dohle	Kauw
Kestrel, Common	*Falco tinnunculus*	Turmfalke	Torenvalk
Kestrel, Lesser	*Falco naumanni*	Rötelfalke	Kleine torenvalk
Kingfisher	*Alcedo atthis*	Eisvogel	IJsvogel
Kite, Black	*Milvus migrans*	Schwarzmilan	Zwarte wouw
Kite, Black-winged	*Elanus caeruleus*	Gleitaar	Grijze wouw
Lammergeier	*Gypaetus barbatus*	Bartgeier	Lammergier
Lapwing	*Vanellus vanellus*	Kiebitz	Kievit
Lark, Calandra	*Melanocorypha calandra*	Kalanderlerche	Kalanderleeuwerik
Lark, Crested	*Galerida cristata*	Haubenlerche	Kuifleeuwerik
Lark, Dupont's	*Chersophilus duponti*	Dupontlerche	Duponts leeuwerik
Lark, Lesser Short-toed	*Calandrella rufescens*	Stummellerche	Kleine kortteenleeuwerik
Lark, Short-toed	*Calandrella brachydactyla*	Kurzzehenlerche	Kortteenleeuwerik
Lark, Thekla	*Galerida theklae*	Theklalerche	Theklaleeuwerik
Linnet	*Carduelis cannabina*	Bluthänfling	Kneu
Magpie, Azure-winged	*Cyanopica cyana*	Blauelster	Blauwe ekster
Mallard	*Anas platyrhynchos*	Stockente	Wilde eend
Martin, Crag	*Ptyonoprogne rupestris*	Felsenschwalbe	Rotszwaluw
Martin, House	*Delichon urbicum*	Mehlschwalbe	Huiszwaluw
Martin, Sand	*Riparia riparia*	Uferschwalbe	Oeverzwaluw
Nightingale	*Luscinia megarhynchos*	Nachtigal	Nachtegaal
Nightjar, Common	*Caprimulgus europaeus*	Ziegenmelker	Nachtzwaluw
Nightjar, Red-necked	*Caprimulgus ruficollis*	Rothals-Ziegenmelker	Moorse nachtzwaluw
Nuthatch	*Sitta europaea*	Kleiber	Boomklever
Oriole, Golden	*Oriolus oriolus*	Pirol	Wielewaal
Osprey	*Pandion haliaetus*	Fischadler	Visarend
Ouzel, Ring	*Turdus torquatus*	Ringdrossel	Beflijster
Owl, Barn	*Tyto alba*	Schleiereule	Kerkuil
Owl, Eagle	*Bubo bubo*	Uhu	Oehoe
Owl, Little	*Athene noctua*	Steinkauz	Steenuil
Owl, Scops	*Otus scops*	Zwergohreule	Dwergooruil
Owl, Tawny	*Strix aluco*	Waldkauz	Bosuil
Parakeet, Monk	*Myiopsitta monachus*	Mönchsittich	Monniksparkiet
Parakeet, Ring-necked	*Psittacula krameri*	Halsbandsittich	Halsbandparkiet
Partridge, Red-legged	*Alectoris rufa*	Rothuhn	Rode patrijs
Peregrine	See Falcon, Peregrine		
Pigeon, Wood	*Columba palumbus*	Ringeltaube	Houtduif
Pintail	*Anas acuta*	Spiessente	Pijlstaart
Pipit, Meadow	*Anthus pratensis*	Wiesenpieper	Graspieper
Pipit, Tawny	*Anthus campestris*	Brachpieper	Duinpieper
Pipit, Water	*Anthus spinoletta*	Bergpieper	Waterpieper
Plover, Golden	*Pluvialis apricaria*	Goldregenpfeifer	Goudplevier
Plover, Grey	*Pluvialis squatarola*	Kiebitzregenpfeifer	Zilverplevier
Plover, Kentish	*Charadrius alexandrinus*	Seeregenpfeifer	Strandplevier
Plover, Little Ringed	*Charadrius dubius*	Flussregenpfeifer	Kleine plevier
Plover, Ringed	*Charadrius hiaticula*	Sandregenpfeifer	Bontbekplevier
Pochard	*Aythya ferina*	Tafelente	Tafeleend
Pochard, Red-crested	*Netta rufina*	Kolbenente	Krooneend

SPECIES LIST & TRANSLATION

Pratincole, Collared	*Glareola pratincola*	Rotflügel-Brachschwalbe	Vorkstaartplevier
Quail, Common	*Coturnix coturnix*	Wachtel	Kwartel
Rail, Water	*Rallus aquaticus*	Wasserralle	Waterral
Raven	*Corvus corax*	Kolkrabe	Raaf
Razorbill	*Alca torda*	Tordalk	Alk
Redshank, Common	*Tringa totanus*	Rotschenkel	Tureluur
Redshank, Spotted	*Tringa erythropus*	Dunkler Wasserläufer	Zwarte ruiter
Redstart, (Common)	*Phoenicurus phoenicurus*	Gartenrotschwanz	Gekraagde roodstaart
Redstart, Black	*Phoenicurus ochruros*	Hausrotschwanz	Zwarte roodstaart
Redwing	*Turdus iliacus*	Rotdrossel	Koperwiek
Robin, Rufous Bush	*Cercotrichas galactotes*	Heckensänger	Rosse waaierstaart
Roller	*Coracias garrulus*	Blauracke	Scharrelaar
Sanderling	*Calidris alba*	Sanderling	Drieteenstrandloper
Sandgrouse, Black-bellied	*Pterocles orientalis*	Sandflughuhn	Zwartbuikzandhoen
Sandgrouse, Pin-tailed	*Pterocles alchata*	Spiessflughuhn	Witbuikzandhoen
Sandpiper, Common	*Actitis hypoleucos*	Flussuferläufer	Oeverloper
Sandpiper, Curlew	*Calidris feruginea*	Sichelstrandläufer	Krombekstrandloper
Sandpiper, Green	*Tringa ochropus*	Waldwasserläufer	Witgat
Serin	*Serinus serinus*	Girlitz	Europese kanarie
Shag	*Phalacrocorax aristotelis*	Krähenscharbe	Kuifaalscholver
Shearwater, Balearic	*Puffinus mauretanicus*	Balearensturmtaucher	Vale pijlstormvogel
Shearwater, Cory's	*Calonectris borealis*	Kanarensturmtaucher	Kuhls pijlstormvogel
Shearwater, Yelkouan	*Puffinus yelkouan*	Mittelmeer-Sturmtaucher	Yelkouanpijlstormvogel
Shelduck	*Tadorna tadorna*	Brandgans	Bergeend
Shoveler	*Anas clypeata*	Löffelente	Slobeend
Shrike, Iberian Grey	*Lanius meridionalis*	Südlicher Raubwürger	Zuidelijke klapekster
Shrike, Woodchat	*Lanius senator*	Rotkopfwürger	Roodkopklauwier
Siskin	*Carduelis spinus*	Erlenzeisig	Sijs
Skua, Great	*Stercorarius skua*	Skua	Grote jager
Skylark	*Alauda arvensis*	Feldlerche	Veldleeuwerik
Sparrow, House	*Passer domesticus*	Haussperling	Huismus
Sparrow, Rock	*Petronia petronia*	Steinsperling	Rotsmus
Sparrow, Spanish	*Passer hispaniolensis*	Weidensperling	Spaanse mus
Sparrow, Tree	*Passer montanus*	Feldsperling	Ringmus
Sparrowhawk	*Accipiter nisus*	Sperber	Sperwer
Spoonbill	*Platalea leucorodia*	Löffler	Lepelaar
Starling, Common	*Sturnus vulgaris*	Star	Spreeuw
Starling, Spotless	*Sturnus unicolor*	Einfarbstar	Zwarte spreeuw
Stilt, Black-winged	*Himantopus himantopus*	Stelzenläufer	Steltkluut
Stint, Temminck's	*Calidris temminckii*	Temminckstrandläufer	Temmincks strandloper
Stonechat	*Saxicola torquata*	Schwarzkehlchen	Roodborsttapuit
Stork, Black	*Ciconia nigra*	Schwarzstorch	Zwarte ooievaar
Stork, White	*Ciconia ciconia*	Weissstorch	Ooievaar
Storm-petrel, European	*Hydrobates pelagicus*	Sturmschwalbe	Stormvogeltje
Swallow	*Hirundo rustica*	Rauchschwalbe	Boerenzwaluw
Swallow, Red-rumped	*Cecropsis daurica*	Rötelschwalbe	Roodstuitzwaluw
Swift, Alpine	*Tachymarptis melba*	Alpensegler	Alpengierzwaluw
Swift, Common	*Apus apus*	Mauersegler	Gierzwaluw
Swift, Little	*Apus affinis*	Haussegler	Huisgierzwaluw

Swift, Pallid	*Apus pallidus*	Fahlsegler	Vale gierzwaluw
Swift, White-rumped	*Apus caffer*	Kaffernsegler	Kaffergierzwaluw
Teal	*Anas crecca*	Krickente	Wintertaling
Tern, Black	*Chlidonias niger*	Trauerseeschwalbe	Zwarte stern
Tern, Gull-billed	*Gelochelidon nilotica*	Lachseeschwalbe	Lachstern
Tern, Lesser Crested	*Thalasseus bengalensis*	Rüppellseeschwalbe	Bengaalse stern
Tern, Little	*Sternula albifrons*	Zwergseeschwalbe	Dwergstern
Tern, Sandwich	*Thalasseus sandvicensis*	Brandseeschwalbe	Grote stern
Tern, Whiskered	*Chlidonias hybrida*	Weissbart-Seeschwalbe	Witwangstern
Thrush, Blue Rock	*Monticola solitarius*	Blaumerle	Blauwe rotslijster
Thrush, Mistle	*Turdus viscivorus*	Misteldrossel	Grote lijster
Thrush, Rock	*Monticola saxatilis*	Steinrötel	Rode rotslijster
Tit, Blue	*Cyanistes caeruleus*	Blaumeise	Pimpelmees
Tit, Coal	*Periparus ater*	Tannenmeise	Zwarte mees
Tit, Crested	*Lophophanes cristatus*	Haubenmeise	Kuifmees
Tit, Great	*Parus major*	Kohlmeise	Koolmees
Tit, Long-tailed	*Aegithalos caudatus*	Schwanzmeise	Staartmees
Tit, Penduline	*Remiz pendulinus*	Beutelmeise	Buidelmees
Treecreeper, Short-toed	*Certhia brachydactyla*	Gartenbaumläufer	Boomkruiper
Vulture, Bearded	See Lammergeier		
Vulture, Black	*Aegypius monachus*	Mönchsgeier	Monniksgier
Vulture, Egyptian	*Neophron percnopterus*	Schmutzgeier	Aasgier
Vulture, Griffon	*Gyps fulvus*	Gänsegeier	Vale gier
Wagtail, Grey	*Motacilla cinerea*	Gebirgsstelze	Grote gele kwikstaart
Wagtail, White	*Motacilla alba*	Bachstelze	Witte kwikstaart
Wagtail, Yellow (Iberian)	*Motacilla flava iberiae*	Iberische Schafstelze	Iberische kwikstaart
Wallcreeper	*Tichodroma muraria*	Mauerläufer	Rotskruiper
Warbler, Bonelli's	*Phylloscopus bonelli*	Berglaubsänger	Bergfluiter
Warbler, Cetti's	*Cettia cetti*	Seidensänger	Cetti's zanger
Warbler, Dartford	*Sylvia undata*	Provencegrasmücke	Provençaalse grasmus
Warbler, Great Reed	*Acrocephalus arundinaceus*	Drosselrohrsänger	Grote karekiet
Warbler, Melodious	*Hippolais polyglotta*	Orpheusspötter	Orpheusspotvogel
Warbler, Moustached	*Acrocephalus melanopogon*	Mariskensänger	Zwartkoprietzanger
Warbler, Reed	*Acrocephalus scirpaceus*	Teichrohrsänger	Kleine karekiet
Warbler, Sardinian	*Sylvia melanocephala*	Samtkopf-Grasmücke	Kleine zwartkop
Warbler, Savi's	*Locustella luscinioides*	Rohrschwirl	Snor
Warbler, Spectacled	*Sylvia conspicillata*	Brillengrasmücke	Brilgrasmus
Warbler, Subalpine	*Sylvia cantillans cantillans*	Westliche Weissbart-Grasmücke	Westelijke baardgrasmus
Warbler, Western Olivaceous	*Iduna opaca*	Isabellspötter	Westelijke vale spotvogel
Warbler, Western Orphean	*Sylvia hortensis*	Orpheusgrasmücke	Orpheusgrasmus
Waxbill, Black-rumped	*Estrilda troglodytes*	Grauastrild	Napoleonnetje
Waxbill, Common	*Estrilda astrild*	Wellenastrild	Sint-Helenafazantje
Wheatear, Black	*Oenanthe leucura*	Trauersteinschmätzer	Zwarte tapuit
Wheatear, Black-eared	*Oenanthe hispanica*	Mittelmeer-Steinschmätzer	Blonde tapuit
Wheatear, Northern	*Oenanthe oenanthe*	Steinschmätzer	Tapuit
Woodlark	*Lullula arborea*	Heidelerche	Boomleeuwerik

SPECIES LIST & TRANSLATION

Woodpecker, Great Spotted	*Dendrocopos major*	Buntspecht	Grote bonte specht
Woodpecker, Iberian Green	*Picus sharpei*	Iberischer Grünspecht	Iberische groene specht
Woodpecker, Lesser Spotted	*Dendrocopos minor*	Kleinspecht	Kleine bonte specht
Wren	*Troglodytes troglodytes*	Zaunkönig	Winterkoning
Wryneck	*Jynx torquilla*	Wendehals	Draaihals

Reptiles and Amphibians

English	Scientific	German	Dutch
Algyroides, Spanish	*Algyroides marchi*	Spanische Kieleidechse	Andalusische kielhagedis
Chameleon, Common	*Chamaeleo chamaeleon*	Chamäleon	Gewone kameleon
Frog, European Tree	*Hyla arborea*	Europäischer Laubfrosch	Boomkikker
Frog, East Iberian Painted	*Discoglossus jeanneae* Scheibenzüngler	(Ost)Iberischer schijftongkikker	Oost-Iberische
Frog, Iberian Parsley	*Pelodytes ibericus*	Iberischer Schlammtaucher	Iberische groengestipte kikker
Frog, Iberian Water	*Pelophylax/Rana perezi*	Iberischer Wasserfrosch	Iberische groene kikker
Frog, Parsley	*Pelodytes punctatus*	Westlicher Schlammtaucher	Groengestipte kikker
Frog, Stripeless Tree	*Hyla meridionalis*	Mittelmeer-Laubfrosch	Mediterrane boomkikker
Frog, West Iberian Painted	*Discoglossus galganoi* Scheibenzüngler	(West)Iberischer schijftongkikker	West-Iberische
Gecko, Mediterranean House	*Hemidactylus turcicus*	Europäischer Halbfinger	Europese tjiktjak
Gecko, Moorish	*Tarentola mauritanica*	Maurischer Gecko	Muurgekko
Lizard, Iberian Wall	*Podarcis hispanica*	Spanische Mauereidechse	Spaanse muurhagedis
Lizard, Iberian Worm	*Blanus cinereus*	Maurische Netzwühle	Moorse wormhagedis
Lizard, Ocellated	*Timon lepidus*	Perleidechse	Parelhagedis
Lizard, Sierra Nevada Ocellated	*Timon nevadensis*	Nevada-Perleidechse	Sierra Nevada parelhagedis*
Lizard, Spiny-footed	*Acanthodactylus erythrurus*	Europäischer Fransenfinger	Franjeteenhagedis
Newt, Bosca's	*Lissotriton boscai*	Spanischer Wassermolch	Iberische watersalamander
Newt, Sharp-ribbed	*Pleurodeles waltl*	Spanischer Rippenmolch	Ribbensalamander
Newt, Southern Marbled	*Triturus pygmaeus*	Zwergmarmormolch	Dwergmarmersalamander
Psammodromus, Large	*Psammodromus algirus*	Algrischer Sandläufer	Algerijnse zandloper
Psammodomus, Spanish	*Psammodromus hispanicus*	Spanischer Sandläufer	Spaanse zandloper
Salamander, Fire	*Salamandra salamandra*	Feuersalamander	Vuursalamander
Skink, Bedriaga's	*Chalcides bedriagai*	Iberischer Walzenskink	Iberische skink
Skink, Western Three-toed	*Chalcides striatus*	Westliche Erzschleiche	Gestreepte hazelskink
Snake, False Smooth	*Macroprotodon cucullatus*	Kapuzennatter	Mutsslang
Snake, Grass	*Natrix natrix*	Ringelnatter	Ringslang
Snake, Horseshoe Whip	*Coluber hippocrepis*	Hufeisennatter	Hoefijzerslang
Snake, Ladder	*Elaphe scalaris*	Treppennatter	Trapslang
Snake, Montpellier	*Malpolon monspessulanus*	Eidechsennatter	Hagedisslang
Snake, Smooth	*Coronella austriaca*	Schlingnatter	Gladde slang
Snake, Southern Smooth	*Coronella girondica*	Girondische Glattnatter	Girondische gladde slang
Snake, Viperine	*Natrix maura*	Vipernatter	Adderringslang

English	Scientific	German	Dutch
Spadefoot, Western	*Pelobates cultripes*	Messerfuss	Iberische knoflookpad
Terrapin, Spanish	*Mauremys leprosa*	Spanische Wasserschildkröte	Moorse beekschildpad
Toad, Common	*Bufo bufo*	Erdkröte	Gewone pad
Toad, Iberian Midwife	*Alytes cisternasii*	Iberische Geburtshelferkröte	Iberische vroedmeester pad
Toad, Natterjack	*Bufo/Epidalea calamita*	Kreuzkröte	Rugstreeppad
Toad, Southern Midwife	*Alytes dickhilleni*	Südiberische Geburtshelferkröte	Andalusische vroedmeesterpad
Toad, Western	*Bufo spinosa*	Mittelmeer-Erdkröte	Iberische gewone pad
Tortoise, Spur-thighed	*Testudo graeca*	Maurische Landschildkröte	Moorse landschildpad
Turtle, Loggerhead	*Caretta caretta*	Unechte Karettschildkröte	Onechte karetschildpad
Viper, Lataste's	*Vipera latasti*	Stülpnasenotter	Wipneusadder

Invertebrates

English	Scientific	German	Dutch
Apollo	*Parnassius apollo*	Apollofalter	Apollovlinder
Argus, Mountain	*Aricia montensis*	Grosser Sonnenröschen-Bläuling	Vals bruin blauwtje
Argus, Southern Brown	*Aricia cramera*	Südlicher Sonnenröschen-Bläuling	Moors bruin blauwtje
Argus, Spanish	*Aricia morronensis*	Spanischer Kleiner Sonnenröschen-Bläuling	Spaans bruin blauwtje
Black-tip, Spanish Greenish	*Euchloe bazae*	Grünlicher Weissling*	Groen marmerwitje
Blue, Adonis	*Polyommatus bellargus*	Himmelblauer Bläuling	Adonisblauwtje
Blue, African Grass	*Zizeeria knysna*	Amethist- Bläuling*	Amethistblauwtje
Blue, Amanda´s	*Polyommatus amandus*	Vogelwicken-Bläuling	Wikkeblauwtje
Blue, Andalusian Anomalous	*Polyommatus violetae*	Andalusischer Esparsetten-Bläuling*	Almijara esparcetteblauwtje
Blue, Black-eyed	*Glaucopsyche melanops*	Schwarz-Auge Blauling*	Spaans bloemenblauwtje
Blue, Carswell's	*Cupido carswelli*	Carswelli's Zwerg-Bläuling*	Carswelli's dwergblauwtje
Blue, Chapman's	*Polyommatus thersites*	Kleine Esparsetten-Bläuling	Esparcetteblauwtje
Blue, Common	*Polyommatus icarus*	Hauhechel-Bläuling	Icarusblauwtje
Blue, Common Tiger	*Tarucus theophrastus*	Andalusischer Christusdorn-Bläuling*	Moors christusdoorn-blauwtje
Blue, Escher's	*Polyommatus escheri*	Escher-Bläuling	Groot tragantblauwtje
Blue, Green-underside	*Glaucopsyche alexis*	Himmelblauer Steinkleebläuling	Bloemenblauwtje
Blue, Idas	*Plebejus idas*	Ginster-Bläuling	Vals heideblauwtje
Blue, Iolas	*Iolana iolas*	Blasenstrauch-Bläuling	Blazenstruikblauwtje
Blue, Long-tailed	*Lampides boeticus*	Grosser Wander-Bläuling	Tijgerblauwtje
Blue, Lorquin's	*Cupido lorquinii*	Morischer Zwerg-Bläuling	Moors dwergblauwtje
Blue, Mother-of-Pearl	*Polyommatus nivescens*	Perlmutt-Bläuling*	Parelmoerblauwtje
Blue, Nevada	*Polyommatus golgus*	Nevada Wundklee-Bläuling*	Nevadaturkooisblauwtje
Blue, Osiris	*Cupido osiris*	Kleiner Alpenbläuling	Zuidelijk dwergblauwtje
Blue, Panoptes	*Pseudophilotes panoptes*	Panoptes-Bläuling	Spaans tijmblauwtje
Blue, Silver-studded	*Plebejus argus*	Geissklee-Bläulling	Heideblauwtje

Blue, Spanish Chalk-hill	Lysandra albicans	Silberweisser Bläuling*	Kwartsblauwtje
Blue, Spanish Zephyr	Plebejus hespericus	Spanischer Tragant-Bläuling*	Spaans saffierblauwtje
Blue, Zullich's	Plebejus zullichi	Nevada Alpenbläuling*	Nevada mansschild-blauwtje
Bluet, Dainty	Coenagrion scitulum	Gabel-Azurjungfer	Gaffelwaterjuffer
Bluet, Mediterranean	Coenagrion caerulescens	Südliche Azurjungfer	Zuidelijke waterjuffer
Bluet, Mercury	Coenagrion mercuriale	Helm-Azurjungfer	Mercuurwaterjuffer
Bluetail, Iberian	Ischnura graellsii	Spanische Pechlibelle	Iberische grasjuffer
Bronze, Geranium	Cacyreus marshalli	Pelargonien-Bläuling	Geraniumblauwtje
Brown, Dusky Meadow	Hyponephele lycaon	Kleines Ochsenauge	Grauw zandoogje
Brown, Meadow	Maniola jurtina	Grosses Ochsenauge	Bruin zandoogje
Brown, Oriental Meadow	Hyponephele lupinus	Südliches Kleines Ochsenauge*	Zuidelijk grauw zandoogje
Burnet, Nevada	Zygaena nevadensis	Nevada-Widderchen*	Nevada sint-jansvlinder*
Burnet, Provence	Zygaena occitanica	Provense-Widderchen*	Provence sint-jansvlinder*
Butterfly, Nettle-tree	Libythea celtis	Zürgelbaum-Schnauzenfalter	Snuitvlinder
Cardinal	Argynnis pandora	Kardinal	Kardinaalsmantel
Cascader, Ringed	Zygonyx torridus	Wasserfall-Kreuzer	Watervallibel
Centipede, Megarian Banded	Scolopendra cingulata	Riesenläufer/Gürtelskolopender	Scolopendra*
Cleopatra	Gonepteryx cleopatra	Mittelmeer-Zitronenfalter	Cleopatra
Clubtail, Pronged	Gomphus graslinii	Französische Keiljungfer	Gevorkte rombout
Clubtail, Western	Gomphus pulchellus	Westliche Keiljungfer	Plasrombout
Clubtail, Yellow	Gomphus simillimus	Gelbe Keiljungfer	Gele rombout
Cochineal	Dactylopius coccus	Cochenilleschildlaus	Cochenilleluis
Comma	Nymphalis c-album	C-Falter	Gehakkelde aurelia
Copper, Purple-shot	Lycaena alciphron	Violetter Feuerfalter	Violette vuurvlinder
Copper, Small	Lycaena phlaeas	Kleiner Feuerfalter	Kleine vuurvlinder
Copper, Violet	Lycaena helle	Blauschillernder Feuerfalter	Blauwe vuurvlinder
Cruiser, Splendid	Macromia splendens	Europäischer Flussherrscher	Prachtlibel
Damsel, Common Winter	Sympecma fusca	Gemeine Winterlibelle	Bruine winterjuffer
Damsel, Small Red	Ceriagron tenellum	Scharlachlibelle	Koraaljuffer
Darter, Desert	Sympetrum sinaiticum	Blasse Heidelibelle	Woestijnheidelibel
Darter, Red-veined	Sympetrum fonscolombii	Frühe Heidelibelle	Zwervende heidelibel
Demoiselle, Beautiful	Calopteryx virgo	Blauflügel-Prachtlibelle	Bosbeekjuffer
Demoiselle, Copper	Calopteryx haemorrhoidalis	Bronzene Prachtlibelle	Koperen beekjuffer
Demoiselle, Western	Calopteryx xanthostoma	Südwestliche Prachtlibelle	Iberische beekjuffer
Dropwing, Orange-winged	Trithemis kirbyi	Gefleckter Sonnenzeiger	Oranje zonnewijzer
Dropwing, Violet	Trithemis annulata	Violetter Sonnenzeiger	Purperlibel
Emerald, Orange-spotted	Oxygastra curtisii	Gekielte Smaragdlibelle	Bronslibel
Emperor, Blue	Anax imperator	Grosse Königslibelle	Grote keizerlibel
Emperor, Lesser	Anax parthenope	Kleine Königslibelle	Zuidelijke keizerlibel
Emperor, Vagrant	Anax ephippiger	Schabrackenlibelle	Zadellibel
Featherleg, Orange	Platycnemis acutipennis	Orangerote Federlibelle	Oranje breedscheenjuffer
Featherleg, White	Platycnemis latipes	Weisse Federlibelle	Witte breedscheenjuffer
Festoon, Spanish	Zerinthia rumina	Spanischer Osterluzeifalter	Spaanse pijpbloemvlinder

English	Scientific	German	Dutch
Fritillary, Aetherie	Melitaea aetherie	Aetherie-Scheckenfalter	Moorse parelmoervlinder
Fritillary, Dark Green	Argynnis aglaja	Grosser Perlmutterfalter	Grote parelmoervlinder
Fritillary, Heath	Melitaea athalia	Gemeine Scheckenfalter	Bosparelmoervlinder
Fritillary, High Brown	Argynnis adippe	Feuriger Perlmutterfalter	Bosrandparelmoervlinder
Fritillary, Knapweed	Melitaea phoebe	Flockenblumen-Scheckenfalter	Knoopkruidparelmoervlinder
Fritillary, Lesser Spotted	Melitaea trivia	Bräunlicher Scheckenfalter	Toortsparelmoervlinder
Fritillary, Marbled	Brenthis daphne	Brombeer-Perlmuttfalter	Braamparelmoervlinder
Fritillary, Marsh	Euphydryas aurinia	Skabiosen-Scheckenfalter	Moerasparelmoervlinder
Fritillary, Silver-washed	Argynnis paphia	Kaisermantel	Keizersmantel
Fritillary, Spanish	Euphydryas desfontainii	Spanische Scheckenfalter	Mozaïekparelmoervlinder
Fritillary, Spotted	Melitaea didyma	Roter Scheckenfalter	Tweekleurige parelmoervlinder
Fritillary, Twin-spot	Brenthis hecate	Saumfleck-Perlmutterfalter	Dubbelstipparelmoervlinder
Gatekeeper, Southern	Pyronia cecilia	Südliches Ochsenauge	Zuidelijk oranje zandoogje
Gatekeeper, Spanish	Pyronia bathseba	Spanischer Ochsenauge	Spaans oranje zandoogje
Goldenring, Common	Cordulegaster boltonii	Zweigestreifte Quelljungfer	Gewone bronlibel
Grasshopper, Long-nosed	Truxalis nasuta	Europaeische Nasenschrecke	Kegelkopsprinkhaan*
Grayling	Hipparchia semele	Ockerbindige Samtfalter	Heivlinder
Grayling, Andalusian False	Arethusana boabdil	Andalusische Samtfalter*	Andalusische steppevlinder
Grayling, Great Banded	Brintesia circe	Weisser Waldportier	Witbandzandoog
Grayling, Nevada	Pseudochazara hippolyte	Nevada-Samtfalter*	Nevadaheremiet
Grayling, Rock	Hipparchia alcyone	Kleine Waldportier	Kleine boswachter
Grayling, Striped	Pseudotergumia fidia	Streifen-Samtfalter*	Gestreepte heivlinder
Grayling, Tree	Hipparchia statilinus	Eisenfarbiger Samtfalter	Kleine heivlinder
Groundling, Northern Banded	Brachythemis impartita	Treuer Kurzpfeil	Noordelijke bandgrondlibel
Hairstreak, Blue-spot	Satyrium spini	Kreuzdorn-Zipfelfalter	Wegedoornpage
Hairstreak, Chapman's Green	Callophrys avis	Erdbeerbaum Zipfelfalter*	Aardbeiboomgroentje
Hairstreak, False Ilex	Satyrium esculi	Südlicher Eichen-Zipfelfalter	Spaanse eikenpage
Hairstreak, Provence	Tomares ballus	Ballusbläuling	Groene klaverpage
Hairstreak, Spanish Purple	Laeosopis roboris	Spanischer Blauer Zipfelfalter	Essenpage
Hawker, Green-eyed	Aeshna isosceles	Keilflecklibelle	Vroege glazenmaker
Hawk-moth, Humming-bird	Macroglossum stellatarum	Taubenschwänzchen	Kolibrievlinder
Hawk-moth, Silver-striped	Hippotion celerio	Grosser Weinschwärmer	Wingerdpijlstaart
Hawk-moth, Southern Pine	Sphinx maurorum	Südlicher Kiefernschwärmer*	Zuidelijke dennenpijlstaart*
Heath, Dusky	Coenonympha dorus	Dorus Wiesenvögelchen	Bleek hooibeestje
Hermit	Chazara briseis	Berghexe	Heremiet
Hermit, Southern	Chazara prieuri	Südlicher Berghexe*	Bonte heremiet
Lacewing, Thread-winged	Nemoptera bipennis	Fadenhaft	Iberische prachtvleugel*

Lady, Painted	Vanessa cardui	Distelfalter	Distelvlinder
Locust, Egyptian	Anacridium aegyptium	Agyptische Wanderheuschrecke	Egyptische treksprinkhaan
Mantis, (European) Dwarf	Ameles spallanzania	Kleine Fangschrecke	Dwergbidsprinkhaan
Mantis, European Praying	Mantis religiosa	Gottesanbeterin	Bidsprinkhaan
Mantis, Hooded Praying*	Empusa pennata	Kapuze-Gottesanbeterin*	Kapbidsprinkhaan*
Monarch	Danaus plexippus	Monarchfalter	Monarchvlinder
Monarch, African	See: Tiger, Plain		
Moth, Cream-spot Tiger	Arctia villica	Schwarzer Bär	Roomvlek
Moth, Crimson Speckled	Utetheisa pulchella	Harlekinbär	Prachtbeer
Moth, Spanish Moon	Graellsia isabellae	Isabellaspinner	Spaanse maanvlinder
Orange-tip	Anthocharis cardamines	Aurorafalter	Oranjetipje
Orange-tip, Desert	Colotis evagore	Wüsten-Aurorafalter	Vals oranjetipje
Orange-tip, Provence	Anthocharis euphenoides	Gelber Aurorafalter	Geel oranjetipje
Orange-tip, Sooty	Zegris eupheme	Dunkler Aurorafalter	Zuidelijk oranjetipje
Pasha, Two-tailed	Charaxes jasius	Erdbeerbaumfalter	Aardbeiboomvlinder
Peacock	Inachis io	Tagpfauenauge	Dagpauwoog
Pennant, Black	Selysiothemis nigra	Teufelchen	Zwarte korenbout
Percher, Black	Diplacodes lefebvrii	Glänzender Schwarzpfeil	Moriaantje
Pincertail, Faded	Onychogomphus costae	Braune Zangenlibelle	Moorse tanglibel
Pincertail, Large	Onychogomphus uncatus	Grosse Zangenlibelle	Grote tanglibel
Pincertail, Small	Onychogomphus forcipatus	Kleine Zangenlibelle	Kleine tanglibel
Processionary, Pine	Thaumetopoea pityocampa	Pinien-Prozessionsspinner	Dennenprocessierups
Red-eye, Small	Erythromma viridulum	Kleines Granatauge	Kleine roodoogjuffer
Ringlet, Spanish Brassy	Erebia hispania	Spanischer Schillernder Mohrenfalter*	Spaanse glanserebia
Satyr, Black	Satyrus actaea	Spanische Waldportier*	Kleine saterzandoog
Scarlet, Broad	Crocothemis erythraea	Feuerlibelle	Vuurlibel
Shell, Noble Pen	Pinna nobilis	Edle Steckmuschel	Grote steekmossel
Skimmer, Black-tailed	Orthetrum cancellatum	Grosser Blaupfeil	Gewone oeverlibel
Skimmer, Epaulet	Orthetrum chrysostigma	Rahmstreif-Blaupfeil	Epauletoeverlibel
Skimmer, Keeled	Orthetrum coerulescens	Kleiner Blaupfeil	Beekoeverlibel
Skimmer, Long	Orthetrum trinacria	Langer Blaupfeil	Lange oeverlibel
Skimmer, Southern	Orthetrum brunneum	Südlicher Blaupfeil	Zuidelijke oeverlibel
Skimmer, Yellow-veined	Orthetrum nitidinerve	Gelbader-Blaupfeil	Geeladeroeverlibel
Skipper, Cinquefoil	Pyrgus cirsii	Spätsommer-Würfel-Dickkopffalter	Rood spikkeldikkopje
Skipper, Lulworth	Thymelicus acteon	Mattscheckiger Braun-Dickkopffalter	Dwergdikkopje
Skipper, Mallow	Carcharodus alceae	Malven-Dickkopffalter	Kaasjeskruiddikkopje
Skipper, Marbled	Carcharodus lavatherae	Loreley-Dickkopffalter	Andoorndikkopje
Skipper, Mediterranean	Gegenes nostrodamus	Grosser Mittelmeer-Dickkopffalter	Groot kustdikkopje
Skipper, Red-underwing	Spialia sertorius	Roter Würfel-Dickkopffalter	Kalkgraslanddikkopje
Skipper, Safflower	Pyrgus carthami	Steppenheiden-Würfel-Dickkopffalter	Witgezoomd spikkeldikkopje
Skipper, Sage	Muschampia proto	Brandkraut-Dickkopffalter*	Klein brandkruiddikkopje

Skipper, Silver-spotted	*Hesperia comma*	Komma-Dickkopffalter	Kommavlinder
Skipper, Small	*Thymelicus sylvestris*	Braunkolbiger Braun-Dickkopffalter	Geelsprietdikkopje
Skipper, Southern Marbled	*Charcharodes boeticus*	Andorn-Dickkopffalter	Malrovedikkopje
Spectre, Western	*Boyeria irene*	Westliche Geisterlibelle	Schemerlibel
Spreadwing, Dark	*Lestes macrostima*	Dunkle Binsenjungfer	Grote pantserjuffer
Spreadwing, Small	*Lestes virens*	Kleine Binsenjungfer	Tengere pantserjuffer
Swallowtail	*Papilio machaon*	Schwalbenschwanz	Koninginnenpage
Swallowtail, Scarce	*Iphiclides podalirius*	Segelfalter	Koningspage
Sweeper, Chimney	*Odezia atrata*	Rouwspanner	Schwarzspanner
Tarantula, European	*Lycosa tarantula*	Apulische Tarantel	Europese tarantula
Tiger, Plain	*Danaus chrysippus*	Afrikanischer Monarch	Kleine monarchvlinder
Tortoiseshell, Large	*Nymphalis polychloros*	Grosser Fuchs	Grote vos
Tortoiseshell, Small	*Aglais urticae*	Kleiner Fuchs	Kleine vos
Underwing, Oak Yellow	*Catocala nymphagoga*	Kleines Gelbens Ordensband*	Klein geel weeskind
White, Bath	*Pontia daplidice*	Reseda falter	Resedawitje
White, Black-veined	*Aporia crataegi*	Baumweissling	Groot geaderd witje
White, Green-striped	*Euchloe belemia*	Grüngestreifter Weissling	Gestreept marmerwitje
White, Iberian Marbled	*Melanargia lachesis*	Iberisches Schachbrett	Spaans dambordje
White, Portuguese Dappled	*Euchloe tagis*	Portugiesische Gesprenkelter Weissling*	Klein marmerwitje
White, Small	*Pieris rapae*	Kleiner Kohlweissling	Klein koolwitje
White, Spanish Marbled	*Melanargia ines*	Spanisches Schachbrett	Moors dambordje
White, Wood	*Leptidea sinapis*	Senfweissling	Boswitje
Widow, Black	*Latrodectus tredecimguttatus*	Europäische Schwarze Witwe	Europese zwarte weduwe
Wood, Speckled	*Pararge aegeria*	Waldbrettspiel	Bont zandoogje
Yellow, Clouded	*Colias crocea*	Postillion	Oranje luzernevlinder

Fish

English	Scientific	German	Dutch
Blennies	*Blennidae*	Schleimfische	Naakte slijmvissen
Bream, Sea	*Sparidae*	Meerbrassen	Zeebrasems
Comber, Painted	*Serranus scriba*	Schriftbarsch	Schriftbaars
Damselfish	*Chromis chromis*	Mönchsfisch	Monniksvis
Moray, Mediterranean	*Muraena helena*	Mittelmeer-Muräne	Europese murene
Mullet, Red	*Mullus surmuletus*	Streifenbarbe	Mul
Ray, Eagle	*Myliobatis aquila*	Gewöhnlicher Adlerrochen	Adelaarsrog
Wrasse, Ornate	*Thalassoma pavo*	Meerpfau	Pauwlipvis
Wrasse, Rainbow	*Coris julis*	Meerjunker	Regenbooglipvis

CROSSBILL GUIDES

IF YOU WANT TO SEE MORE

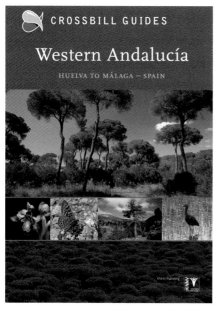
CROSSBILL GUIDES
Western Andalucía
HUELVA TO MÁLAGA – SPAIN

CROSSBILL GUIDES
Finnish Lapland

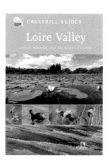
CROSSBILL GUIDES
Loire Valley

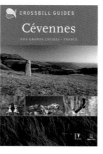
CROSSBILL GUIDES
Cévennes
AND GRANDS CAUSSES – FRANCE

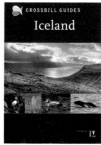
CROSSBILL GUIDES
Iceland

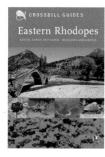
CROSSBILL GUIDES
Eastern Rhodopes

CROSSBILL GUIDES
North-east Poland

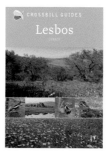
CROSSBILL GUIDES
Lesbos

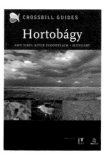
CROSSBILL GUIDES
Hortobágy
AND TISZA RIVER FLOODPLAIN – HUNGARY

CROSSBILL GUIDES
Canary Islands - I

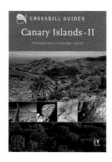
CROSSBILL GUIDES
Canary Islands - II

CROSSBILL GUIDES
Extremadura

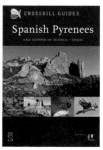
CROSSBILL GUIDES
Spanish Pyrenees
AND STEPPE OF HUESCA – SPAIN

More titles are in preparation. Check our website for further details and updates.
WWW.CROSSBILLGUIDES.ORG